Charles Crichton

**BRITISH
FILM
MAKERS**

Manchester University Press

BRIAN MCFARLANE, NEIL SINYARD series editors
ALLEN EYLES, SUE HARPER, TIM PULLEINE,
JEFFREY RICHARDS, TOM RYALL
series advisers

already published

Lindsay Anderson: Cinema Authorship JOHN IZOD, KARL MAGEE, KATHRYN MACKENZIE, ISABELLE GOURDIN-SANGOUARD

Anthony Asquith TOM RYALL

Richard Attenborough SALLY DUX

Roy Ward Baker GEOFF MAYER

Sydney Box ANDREW SPICER

Jack Clayton NEIL SINYARD

Lance Comfort BRIAN MCFARLANE

Terence Davies WENDY EVERETT

Terence Fisher PETER HUTCHINGS

Terry Gilliam PETER MARKS

Derek Jarman ROWLAND WYMER

Humphrey Jennings KEITH BEATTIE

Launder and Gilliat BRUCE BABINGTON

David Lean MELANIE WILLIAMS

Mike Leigh TONY WHITEHEAD

Richard Lester NEIL SINYARD

Joseph Losey COLIN GARDNER

Carol Reed PETER WILLIAM EVANS

Michael Reeves BENJAMIN HALLIGAN

Karel Reisz COLIN GARDNER

Tony Richardson ROBERT SHAIL

J. Lee Thompson STEVE CHIBNALL

Michael Winterbottom BRIAN MCFARLANE AND DEANE WILLIAMS

Four from the Forties: Arliss, Crabtree, Knowles and Huntington BRIAN MCFARLANE

Charles Crichton

QUENTIN FALK

Manchester University Press

Copyright © Quentin Falk 2021

The right of Quentin Falk to be identified as the author of this work has been asserted by them in accordance with the Copyright, Designs and Patents Act 1988.

Published by Manchester University Press
Altrincham Street, Manchester M1 7JA
www.manchesteruniversitypress.co.uk

British Library Cataloguing-in-Publication Data
A catalogue record for this book is available from the British Library

ISBN 978 1 5261 4995 4 hardback

First published 2021

The publisher has no responsibility for the persistence or accuracy of URLs for any external or third-party internet websites referred to in this book, and does not guarantee that any content on such websites is, or will remain, accurate or appropriate.

Typeset
by Newgen Publishing UK

To Alison Valentine and Joseph Peter
& for the Crichton family

Also by Quentin Falk

Travels in Greeneland: The Cinema of Graham Greene, Quartet Books, 1984; revised and updated 1990; 3rd edition revised and updated, Reynolds & Hearn, 2000; 4th edition revised and updated, UPNG, 2014

The Golden Gong: Fifty Years of the Rank Organisation, Its Films and Its Stars, Columbus Books, 1987

Last of a Kind: The Sinking of Lew Grade (with Dominic Prince), Quartet Books, 1987

Anthony Hopkins: Too Good to Waste, Columbus Books, 1989; 5th edition revised and updated, Virgin Books, 2004

Albert Finney: In Character, Robson Books, 1992; 3rd edition revised and updated, Endeavour Press (online only), 2015

Cinema's Strangest Moments, Robson Books, 2003

Television's Strangest Moments (with Ben Falk), Robson Books, 2005

Mr Hitchcock, Haus Publishing, 2007

The Musical Milkman Murder, Blake Publishing, 2012

Mr Midshipman VC: The Short, Accident-Prone Life of George Drewry, Gallipoli Hero, Pen & Sword, 2018

Contents

LIST OF FIGURES	*page* viii
SERIES EDITORS' FOREWORD	x
ACKNOWLEDGEMENTS	xi
Introduction	1
1 **Cutting for Korda: 1932–35**	7
2 **Cutting for Korda: 1936–40**	19
3 **The forties: Enter Ealing, 1940–45**	35
4 **The forties: 1946–49**	59
5 **The fifties: 1950–54**	85
6 **The fifties: Exit Ealing, 1954–59**	124
7 **The sixties: 1960–64**	154
8 **The sixties: 1965–69**	185
9 **The seventies: Downsizing**	202
10 **The eighties: Ealing regained**	217
APPENDIX 1: **An attitude to direction**	240
APPENDIX 2: **Memories of a mentor**	247
FILMOGRAPHY	251
SELECTED BIBLIOGRAPHY	261
INDEX	264

Figures

Frontispiece: Crichton in profile (credit: David Crichton)		xiv
1.1	Denham Film Studios (credit: Batsford/Patricia Warren)	14
2.1	Ealing Studios (credit: Batsford/Patricia Warren)	32
3.1	David Farrar (left) and Ralph Michael in *For Those in Peril* (credit: Studiocanal)	44
3.2	Crichton (left) with T.E.B. Clarke (credit: Studiocanal)	45
3.3	Crichton (left) with Douglas Slocombe (credit: Studiocanal)	47
3.4	Bill Blewitt and May Hallatt (centre) in *Painted Boats* (credit: Studiocanal)	50
3.5	Basil Radford (left) and Naunton Wayne in *Dead of Night* (credit: Studiocanal)	55
4.1	Harry Fowler (centre) with Joan Dowling (left), Douglas Barr and Stanley Escane in *Hue and Cry* (credit: Studiocanal)	62
4.2	Simone Signoret and Jack Warner in *Against the Wind* (credit: Studiocanal)	69
4.3	Robert Beatty (left) with Crichton on the set of *Another Shore* (credit: Studiocanal)	76
5.1	(Left to right) Jane Hylton, Petula Clark, Diana Dors and Natasha Parry in *Dance Hall* (credit: Studiocanal)	87
5.2	Pendlebury (Stanley Holloway) and Holland (Alec Guinness) embrace in *The Lavender Hill Mob* (credit: Studiocanal)	95
5.3	Dirk Bogarde and Jon Whiteley in *Hunted* (credit: Moviestore Collection/Alamy Stock Photo)	103
5.4	Godfrey Tearle and George Relph in *The Titfield Thunderbolt* (credit: Studiocanal)	111
5.5	Flanked by Michael Truman (left) and Crichton (right), Sir Michael Balcon (centre) visits the set of *The Titfield Thunderbolt* (credit: Studiocanal)	113

5.6 Crichton (centre) flanked by Herbert Lom and David
     Niven on the set of *The Love Lottery* (credit: Studiocanal)   117
6.1 Yvonne Mitchell and Michel Ray in *The Divided Heart*
     (credit: Studiocanal)   128
6.2 Jack Hawkins in *The Man in the Sky* (credit: Studiocanal)   138
6.3 Anne Heywood and Howard Keel in *Floods of Fear*
     (credit: Christopher Weedman)   150
7.1 Maurice Reyna as *The Boy Who Stole a Million*
     (credit: Maurice Reyna)   167
7.2 Crichton (rear) with camera crew, including director
     of photography Douglas Slocombe (second left),
     camera operator Chic Waterson (front centre)
     and focus puller Robin Vidgeon (front right),
     track Pamela Franklin on *The Third Secret*
     (credit: 20th Century Fox/powerhousefilms.co.uk)   175
7.3 Crichton relaxes on *The Third Secret* (credit: 20th
     Century Fox/powerhousefilms.co.uk)   177
8.1 Tom Bell and Judi Dench in *He Who Rides a Tiger*
     (credit: Moviestore Collection/Alamy Stock Photo)   189
9.1 Crichton with director of photography Peter Middleton
     (left) on a Video Arts shoot (credit: Video Arts)   215
10.1 Crichton and John Cleese on the set of *A Fish
     Called Wanda* (© MGM/courtesy Everett Collection)   218
10.2 Kevin Kline menaces Michael Palin in *A Fish
     Called Wanda* (© MGM/courtesy Everett Collection)   233

Series editors' foreword

The aim of this series is to present in lively, authoritative volumes a guide to those film-makers who have made British cinema a rewarding but still under-researched branch of world cinema. The intention is to provide books that are up to date in terms of information and critical approach, but not bound to any one theoretical methodology. Though all books in the series will have certain elements in common – comprehensive filmographies, annotated bibliographies, appropriate illustration – the actual critical tools employed will be the responsibility of the individual authors.

Nevertheless, an important recurring element will be a concern for how the *oeuvre* of each film-maker does or does not fit certain critical and industrial contexts, as well as for the wider social contexts that helped to shape not just that particular film-maker but the course of British cinema at large.

Although the series is director-orientated, the editors believe that reference to a variety of stances and contexts is more likely to reconceptualise and reappraise the phenomenon of British cinema as a complex, shifting field of production. All the texts in the series will engage in detailed discussion of major works of the film-makers involved, but they all consider as well the importance of other key collaborators, of studio organisation, of audience reception, of recurring themes and structures: all those other aspects that go towards the construction of a national cinema.

The series explores and charts a field that is more than ripe for serious excavation. The acknowledged leaders of the field will be reappraised; just as important, though, will be the bringing to light of those who have not so far received any serious attention. They are all part of the very rich texture of British cinema, and it will be the work of this series to give them all their due.

Acknowledgements

I am particularly grateful for the support, encouragement and active assistance of many distinguished contemporary chroniclers of British cinema, and Ealing Studios in particular, including Professors Charles Barr, Robert Murphy, Andrew Spicer and John Wyver, but especially Professor Neil Sinyard and Dr Brian McFarlane who together first championed this project. When I finally began to put finger to keyboard, I would recall Steven Spielberg who once wrote, 'we steal from the same people, providing of course they are the *best* people'.

Researching and writing a biography before and during the time of COVID-19 about a man who died more than twenty years ago on the cusp of ninety years of age required in many cases impressive feats of memory, so many thanks to the following, who worked with Charles Crichton front and back of camera, for their recall: Steve Abbott, Steven Webb, Jonathan Benson (1939–2020), Andrew Birkin, Christian 'Kits' Browning, Michel Ray de Carvalho, Petula Clark, John Cleese, Gregory Dark, Dame Judi Dench, Simon Hume, Paul Knight (1944–2020), Robert McKee, Peter Middleton, Sir Michael Palin (and for his kind permission to quote from two volumes of his diaries, *Halfway to Hollywood, 1980–88* and *Travelling to Work, 1988–98*), Miguel Pereira, Maurice Reyna, Edina Ronay, Martin Stephens, Linda Thorson, Maggie Tree, Robin and Angela Vidgeon, and Dr Jon Whiteley (1945–2020).

For their help with research and access: Jeff Billington, Paul Brown Constable, Drummond Challis, Mike Dick, Dr Ben Falk, Alan Lowne, C.J. Kuhl and Said Mosteshar, Muirne Mathieson; Massimo Moretti of Studiocanal for the use of Ealing Studios material (permission for the use of other photographs was sought and obtained where possible); Roger Moston; Storm Patterson, special collections co-ordinator, British Film Institute (BFI) Reuben Library; Tilly (Tremayne) Peacock, Professor Duncan Petrie, David (Lord) Puttnam; Caitlin Quinlan, London Film School; Patricia Warren; and Dr Christopher Weedman.

For the following extra research 'tools': *Tuesday Documentary: Ealing Comedies*, BBC, 1970; *Omnibus: Made in Ealing*, BBC, 1986; British Library and British Newspaper Archive; Times Digital Archive; Internet Archive Digital Library; iMDB.co.uk; Talking Pictures TV; Brian McFarlane's towering *An Autobiography of British Cinema*; and most crucially of all, Crichton's interview with Sidney Cole and Alan Lawson on 14 December 1988, for the remarkable, still ongoing, *British Entertainment History Project* (historyproject.org.uk). The extensive extracts I have used were, on occasion, subject to (I hope) sensitive amendments on spelling, punctuation and syntax for greater ease of reading.

Final thanks must be reserved for my regular library research assistant, Richard Tedham; Matthew Frost and Jen Mellor at Manchester University Press; at Newgen Publishing, project manager Charlie Clark and copy editor Kelly Derrick; my agent Jane Judd for her advice and friendship across thirty years; and David and Jamie Crichton, who also kindly allowed me to reproduce 'An Attitude to Direction' as well as use some private family correspondence dating from 1929 that helped put some extra flesh on the bones.

Little Marlow, 2021

Frontispiece: Crichton in profile

Introduction

Beyond respectable, albeit mostly respectful, entries in various film reference books, Charles Crichton, despite being one of Ealing Studios' most prolific and successful directors, has tended to be regarded more as a footnote than at the forefront of British cinema in the forties and fifties. If he had not, so belatedly, achieved such a startling success aged seventy-eight with *A Fish Called Wanda* in the eighties, one fears he may well have been ignored altogether by some serious film historians. But not even that late flowering has been enough to convince, say, the venerable David Thomson who, after finding space for other Ealing alumni such as Robert Hamer, Alexander Mackendrick, Cavalcanti and Basil Dearden, still considers Crichton unworthy of mention after nearly forty years and six weighty editions of his influential *New Biographical Dictionary of Film*.

Happily, *The Encyclopedia of British Film* does try to restore the balance, citing Crichton as 'the quintessential Ealing director, the man who made the films most affectionately associated in the public mind with the studio, combining a whimsical imagination with a flair for surface realism ... His was a gentle talent but at its best his work also exhibited an underlying structural shrewdness and a sharp observer's eye.'[1] Philip Kemp in *Directors in British and Irish Cinema* is also happy to give credit where it is due, even pausing to praise some of the film-maker's less well-known titles among his baker's dozen for Ealing, as well as noting his editing skills 'letting a scene tell its story with terse economy but no loss of lucidity'.[2]

Yet, for the most part, Crichton still remains for many just a directorial bit player, a journeyman at the creative end of British cinema, almost as if helping to craft a few Ealing comedies, perhaps most notably *Hue and Cry* and *The Lavender Hill Mob*, on the one hand and, more than thirty years later, keeping an Anglo-American cast on track in *A Fish Called Wanda*, a sort of Ealing-style reboot, on the other, somehow comprised the sum total of his cinematic contribution. So perhaps the problem, as some might still see it, is that Crichton was less an artist, rather more just an effective, collaborative, craftsman without a describable style or vision, simply a contributor to a canon rather than one of its defining lights. But why should 'craftsman' and 'artist' be mutually exclusive anyway? For Crichton, however, I would instead like to offer a phrase, 'gifted workhorse', coined by my favourite film critic, the late Roger Ebert, when he once described the great Michael Curtiz.

I will also argue that not only is Crichton's own sixty-year career ripe for an in-depth review and reassessment in its own versatile right, but that, in its entirety, it serves as an almost perfect barometer for the vagaries of British cinema's 'climate' across almost seven decades following fast on the advent of talkies in this country.

Crichton's film 'school' was Denham Film Studios where, under a foreign-born mogul, Alexander Korda, domestic movie-making grew up and first attained international recognition; his postgraduate 'academy' was Ealing Studios, soon to become firmly in the vanguard of indigenous independent production as cinemagoing boomed during, and immediately after, the war years. Then, as American film finance began to flee the UK industry while, at the same time, 'youth' became the creative prerequisite, Crichton, like so many others of an age, found some solace, first, in independent production, then in filmed television. Eventually, having, as a working director, long outlasted all his contemporaries, Crichton returned triumphantly to the big screen for a home-grown comedy, funded – naturally – by Hollywood.

I met Crichton for the first and only time after I had been commissioned by the *Guardian* to write an article about *A Fish Called Wanda* when it was filming court scenes in Oxford. Thirty-something years later, my precise recollection of the occasion would probably have remained quite hazy if it had not been for vivid reminders of that set visit and, in particular, my close encounter with Crichton, conjured up again during separate interviews with John Cleese and Sir Michael Palin in the course of researching this book.

Cleese explained how it seemed that after just three days on the set directing *Wanda*, it was as if Crichton had somehow 'shed seven years. He just loved directing'.[3] Suddenly I could recall Crichton's almost palpably youthful enthusiasm for the job in hand, which was complemented by, in my mind's eye, Palin's colourfully accurate physical description of the man himself, who had some years earlier suffered a stroke and since been plagued by a bad back. Said Palin: 'He walked with a stick, smoked a pipe and spoke as if he had a mouthful of something he couldn't quite swallow, firing his words out preceded by a certain juggling of the jaw.'[4]

Cleese had, of course, been very much responsible for Crichton's renaissance having, more by good luck than judgement, first collaborated, albeit abortively, with him, at the back end of the sixties. Then, when, at the height of Python's success, Cleese co-founded Video Arts in the early seventies, he eventually made sure that Crichton, now in a long and apparently endless dry patch between features, came on board to direct some of Video Arts' most successful corporate and training films. These along with his prolific TV work through the seventies and early eighties, became a sort of extra showreel for Crichton ahead of what would then, thanks to Cleese's continuing support and encouragement, turn out to be the box office phenomenon that was *Wanda*.

But for all *Wanda*'s remarkable success, Crichton's reputation still, for most people, principally revolves around his long involvement years earlier with Ealing Studios and, in particular, the brand that became known as 'Ealing comedy'. 'Our theory of comedy – if we had one,' Sir Michael Balcon wrote in his memoirs, 'was ludicrously simple. We took a character – or group of characters – and let him or them run up against an apparently insoluble problem, with the audience hoping that a way out would be found, which it usually was. The comedy lay in how the characters did get around their problem.'[5]

If that definition then suggests a degree of homogeneity with the comic results, or that somehow its principal practitioners were creatively cut from exactly the same cloth, nothing could be further from the truth. Ealing's four best comedies – *Kind Hearts and Coronets*, *The Lavender Hill Mob*, *The Man in the White Suit* and *The Ladykillers* (five, if you also count *Hue and Cry*, which actually spawned the term 'Ealing comedy'), while adhering loosely to Balcon's comic criteria could not be more different in their content and execution.

While it may be convenient to ascribe a group identity to Ealing's creatives beyond the general similarity in age and experience, it is, certainly as far as Crichton was concerned, misleading, as he told *Sight & Sound* magazine in 1951 during a round-table discussion among a number of the film-makers: 'I don't accept the premise of this discussion implying that all our pictures have the same "signature tune". Bob's [Hamer] personal style is as different from mine as Charles Frend's from Basil's [Dearden]. We choose different kinds of subjects and treat them in a completely different way.'[6]

Two of Crichton's best if, generally, long-forgotten Ealing films were most definitely not comedies, *Against the Wind* and *The Divided Heart* – actually, best films, period – both had a World War II background. Also both featured, unusually for Ealing fare, very strong female roles. Although lighter in tone but still spiced with some realism is his *Dance*

Hall, set post-war and, arguably, the studio's most significant addition to the distaff stakes.

Crichton's versatility clearly extended way beyond just 'Ealing comedy' and any subsequent forays into humour and satire (*Law and Disorder, The Battle of the Sexes*, etc). Starting with *Hunted* in 1952, about a killer on the run, followed by *Floods of Fear, The Third Secret* and *He Who Rides a Tiger*, Crichton also established an extremely significant niche in Brit 'film noir', deliciously redolent in all those titles. But they, along with his later contribution to hours and hours of popular filmed television, including *Danger Man, The Avengers, The Adventures of Black Beauty* and *Space: 1999*, tend to remain, for the most part, unacknowledged.

'Wirral-born movie legend dies', the *Liverpool Echo*, the family's 'local' paper, recorded hyperbolically on 15 September 1999, the day after Crichton died in London aged eighty-nine. But beyond newspaper headlines, a rash of generous obituaries, and my own short encounter, it has been quite tough to try and nail down the man himself behind such prolific credits in film and television. Even the two long and often fascinating interviews he gave post-*Wanda* to the *British Entertainment History Project* (then known as the *BECTU Project*) and to Dr Brian McFarlane for his *Autobiography of British Cinema* tended to be long on modesty yet a little short on process.

The testimony from surviving colleagues and collaborators dating back from between thirty to all of seventy years has inevitably been sketchy at times. It was therefore with some excitement that, thanks to Crichton's surviving family, I suddenly found myself in possession of two invaluable documents. The first, from the turn of the sixties, was a speech he gave to students in Liverpool about film-making in general, and *The Lavender Hill Mob* in particular; the second, dated a decade later, appears self-explanatory, 'An Attitude to Direction', and reveals more about his modus operandi than any interview.

'There is no room for egotism in cinema,' he writes.

> The more selfless a director may be, the more forcefully will his personality emerge on the screen. The novice director is sometimes confused by his reverence for the *cinema d'auteur* and feels that it implies a need to exercise a tyrannical control over his colleagues.
>
> But I take it that it that *cinema d'auteur* is a term used to describe a film dominated by the creative vision of one personality in contradistinction to the slick machine-made picture, which used to come from the Hollywood factory.
>
> This vision is not impressed upon the film by the use of strong-arm methods. Film is a gregarious medium and the director should be sensitive to the artistry of others and create for them a sense of freedom

so that their talents can be fully expressed within the framework of his conception of the whole.

The whole essay is included at the end of this book in Appendix 1, outlining a no-nonsense approach to film-making, which would prove so helpful to aspiring directors like Argentina's Miguel Pereira who benefited from Crichton's expertise when the latter taught classes at the London International Film School (later London Film School) around the turn of the eighties. Pereira, who would go on to become an award-winning film-maker in his own right, recalls the Crichton 'touch' in Appendix 2.

Other clues to Crichton's preferred career path and mindset were contained in a short but informative eulogy written at the time of his death by his younger brother, Patrick. The child of parents both sharing Scots heritage, his mother Hester was the niece of a one-time president of the Royal Scottish Academy. This, suggested Patrick, helped his brother 'inherit the ability to see in pictures.' When the family went on holiday it was often to Ballachulish, set spectacularly in the Highlands, where Crichton's 'pictorial ability developed fast by taking photographs which were memorable'.[7]

At university, 'Charles became more and more interested in the cinema as an art form; his fascination with comedy owed much to the films of René Clair, but he was also drawn by the documentaries of Cavalcanti and John Grierson.' Continued Patrick: 'Charles regarded comedy seriously; he would say, "Comedy is creation; tragedy is all too easy, it is but a reflection of life." When he did direct films of serious content he was deeply involved emotionally, as with *The Divided Heart*. But in some ways he despised himself for showing that emotion; perhaps it was all part of his distaste of pomposity.'

The late Alexander Walker, one of Britain's best and acutest post-war film commentators, who had followed Crichton's career from the critic's own journalistic origins in Birmingham, provided a typically idiosyncratic epitaph, when he wrote: 'Crichton himself was a bit of a rebel against respectability ... but always within limits, dear boy, nothing to smash the furniture.'[8]

Robert McKee, the American screenwriting 'guru', whose Story Seminars have attracted a legion of film-makers for well over thirty-five years, first met Crichton in 1992 when they were invited to work together on an ultimately abortive film project. McKee had, coincidentally, been using *A Fish Called Wanda* as his ultimate comedy teaching tool ever since first seeing it four year earlier and revelling in the way 'it demonstrated,' he told me, 'every single brilliant principle of comic execution'.[9]

McKee said: 'Because he began as an editor, he was a genius *of precision*. In terms of comedy he understood the underlying dynamics of a laugh, plus the integrity of the characters. He was always asking, is this true, is this honest? Can I believe this? With comic exaggeration, of course. From the bottom up, he understood the personal and social tensions of great comedy, and he had that precise execution of jokes.'[10]

I cannot resist ending by reproducing in full the contents of a handwritten letter sent by Crichton to Dr Brian McFarlane who, a year earlier, in 1992, had interviewed the film-maker in London for his book, which was still some years away from publication. Based in Australia, Dr McFarlane had mailed Crichton his interview comprising a short introduction followed by a Q & A format.

> Dear Dr McFarlane,
> Many thanks for sending me the material about ME, which you wish to use in your forthcoming book.
> I am returning the first two pages with minor corrections, which I think should be made. I am, of course, flattered by your assessment of my work though I think you are a wee bit harsh about *The Titfield Thunderbolt* – I have just heard from a chap who has seen it 124 times!!! (The poor railway buff)
> I do not like those pages, which deal with our meeting. The edited version of the interview may make sense to you and me but I think not to the reader.
> I would eliminate them but understand you do not wish to reduce your word count and so I will try hard to send you suggested amendments in time for your February deadline. Unfortunately I have just had a seriously unpleasant operation and my head is full of porridge.
> Very best wishes for the success of your book.
>
> Yours sincerely,
> Charles Crichton
> (PS Have not included your page 2 as it seems okay)

Even at eighty-three, ever the editor.

Notes

1 Brian McFarlane (ed.), *The Encyclopedia of British Film* (Methuen, 2003), p. 169.
2 Philip Kemp, 'Charles Crichton' in Robert Murphy (ed.) *Directors of British and Irish Cinema: A Reference Companion* (BFI, 2006), p. 127.
3 Interview with the author, 14 August 2019.
4 Interview with the author, 11 February 2020.
5 Michael Balcon, *A Lifetime of Films* (Hutchinson, 1969), p. 158.
6 *Sight & Sound*, studio supplement, Spring 1951, p. 9.
7 Interviews with David Crichton throughout 2019 and 2020.
8 *Evening Standard*, 22 September 1999.
9 Interview with the author, 20 November 2019.
10 *Ibid*.

Cutting for Korda: 1932–35

On 17 March 1936, following a severe winter, and just weeks before Alexander Korda's extravagantly oversized new studio complex at Denham was officially due to open, fire 'tore through two of the newly erected sound stages, destroying the roofs and sound-proofing'.[1] Anything between ten and fifteen fire brigades from all over Buckinghamshire, depending on which breathless report you believed – including dramatic aerial newsreel footage with its barked narration – attended the spectacular blaze that had started in the early hours of that Tuesday morning, eventually causing nearly £50,000 worth of damage, another severe financial blow – over £3m in today's terms – to Korda's already cash-stretched film empire.

Writing to his mother a month later, on 19 April, Crichton noted:

> The studio is quiet. They are shooting in it for the first time tomorrow – some retakes of the 'Miracle Man' [HG Wells's *The Man Who Could Work Miracles*]. Unfortunately they have not yet tried out the lighting apparatus and everybody is terrified we may have a fire again. So besides the ordinary call for the unit and actors, there is a call for all the local fire brigades. It would be a pity for Korda and Co. to be roasted alive.

Whether it was the spectre of fire or, more likely, the imminent, increasingly nightmarish prospect of editing over fifty-five hours of location footage from India on Robert Flaherty's much-vaunted new feature project, *Elephant Boy* (based on Kipling's original story, *Toomai of the Elephants*), Crichton was to be found musing, rather too world-wearily for a twenty-five-year-old, on the meaning of life – his in particular – earlier in that same letter to his mother:

> Would you kindly explain to me 1. Why are there so many good things to do? 2. Why there is so little time to do them in? 3. Why it is necessary to work at fixed hours? Work is alright only one should just do it when one feels like it. It seems a shame to waste one's life inside when one could be doing all sorts of peculiar things in all sorts of corners of the world.

In his fifth year of cutting for Korda, a claustrophobic occupation if ever there was one, Crichton, still months away from marriage later that same year, might well have been pining for the great outdoors of Canada where a few years earlier, before going to university, he had spent some months gold prospecting near St Felicien in the Province of Quebec. He wrote home at the time: 'It is cold, it rains hard and we are working at the bottom of a bottomless pit which is full of mud ... We have had to timber the sides to prevent them falling in. Every now and then somebody cries despairingly as he sinks beneath the mud, but always the relentless work in search of gold goes on.' On reflection, his youthful observations seem now perfectly to serve as a metaphor for his future work as a film editor then later as a director.

Born on 6 August 1910, in Wallasey, just across the river from Liverpool, and less than a mile from the Irish Sea, Crichton was the second of four children (there were also twins who died tragically young) to John Douglas Crichton, known as 'J.D.', who, like his wife Hester, was of Scottish stock. Crichton senior, an unconventional man who often jauntily sported a black Basque beret rather than the traditional bowler on his way into the city, where he worked in shipping middle management, went off to war in 1914, fell down a hole and was wounded.

Crichton first attended a neighbourhood prep school within spitting distance of the Cheshire shore where he and his friends excitedly spotted the first camouflage ship ever seen in the Mersey, as well as scarred troops returning from the disastrous Zeebrugge Raid six months before the Armistice in 1918. He was then sent south to board at a boys' prep school, St Piran's, outside Maidenhead, where he was an exact contemporary of F.R. 'Freddie' Brown, who became an England Test cricketer. St Piran's, which two of his grandsons would attend some seventy years later, had a fine reputation despite, it is said, the headmaster having a penchant for whisky, not to mention an abiding passion for the matron with whom he eventually ran away to open a hotel in Mousehole, Cornwall.

After public school at Oundle in Leicestershire – where fellow pupils included Peter Scott, Harry Llewellyn, John Whitworth, Michael Ashby and Kenneth Robinson, later, respectively, naturalist, show jumper, ace pilot, neurologist and Labour cabinet minister – then New College, Oxford, reading modern history, Crichton began to ponder various careers including journalism. He might well have proved a harsh theatre critic judging by an excerpt from one of a number of student letters to his mother in 1929 in which he criticised some of the performers and even a famed Russian playwright of a farce about matrimony and matchmaking: 'We went to the Playhouse on Friday to see the Cambridge

Festival Co perform "Marraige" [sic] by Gogol. It was rather disappointing, the acting was very badly overdone, only two actors one of whom was Robert Donat were any good. The costumes were hectic. The plot was poor. I understand that the Oxford Players are infinitely superior.' Little could he have known then that within a couple of years he would find himself working in much closer proximity to the same Donat, then an emerging British stage actor, five years Crichton's senior, who was about to make his screen debut for Alexander Korda. A regular filmgoer as silent cinema began to be overtaken by the talkies, mostly 'terrible, awful films to which I used to drag my mother,'[2] said Crichton. There were shining exceptions to the mediocrity, notably, he would later recall, two of René Clair's early masterpieces, the musical comedies, *Sous les toits de Paris* (1930), followed a year later while he was still up at Oxford, by *Le Million* (1931).

Asked years on what films or film-makers had influenced him, he would regularly cite Clair and 'the soufflé-like quality' of those two particular titles.

He was also an enthusiastic member of the university's film club, and it is also likely he regularly attended screenings of the Film Society, which had been established in 1925 with among its founder members, another Oxford man, Anthony 'Puffin' Asquith, whose own distinguished screen career began in earnest shortly before Crichton's.

The Film Society's brief was 'to encourage "the production of really artistic films" by showing those which the trade deemed un-commercial or which the censor refused'.[3]

Considering retrospectively some of Crichton's own credits, which would often embrace a gritty, drama-documentary feel, it is fascinating to speculate whether he might have been present at, say, one of the Society's most famous, silent, double bills, in 1929, at the New Gallery cinema in Regent Street: Eisenstein's epic *Battleship Potemkin* (1925) paired with John Grierson's brand new *Drifters*, an influential documentary about North Sea herring fishermen. The great Russian director also lectured at the same event.

If cinemagoing during, arguably, the medium's most significant and thrilling transition, was the initial spark, then the fire seems properly to have been lit in the young man following a fateful confrontation when Korda and Co. came to Oxford. Thoughts of any other possible career path were now swiftly swept aside as Crichton 'suddenly thought, to hell with it, all I'm interested in is films'.[4] Gone were any doubts expressed mildly in another student letter to his mother: 'I am not so sure it is going to be worth my while studying the flicks after all. It is rather a crowded business. I was talking to an undergrad yesterday who told me he had been to every flick in Oxford this week – there are five. I understand the night he didn't go was Nov. 5th when more was happening outside than in.' After film-making in his native Hungary beginning way back in 1914, followed by, variously, Vienna, Berlin, Hollywood and Paris, Alexander Korda, born Sandor Laszlo Kellner, and his much-travelled cinematic troupe, principally fellow expatriates like his brothers, Zoltan and Vincent, as well as scenarist Lajos Biro, finally fetched up in England at the turn of the 1930s.

'If Korda had not come to England, the British cinema of the thirties,' noted Karol Kulik, one of his biographers, 'might well have taken a different course. For the rest of his career, Korda brought ambition, recognition, imagination and glamour to an industry that needed his optimism and his showman's talent.'[5]

The essential Englishness of Korda's new British-based adventure would be epitomised in the screen logo he dreamed up for his company – Big Ben, sited at the very heart of parliamentary democracy. But London Film Productions' first great success, *The Private Life of Henry VIII*, was still more than eighteen months away as 'the foundations of British hopes for waging a successful campaign against Hollywood's domination of world markets',[6] were initiated by the much-travelled would-be mogul then still at the comparatively young age of thirty-eight.

As plans for *Henry VIII* gestated slowly, London Films dived headlong into production with a series of films, so-called 'quota quickies', in a deal with Paramount. The first of these was *Men of Tomorrow*, about a group of Oxford undergraduates and their aftermath, played by, among others, Emlyn Williams, Merle Oberon – who would become the second Mrs Korda in 1939 – and the aforementioned Robert Donat. Korda signed up the forty-two-year-old German actress-turned-director Leontine Sagan, then a very rare woman in an almost wholly male-dominated profession, probably because of her film, *Maedchen in Uniform*, set in an all-girls boarding school, which with its hothouse blend of homoeroticism and brutality had caused quite a stir on release in 1931.

As Sagan was shooting locations on *Men of Tomorrow* in Oxford, Crichton, still 'up', decided to try and get some useful advice from her about how to pursue his now chosen profession. 'She was very unhelpful,' he recalled. 'She said I could be an extra if I liked but I wouldn't get any pay.'[7] No use to Crichton as he explained to Sagan he had to earn a living, 'but there was also this funny chap with his hat pulled over his eyes, a Hungarian, who turned out to be Zoli. Eventually he asked what did I want, Sagan explained, so he gave me a job.'[8] The rather mysterious reason he gave Crichton a job, 'Zoli' told him later, was 'because you don't wear Oxford bags and you'd got a big hole in your shoes'.⁹

'Zoli' was, of course, none other than Zoltan Korda, two years younger than Alex, and credited as co-director of the film, primarily, it seems, to keep a very tight rein on any excesses Sagan, a complete newcomer to English-language cinema, might have contemplated in her execution of what was after all just a 'quota quickie', by its very definition to be made at maximum speed and at minimum cost to satisfy the requirements of the 1927 Cinematograph Films Act.

The exact chronology after that of Crichton's actual debut in the industry is rather murkier. The job was, yes, in the cutting room, but, principally it seems, involved 'carrying tea to Mr Young, who was their [Korda's] editor'.¹⁰ Oregon-born Harold Young had first joined Korda during the Hollywood phase of the travelling film circus and continued to work on and off for him through Paris before becoming in-house as supervising editor at newly launched London Films.

Crichton's tea-carrying after Oxford was initially undertaken at Wembley Studios where London Films was embarked on its inaugural production, *Wedding Rehearsal*, set among the upper crust, a faintly Wodehousian comedy about 'a bachelor who defies his mother's matrimonial plans for him by marrying off the girls she proposes to his friends'.¹¹ The cast included Roland Young along with ingénues Wendy Barrie, Joan Gardner and Merle Oberon as a bevy of eligible beauties. Seventy-two-year-old Lady Tree, as the Countess of Stokeshire, lent the credits an authentically aristocratic twang.

Although consigned solely to tea duties at the outset, Crichton was officially part of the cutting room staff. 'They didn't like me at first because I'd been put in by Zoli without consultation. For the first three weeks, from nine in the morning to nine at night, I was given nothing to do. Then Hal [Young] said, "Charlie, we didn't want you here, but as you've stood there for three weeks doing nothing, now we're really going to give you a job."'¹² That job was 'rolling up cuts'¹³ – collecting bits of edited material. A start but not exactly creative.

When *Men of Tomorrow* returned from shooting exteriors in Oxford, Crichton moved from Wembley to the British & Dominions (B & D) sound stages at Elstree where Sagan continued filming, but not without problems especially in the latter stages of production.

Although she was finally credited as editor, and indeed fashioned one cut herself, the film would be extensively re-edited by others including, he later claimed, an uncredited Crichton who listed the title as his first in a flurry for Korda's company over the next eight years. Wrote Karol Kulik: 'Sagan complained that this re-editing ruined the rhythmic balance of the editing and shifted the emphasis of the story. This is the first of several instances where Korda was criticized for damaging the work of other directors in his employ.'[14]

Having cut his teeth, among other things, on Korda's first Quota film, Crichton was next involved as an uncredited assistant on *Cash*, the last of the five, which also marked Zoltan Korda's solo directing debut. This fast-moving farce, reuniting Wendy Barrie and Robert Donat, starred the ever-lovable Edmund Gwenn, as a debt-ridden schemer living way beyond his means. As Crichton was fully occupied assisting the editing of both *Cash* – whose plot was about to presage an imminent reality as 1933 dawned – and, simultaneously, the rather more ambitious Paris-based *The Girl From Maxim's*, like *Wedding Rehearsal*, directed by Alex – he may not have been wholly aware of now gathering clouds over the very future of London Films following a falling out with Michael Balcon's Gaumont-British, one of Korda's key financial backers.

Korda's money troubles also happened to coincide with a bad flu epidemic, which required *Cash* – along with *Counsel's Opinion*, another of the 'Quota' quintet – to halt filming for several days when some cast and crew fell ill. Crichton recalled later, 'there were one or two very awkward moments when we went home unpaid'.[15] Noted Charles Drazin, another of Korda's biographers: 'Alex struggled on, looking for new backers and continuing to pay his employees with IOUs and charm instead of cash. The trick, he learned, was always to smile and to pretend everything was all right. *Sursum corda.* Only confidence could keep the enterprise moving, and so long as it was moving there was always the hope that help might be found.'[16]

That hope was to be fulfilled in spades along with the overall fortunes of London Films towards the end of that same, fateful, year when, after a dicey start, Korda's first magnum opus, *The Private Life of Henry VIII*, was eventually launched in October 1933, on, most importantly, delighted audiences *both* sides of the Atlantic.

The fact that *Henry VIII* ever made it to the screen in the first place was in itself a minor miracle. With Gaumont-British out of the picture and the subject matter regarded as unfashionable, it finally required a significant slab of Hollywood money – courtesy of United Artists – to ignite the project on which, once again, Crichton worked uncredited with senior editors Stephen Harrison and Harold Young.

Part of a complicated deal required Korda to film at Elstree's B & D studios which, due to inadequate financing, necessitated less than robust sets, designed ingeniously if economically, by Vincent Korda, youngest of the film-making siblings. According to Karol Kulik: 'The cast and film crew had faith in [Alex] Korda and what he was trying to do, and many of them agreed to share the risks with Korda, either going without or reducing their salaries and waiting until the film was released to receive proper compensation."[17]

While some of the constructed interiors might have been flimsy, they, along with some authentic locations like Hampton Court and a beautiful fourteenth-century manor house at Long Crendon in Buckinghamshire, were quite literally glossed over thanks to exquisite lighting by imported French cinematographer, Georges Périnal – 'with a face like a weary saint', as memorably described by Michael Powell – continuing his collaboration from Paris with Korda on *The Girl From Maxim's*.

For Crichton it must also have been some kind of dream come true to be handling material photographed by the magician behind those two René Clair films, which would remain such an influence on his own film-making ambitions. Clair himself would come almost within reach of Crichton just a year or so later when the French master directed *The Ghost Goes West* (1935) for Korda.

If United Artists could be regarded as a conventional 'patron' of the *Henry* project, Korda's other, altogether less orthodox, indeed last-minute, investors were Ludovico Toeplitz de Grand Ry, outsize and heavily bearded – nicknamed 'Henry IX' – and his Italian banker father, Giuseppe, as the budget doubled to over £93,000 (more than £4m in today's money).

Korda would claim that the film earned the equivalent of nearly £25m on its first run; the truth is probably nearer half that total. Enough, though, to set London Films up for a future slate of ambitious film-making thanks to an ongoing United Artists distribution deal, and, thanks to the intervention of a brand new, if unlikely, source of funding in the shape of the Prudential Assurance Company, Korda's own, brand-new, studios at Denham (Figure 1.1).

Although most of the resulting critical attention for *Henry VIII* was inevitably on Charles Laughton and his hugely enjoyable, international star-making turn as the rambunctious monarch, the production itself won deserved praise, especially in the States: 'A remarkably well-produced film, both in the matter of direction and in the settings and in the selection of scenes', purred Mordaunt Hall in the *New York Times*.[18] The trade paper *Variety*, always a useful barometer for box office potential, also offered an unequivocal thumbs-up.

In its own backyard, the reviews mostly gushed, too. After, unsurprisingly, paying generous tribute to Laughton, its native son, the *Yorkshire Evening Post* tried to express what became a sort of recurring jingoistic theme in many of the domestic reviews: the sense that *Henry VIII* was not just an instant home-grown classic but also, thanks to Korda,

Figure 1.1 Denham Film Studios

somehow signalled the sudden rebirth of the entire British film industry as a genuine global player: 'The British film industry owes him [Korda] a debt of gratitude which I hope will not be forgotten.'

The following March, in the Fiesta Room of the Ambassador Hotel, the sixth annual Academy Awards named Laughton best actor, the first time a performer in a British-made film had been an Oscar winner. The film itself was also one of the ten nominees for the year's outstanding production. Ironically, the winner, up against *Henry VIII* along with more traditional American fare such as *I Am A Fugitive From a Chain Gang*, *42nd Street* and *Little Women*, turned out to be another, albeit more contemporary, mirror of England – Noel Coward's *Cavalcade*, a sprawling, episodic, account of society between 1899 and 1933 with British actors – made entirely at the Fox studios in Hollywood.

Though Korda's corporate fortunes would continue as ever to fluctuate dramatically from film to film over the next five years or so, Crichton's own immediate future now seemed secure as his editing stock rose in the London Films 'family'. Crichton admitted, 'After *Henry VIII*, things began to expand very, very quickly and I was lucky because I was carried up on the tide, as it were.'[19]

Although Harold Young was Crichton's first boss in the Korda cutting rooms, it was his replacement after Young graduated, haltingly, to director on *The Scarlet Pimpernel* (1934) that Crichton would regularly recall as his 'mentor'.[20] William 'Bill' Hornbeck. Hornbeck was just fourteen when he entered the industry in New York as a film winder before joining Mack Sennett's Keystone Company where he worked for twelve years as chief editor on a mass of two-reel comedies. Hornbeck worked with Korda for six years before returning to his native Los Angeles after America entered World War II in 1941. He would go on to edit some of Hollywood's greatest movies including *It's a Wonderful Life*, *A Place in the Sun* – for which he won the Oscar – and *Shane*. In 1977, six years before he died aged eighty-two, he was 'voted by one hundred of his peers as the best his profession has ever produced'.[21]

Hornbeck, said Crichton, 'had a very direct approach to editing, which was that matching didn't matter. He couldn't be bothered with fitting. He said that you could cut from a man standing up to a man sitting down, or from a lady standing on her head to a lady sitting down; as long as the thought goes through, nobody will notice the match or anything of that nature.'[22] It was always more about continuity of the thought rather than of the action. Crichton added: 'The reason I became a director was because of what I learned from him. He knew how to tell a story; he taught me everything.'[23]

Crichton's first credits as a full-blown editor, albeit carefully supervised by Hornbeck and – it will also be become clear – with no little interference from Kordas various, were *Sanders of the River* (1935) and, jointly with Francis Lyon, *Things to Come* (1936), two films that in prospect at least perfectly demonstrated the company's admirable ambition, and about as far removed as one could possibly imagine from the kind of bland drawing room comedies that had been pretty much the indigenous industry's norm since the advent of the talkies.

As Crichton would later find when first confronted on *Elephant Boy* with hours of documentary-style footage garnered assiduously in exotic foreign climes, so it was also with *Sanders of the River*, an adaptation of Edgar Wallace's 1911 collection of short stories set in colonial West Africa. Wallace's first-hand experience of the 'Dark Continent' had been gained in Congo Free State when as a journalist he was investigating atrocities committed against the native population by Belgian interests.

Beginning filming just a year after Wallace had died in Hollywood while collaborating on *King Kong*, the screen version of *Sanders*, with the working title *Kongo Raid*, was part of Anglophile Korda's continuing plan – later would come films like *The Drum*, *The Four Feathers* and, of course, *Elephant Boy* – to extol the virtues of the British Empire, which, in the mid-thirties, was still very much in its pomp. For the film of *Sanders*, directed by Zoltan and designed by Vincent, Wallace's undefined corner of West Africa became, more specifically, Nigeria, and in order to try and make the action seem as authentic and believable as possible, Zoltan, together with two units, left in December 1933 for location shooting in Nigeria, Central and East Africa. Zoltan ran one based out of Lagos while a second, supervised by a game hunter, Herr Grosse, headed for Tanganyika. In addition, Ernst Udet, a former World War I German fighter ace, who boasted no fewer than sixty-two kills, was charged with obtaining dramatic aerial wildlife footage.

Many, many months later – location shooting unnecessarily extended because of poor communication between the competing units – the production finally returned to England. There was, explained Karol Kulik, 'enough material to make a dozen ethnographic films – hours and hours of film and soundtrack of native music and native dances – but the problem was how to make a feature film out of all this documentary material'.[24]

As if Crichton and supervisor Hornbeck's editing assignment wasn't already daunting enough, it was about to be seriously augmented as footage to fit a coherent storyline now had to be devised incorporating, with a combination of back projection and careful cutting, the best and most appropriate of the African material. Following a flurry of story conferences, a script was hastily cobbled together with contributions from Korda regular Lajos Biro and Jeffrey Dell, just starting out on a long career in the film industry. The tale is of the eponymous, all-powerful, district commissioner, locally deferred to as 'Lord Sandi' (Leslie Banks), who enlists the aid of a tribal chief, Bosambo, to help quell slave raids sponsored by wicked King Molofoba, who has also kidnapped Bosambo's new wife Lilongo.

From interiors at B & D, Elstree, then Worton Hall Studios at Isleworth, followed by carefully selected if unlikely corners of Home Counties countryside to a quiet tuck of the Thames near Shepperton, everything was done to try and recreate the Africa settings, and 'to populate the African villages, Negroes were imported from as far away as Cardiff and put in camps close to the studio'.[25]

What was likely to be the tone of the eventual film can be probably be gauged from an explanation offered by Vincent Korda's son, Michael, in *Charmed Lives*, his bestselling memoir about the family. Reflecting generally on his uncle's respective approach to the material, he noted:

> His [Alex's] earlier movies about Africa had been struggles between Zoli's own desire to show the reality of the Africans' lives and aspirations in the bondage of colonialism, and Alex's determination to make films that would present the empire to the British audience in a positive and patriotic light. Not that Alex was unaware of the black man's burden or

even unsympathetic to it; he simply felt that the white man's burden was more acceptable and commercial to Anglo-American audiences.[26]

Crichton may have been accorded the sole 'Editor' credit on the film but as, Karol Kulik, points out, 'the final product reveals the mixed and confused intentions of director and producer'.[27] Even by 1935 standards, the film must have been for many a difficult watch.

Today, despite some eye-catching African footage and clearly well-meaning performances by the distinguished principal cast on either side of the racial divide, not even some historical justification – the 'that's how it was' defence – can make up for the tone (here Alex truly trumped Zoli) of condescension and tired tropes that render much of the film not so much unwatchable as unbearable.

In Crichton's own, now rather battered, Souvenir Programme for the film's world premiere at the Leicester Square Theatre on 2 April 1935, there are all kinds of contemporary gems. 'Even the hair-raising thrills in "Sanders of the River" won't disturb your hair if you use ... Julysia Hair Cream', proclaims one of a flurry of advertisements. Jeffrey Dell contributes 'The Story of the Film', while Zoltan Korda writes revealingly about 'Filming in Africa'. Then in a couple of columns titled 'Interesting Facts about "Sander of the River"', we learn, for instance, that 'the 20,000 African Negroes who take part in this picture received most of their wages in the form of cartons of cigarettes,' and Paul Robeson wears a costume that 'cost less than five shillings'.

'I wonder what Paul Robeson thought of it?' enquired journalist Hannen Swaffer in his 'I Heard Yesterday' column about *Sanders* – headlined 'Just the Same Old Bunk' – for the *Daily Herald* on 26 April 1935. History famously relates that the film's most high-profile victim was undoubtedly its charismatic African American singing star scantily clad in leopard skin loincloth and draped in native bling as pliant Bosambo. Robeson, and his fellow transatlantic import, Nina Mae McKinney, as Lilongo (who, wrote Swaffer, 'looks like the product of a Harlem beauty parlour') were likely lured into service on the film after being beguiled by the documentary footage and Korda charm.

For Robeson in particular, who was at the time based in London studying, among other things, Swahili, at the School of Oriental and African Studies, his avowed wish to embrace his ancestry seemed perfectly to coincide, in prospect at least, with the project.

Crichton later recalled, with some understatement: 'Robeson didn't like the picture at all. I don't know how Alex sold it to him, but on the first night he stormed out of the cinema, because I think *he* thought he was making a picture about the marvellous cooperation between the two races. But, of course, the poor old black man turned out to be very much the underdog.'[28] In fact, Robeson completely disowned the film, declaring still bitterly some years on as Europe headed towards world war: 'It is the only film of mine that can be shown in Italy or Germany, for it shows the negro as Fascist states desire him – savage and childish.'[29]

Notes

1. Charles Drazin, *Korda: Britain's Movie Mogul* (I.B. Tauris, 2011), p. 141.
2. Interview with Crichton, *British Entertainment History Project*, December 1988 (henceforth *BEHP*).
3. *BFI Screenonline*, www.screenonline.org.uk/film/id/454755/index.html (accessed 16 January 2021).
4. *BEHP*.
5. Karol Kulik, *Alexander Korda: The Man Who Could Work Miracles* (Virgin Books, 1990), p. 69.
6. *Ibid.*
7. *BEHP*.
8. *Ibid.*
9. *Ibid.*
10. *Ibid.*
11. Drazin, *Korda*, p. 88.
12. *BEHP*.
13. *Ibid.*
14. Kulik, *Alexander Korda*, p. 80.
15. *BEHP*.
16. Drazin, *Korda*, p. 95.
17. Kulik, *Alexander Korda*, p. 87.
18. *New York Times*, 13 October 1933.
19. *BEHP*.
20. *Ibid.*
21. IMDB.co.uk (accessed 10 September 2020).
22. *BEHP*.
23. *Ibid.*
24. Kulik, *Alexander Korda*, p. 136.
25. *Ibid.*
26. Michael Korda, *Charmed Lives: A Family Romance* (Random House, 1979), p. 306.
27. Kulik, *Alexander Korda*, p. 137.
28. *BEHP*.
29. Martin Duberman, *Paul Robeson: The Discovery of Africa* (Random House, 1989), p. 180.

Cutting for Korda: 1936-40

If extolling empire was one of Korda's abiding passions, then another was for cosying up to eminent literary and political figures of the day. As for the latter, although Winston Churchill was in his so-called 'wilderness years' as an influential parliamentarian, Korda clearly felt he had his uses so put him on salary to contribute story ideas. He also thought sagely that with such a rollercoaster career to date, Churchill's was more than likely to soar again at some point in the near future. It would prove to be a lifelong association.

H.G. Wells was already in his mid-sixties and one of the world's most celebrated visionary writers when, in early 1934, he and Korda met for the first time in a Bournemouth tea shop where a deal was struck instantly for Wells to adapt for the screen his 1898 short story, *The Man Who Could Work Miracles*, and 1933 novel, *The Shape of Things to Come*. Filmed simultaneously, neither, for various reasons – not unakin to Wells's own constant interference in a medium he didn't really understand despite his creative flair and imagination – would be especially successful, but in the case of the latter, it would at least prove to be a rather magnificent failure. For Crichton, though, it was to be the film that firmly cemented his status in Korda's burgeoning empire.

While *Sanders* had been, at its most simplistic, a straightforward cut-and-paste job with its occasionally clumsy blend of fiction and non-fiction footage, *Things to Come* was, as the title might suggest, an extraordinarily ambitious and, for the still nascent indigenous industry still only five years into the talkies, a truly trailblazing piece of science-fiction cinema, unravelling as it did Wells's vision of future 'history' and humanity from 1940 to 2036 and beyond. Or *Whither Mankind?*, as Wells's preferred working title for the project had it.

Starting with the outbreak of World War II – more than four years ahead of the actual event but presumably deduced by the rapid growth of fascism in Europe as practised by Mussolini and Hitler from the early thirties – the writer's nightmarish scenario continues with the city, Everytown, London by any other name, bombed-out, semi-derelict and prey to the 'wandering sickness', this pestilence the result of germ warfare. The year 1970 signals 'social vitality' returning with Everytown now in the grip of a local warlord known as 'The Boss', played by Ralph Richardson clad in a series of moth-eaten ermine capes. Suddenly, the now elderly but still sprightly John Cabal (Raymond Massey) whom we first met back in 1940, swoops down in his aircraft to unveil an optimistic vision of a 'new world of united airmen' leading to the overthrow, from the air, of 'The Boss' and, via the judicious use of some kind of 'peace gas', the old order. With Everytown reconstructed as a shimmering, futuristic, metropolis, the action concludes with a spectacular moon shot from a giant space gun into a star-filled sky.

To help realise Wells's vision, which in the great Korda tradition eventually featured the hands of many others including him, his brothers and Lajos Biro, Alex imported three key Americans: director William Cameron Menzies, already an experienced art director, plus a pair of seasoned special effects men, Harry Zech and Ned Mann. In addition, he hired the Hungarian artist Laszlo Moholy-Nagy to design some of the future Everytown (in the event, less than two minutes of his work was retained in the final cut).

Utilising trick photography, full-size and miniature sets and elaborate model work, the production began shooting at Isleworth in March 1935 before moving to Denham where Korda's new studios on a 165-acre site by the River Colne had barely begun construction. No sooner had the set been built for Everytown, circa 1940 through 1970, featuring a St Paul's Cathedral-like dome and a Piccadilly Circus-style thoroughfare, when high winds in early June blew down part of the structure killing one man and injuring several others. There was also to be location filming at Brooklands Aerodrome and, added film historian Nick Cooper, at 'a disused colliery in Wales where unemployed miners played both The Boss's attacking troops and the defenders'.[1]

These rather bare bones of an epic storyline and its elaborate logistics do require some emphasis just to explain the magnitude of the task facing Crichton, Hornbeck and Lyon, another imported American, as they attempted to create a coherent film with such diverse elements. And it does not even take into account another serious glitch following the only significant change Wells effected, claimed Cooper, during filming. Wells objected that Ernest Thesiger's 'reedy and cultured voice did not fit a character [the dissident Theotocopoulos in the film's final section] supposedly appealing to the masses, and despite the fact that all Thesiger's scenes had been shot, Korda ... agreed to a recasting'.[2]

So the fuller-throated, recently knighted Sir Cedric Hardwicke, who also just happened to be an old friend of Wells, stepped into the role that then had to be partially rewritten for him.

For Crichton, the cutting process would not only prove an extremely fruitful if testingly complex phase of his continuing editing education at Denham but also, certainly as far as he was concerned, help to confer on him the great man's own seal of approval.

As he explained:

> At the beginning, Alex was, to me, a remote and formidable figure. When I became one of the editors on *Things to Come*, I showed him a rough cut of a sequence showing London under attack from the air. The sequence was full of violence, gunfire, bombs, and people running for their lives. Alex said, 'Charlie, you have made a bloody mess of this. It should be that everyone is standing there worried, waiting, because they know something is going to happen, and you haven't put that in the cut at all.'
> And I said, 'But the director didn't shoot such a scene.' So he said, 'You are a bloody fool, Charlie! You take the bits before he has said "Action!" and you take the bits after he has said "Cut!" and you put them all together and you make a marvellous sequence. What's wrong with you?' From the moment I was called 'a bloody fool', I knew that my job was safe! I was a member of the Korda team. But what was more important was that I was beginning to learn that a script is not the Bible, it is not a blueprint, which must be followed precisely, word for word, to the very last detail.[3]

As the premiere date of Friday 21 February 1936 beckoned – almost a year after production had first begun at Worton Hall – the editing process was still in train as Korda, Menzies and others started to be very concerned about the film's excessive running length. The rough cut of 130 minutes was reduced, first, to 117 minutes and then by a further 9 minutes – to 108 mins 40 seconds – for the official London trade show. This, said Nick Cooper, 'was probably the length at the premiere and initial release, although by November, a shorter 98m 06s version was in circulation. The American print suffered even more, running to just 96m 24s.'[4]

Crichton vividly recalled some of those last-minute editing problems, which came to a head when, three nights before the premiere, they had a run-through at the Leicester Square Theatre at 11 o'clock at night after the main feature had finished and the paying public had departed. In this rather more select, late-night audience was Winston Churchill.

In the opening reel, Everytown is being bombed; guns are going off, people screaming, rushing around the streets, Piccadilly collapsing under attack and so on. Suddenly a great big fish appeared on the screen and blew bubbles; this was because we never had previews or anything like that. We were always working right up to the last minute, and nobody had seen the picture all the way through until that night. Nobody liked the picture much, so we came out, bundled the film into a car, and went straight back to the studio.[5]

There, they worked for, as Crichton would delight in retelling years after, forty hours straight in order to get the film back into decent shape for the big night.

But what even the finest editing could not ease or erase in an otherwise seamless blend of startling special effects and truly fabulous futuristic design, aided in no small measure by Arthur Bliss's pounding score, were the deficiencies of the film's human factor subservient to often risibly portentous dialogue. Compared with the rampant theatricality of all the acting, without exception, the performances in, for instance, *Sanders*, seem almost naturalistic by comparison. Never was G.K. Chesterton's famously clever put-down of his fellow author and literary rival better suited when he quipped: 'Mr Wells is a born storyteller who sold his birth right for a pot of message.'

Weighing up very mixed reviews ('An astounding piece of work – paralysing in its prophecies, noble in conception, and magnificent in achievement', *Daily Herald*; 'It is completely humourless: at times it is almost unendurably prosy', *Illustrated London News*) and its poor box office, which two years after release had earned back just a shade over half its projected cost, Michael Korda reflected: 'Audiences either found the destruction of London by foreign bombers absurd or too terrifyingly real to sit through, and Wells' vision of the future seemed to most people cold and inhuman. The film did poorly in the US where, as one distributor said, "Nobody is going to believe that the world is going to be saved by a bunch of people with British accents." '[6]

From the frying pan of Wellsian future shock into the fire of Robert Flaherty's flight of Indian fancy, Crichton's next assignment, as hinted at right at the start of this chapter, shaped up from the outset as yet another helping of ambitious yet utterly disorganised Korda free-for-all. Signing up the fifty-year-old American director of acclaimed documentaries like *Nanook of the North* (1922) and, most recently, *Man of Aran* (1934) for his first narrative feature was a decidedly bold move but then to send him off to India on a kind of timeless, exploratory, cinematic safari without any specific storyline apart from the vague outline of Kipling's 1893 short story of a young elephant handler seemed foolhardy in the extreme, especially in a climate when Korda's financial stability was, to say the least, unreliable.

Accompanied by Korda's ever-reliable cameraman Osmond Borradaile, Flaherty's small team, including his wife Frances, arrived in India in March 1935. Almost a year later, Alex, now ensconced in his other even more extravagant 'production', Denham Film Studios – which was still under construction – contemplated the ramifications of a subcontinental shambles. The previous autumn, after months of non-communication, he'd despatched the American director Monta Bell to assist Flaherty. Fruitlessly, as it turned out, including more time-wasting footage of, thanks to a serious piece of miscommunication, a white-washed elephant.

'In desperation,' Michael Korda noted,

> Alex finally sent Zoli to India and there were soon two different units shooting elephant footage, each with a different notion of the story and each in a different location. Flaherty wrote back in delight to announce the discovery of a natural actor in Sabu, the elephant stable boy of the Maharajah of Mysore, but apart from that cheerful piece of news, Alex knew nothing about what was taking place except that he signed a large cheque every month to cover the expenses.[7]

In June 1936, with the studios now officially open for business – the damage from the March fire having also been attended to – the film crew finally returned from India to South Bucks.

John Collier, among others, was hired to create a simple storyline that could be shot at Denham and then be carefully edited to interweave with the best of Flaherty's footage. Using elephants imported from Whipsnade Zoo, hastily hired actors like Walter Hudd and Allan Jeayes alongside twelve-year-old Sabu and shooting some scenes on distinctly un-Indian autumn nights by the banks of the River Colne and in Denham Woods, Zoli completed the film in just six weeks. Now Crichton and Hornbeck settled down to the task of shaping more than three hundred thousand feet of material into a manageable, hopefully commercial, film of seven thousand feet, 'half of which,' wrote Karol Kulik, 'was pure Flaherty, half of which was pure Korda'.[8]

As the cutters set about their mammoth task, it might just be worth considering more closely the new Gropius-designed environment in which they were now working. According to film historian Patricia Warren:

> By Korda's own admission there was just one thing wrong with this magnificent achievement – it was too big. The workshops were too far away from the stages; the powerhouse was too close to the stages, creating noise and dirt; the cutting rooms were a bike ride away from the

theatres; and dressing rooms and offices were linked to stages by long, draughty corridors.⁹

It was, however, all had to agree, the best equipped – boasting everything from a French chef to its own zoo – and most up-to-date studio complex in Europe.

For Crichton, editing *Elephant Boy* was, he'd recall later,

> a nightmare. I had a big, long cutting room with two doors. Flaherty would put his nose in and say, 'Charlie, I am the director of this picture, don't take any notice of those other two cunts' [referring also to the ever-interfering Alex]. Then Zoli would come in, just like a cuckoo clock, and say, 'Charlie, Flaherty doesn't know what he's doing ...' That went on and on. Zoli used to cut with his teeth. He'd grab a piece of film, bite it and say, 'Hold that, Charlie!' Alex was rewriting the story all the time. The interesting thing was that there were all these Hungarians together, Alex, Biro, and Zoli [as well as Akos Tolnay, another credited screenwriter] and they'd all be arguing the toss in extremely bad English; none of them could understand each other at all. You sat in the middle knowing bloody well that if they'd only speak Hungarian they might reach some kind of agreement.¹⁰

Crichton's last, recorded, words at the time on Flaherty appear in a letter home to his mother in which, deducing from some remarks about his impending engagement to his first wife Pearl, a former dancer, would have been sent during his editing stint on *Elephant Boy*. 'The rest of my news is – on Thursday, Flaherty asked me whether I would like to go to Greenland with him. If the chance ever did come, it would mean the devil of a lot to me as he is so damned incompetent in some ways that I would more or less have to show him how to direct his film. But it was only a very vague remark.' As well as hinting at his possible future as a director, which was still eight years off, he also revealed something of his current status at Denham: 'On Friday I learnt that the London Films people want to put me under contract but that the Prudential "financial experts" are against it because it will cost them more. That is a thing which it is useful to know about.' Finally, in April 1937, fully two years after Flaherty had first set out to India, the film was released to much acclaim, including, rather ironically, an award for 'best direction' at the Venice Festival and some commercial success. The reviews, as ever for a Korda production, were mixed but there was absolutely no argument about the real stars of *Elephant Boy* – Sabu, a natural scene-stealer, and Flaherty's footage.

There was nothing remotely mixed about Graham Greene's assessment of the film for the *Spectator* – where he moonlighted in between his day job as one of the country's coming novelists – which was mainly withering: 'The more positive crimes, the bad cutting, the dreadful studio work, the pedestrian adaptation so unfair to Kipling's story, must be laid at Denham's door.'[11] This appraisal wouldn't have been entirely unexpected as Korda's output was one of his pet peeves; the 'traditional Denham mouse' was a frequent Greene epithet.

Ever the pragmatist, Korda decided that instead of being constantly attacked by Greene perhaps he could actually persuade the thirty-three-year-old to join him at London Films so invited the author to a meeting at Denham. 'When we were alone,' wrote Greene, 'he asked if I had any film story in mind. I had none, so I began to improvise a thriller ... I left Denham half an hour later to work for eight weeks on what seemed an extravagant salary.'[12] So Korda had his man and Greene's spontaneous sketch turned into a decent little sixty-five-minute quota quickie, with John Mills and Rene Ray, called *The Green Cockatoo* after the working title of *Four Dark Hours* (the action was set between one and five in the morning) was changed.

Intriguingly, some might suggest a little suspiciously, Greene's critical stance on Korda seemed to change rather dramatically after that meeting, as he would positively rave about *Knight Without Armour* (1937) and *The Four Feathers* (1939), two of Denham's most prestigious productions in the second half of the decade.

There is no record of whether Crichton had either read, or been especially stung by, Greene's 'cutting' criticism of *Elephant Boy* but their working lives were, amusingly, then to coincide on the writer's next project for Korda – an adaptation of John Galsworthy's short story, *The First and the Last*, eventually retitled *21 Days* for the screen. On this occasion at least, Crichton didn't have to cope with a mass of overseas material as the subject, a romantic melodrama set in London and Southend, was very firmly parochial. But that, of course, didn't prevent Korda and Co. from indulging their traditional, often time-consuming, meddling, as Crichton would recall years later: 'He was always rewriting it. And then of course there was the other thing: every picture started off and the first week was thrown away, always. I never remember any picture when the first week's work wasn't thrown away, and we'd started again, usually with Alex now directing second-hand, from behind the scenes.'[13]

The film was directed by Basil Dean, who had supervised a stage version by Galsworthy himself some fifteen years earlier. Initially stalled because the proposed star, Clive Brook, took a sudden dislike to the subject, it finally ignited when Korda offered to take over the whole show, possibly as director, too. Which is how Dean, who successfully managed to retain the directorial reins because of Galsworthy family backing, came to be making the film at Denham, with rising star Laurence Olivier and Leslie Banks in Brook's role, and, on Korda's insistence, a very inexperienced Vivien Leigh as Olivier's love interest.

21 Days was belatedly released in 1940 having sat on a shelf for two years, and in the wake of Leigh's new-found stardom as Scarlett O'Hara in *Gone with the Wind*. The hope, forlorn as it transpired, was that something of MGM's blockbuster might somehow rub off on a tiny British offering.

The final insult was when Greene, briefly reversing his pro-Korda policy, laid into *21 Days* with an astonishing, surely unprecedented, *mea culpa* contained in his *Spectator* review of 12 January 1940:

> Perhaps I may be forgiven for noticing a picture in which I had some hand, for I have no good word to say of it ... Galsworthy's story ... was peculiarly unsuited to film adaptation, as its whole point lay in a double suicide (forbidden by the censor), a burned confession, and an innocent man's conviction for murder (forbidden by the great public).
> For the rather dubious merits of the original the adaptors have substituted incredible coincidences and banal situations. Slow, wordy and unbearably sentimental, the picture reels awkwardly towards the only suicide the censorship allowed ... and that, I find with some astonishment, has been cut out. I wish I could tell the extraordinary story that lies behind this shelved and resurrected picture involving a theme song, and a bottle of whisky, and camels in Wales ... Meanwhile, let one guilty man, at any rate, stand in the dock, swearing never, never to do it again.[14]

I had the pleasure of disclosing details of that 'extraordinary story' – apart from the still mysterious reference to 'whisky' – some years ago in a sort of cinematic biography of Greene, but none of those were seriously to affect the shooting schedule compared with the constant interference by Korda.

There were already problems enough for Dean: Olivier and Leigh, who would marry three years later, were in the first flush of their steamy affair, forever giggling and laughing on set, often at the expense of an increasingly frustrated director; then there was fellow actor Robert Newton's unrestrained drinking – maybe that explains the 'bottle of whisky' – which seriously disrupted his line-learning especially in a key court scene as counsel for the defence; and Dean himself was responsible for another time-consuming hiatus when he halted a dinner party scene at the studio because the table setting didn't include the right kind of sugar so a car had to be sent to London from Denham to acquire a suitable sweetener.

As for Korda, he rearranged the shooting schedules at the last moment so Olivier and Leigh could go to Denmark to play *Hamlet* together, ordered an elaborate Old Bailey Number One court set dismantled after just a single shot when Dean had been promised four days of filming because he had other plans for the space and then added a new sequence, which he directed himself to give the film, it was said, more of a continental atmosphere. And the title change was his, too, which both Dean and Mrs Galsworthy thought 'pointless'.[15]

All of which sorting and matching was, presumably, in a typical Denham day's work for the editor.

As well as Korda's indefatigable meddling, another recurring motif was his fondness for foreign-language film remakes. During the thirties, the vaults at Denham were apparently full of acquisitions, a number of them foreign language, some of which, Karol Kulik explained, 'Korda had bought and imported for the express purpose of filming an English version. This was a most expeditious and inexpensive way to make films, for the English film-maker could both use the original film as a model and, if need be, keep large portions of the original footage in the adapted version.'[16]

In the event, just four such remakes were completed by London films, among them *Moscow Nights* (1936) and, next on Crichton's schedule, *Prison Without Bars*, which eventually found its way into British cinemas just a little over a year after the 1938 release in continental Europe of its award-winning Gallic original, *Prison sans barreaux*. Korda imported eighteen-year-old Corinne Luchaire – dubbed the 'new Garbo' by Mary Pickford – to repeat her role, in among an otherwise wholly British cast, as one of the wilder inmates of a French girls' reformatory, with just a simple name change from 'Nelly' to 'Suzanne'.

According to the *Times* critic, 'to adapt an English from a foreign film is a tame undertaking and often leads to serious incongruities. Moreover life in a French reformatory for girls is not exactly the best subject for English actors and actresses, who so often excel in representing the niceties of social conduct and seem to require a precise and familiar background before they are at ease.' That said, the review was generally positive saving its main praise for Mlle Luchaire and the film's 'essentially liberal intentions'.[17]

Little could Korda and Co. have known at the time how much more fascinating and tragic their young star's real life would eventually turn out to be. She and her newspaper editor father were accused of collaborating with the Nazis following the occupation in 1940; he was executed for treason in 1946 and she was jailed the same year for 'national disgrace'. Four years later she died of tuberculosis aged just twenty-eight.

As Korda's own Denham fortunes were starting to wane so also, as the prospect of war loomed large, the first phase of Crichton's career began to wind down. As 1938 turned into 1939, Korda's control of the studios was wrested from him when Denham was officially amalgamated with nearby Pinewood, which had been opened by the Rank Organisation four months after Alex's dream complex. By this time Crichton, Pearl and their baby son, David, were living almost over the shop, as it were, having moved into a pretty cottage in Denham village, about a ten-minute drive away from the cutting rooms.

Crichton's closest chum at the studios was Muir Mathieson, the company's Scots-born music director, who had joined London Films in 1933 as assistant music director as he was about to graduate from the Royal College of Music after four years of study. He and Crichton, a year older than Mathieson, both had a Scottish heritage and became firm friends. Together with two others they also shared a little mews house in London off the Brompton Road until Mathieson, later to become a distinguished conductor and, eventually, composer too, married Hermione at the end of 1935. Two years later, the Mathiesons moved to Higher Denham only about a mile or so cross-country from the Crichtons.

In March 1939, work began on the film, which, along with *The Private Life of Henry VIII*, arguably ensured Korda's long-term legacy as a British film-making treasure. Not that the actual production process on *The Thief of Bagdad* was to prove, as Crichton would soon discover, any less fraught than many of Korda's earlier films, and further complicated and inevitably dragged out by the outbreak of war less than six months later, in September. While Korda dreamed of a Technicolor epic full of spectacle on lush sets by brother Vincent and with a sweeping musical score, it seemed his first choice as director, the German Dr Ludwig Berger, had other ideas; well, first choice if you don't actually count Marc Allegret, who had directed *Fanny* in 1932, the second instalment of Marcel Pagnol's bucolic trilogy following Korda's own, very successful, *Marius* a year earlier. Allegret quickly departed in the February after failing to produce what was regarded as a satisfactory script.

An experienced theatre and music man, Berger believed 'the entire look and action should be dictated by the music, which contrary to usual practice would be composed before filming began'.[18] To this end he insisted on hiring the Viennese Oscar Strauss with whom he'd collaborated on his earlier films. Little did he know, however, that Korda had already signed up Mischa Spoliansky – composer of Paul Robeson's two popular songs in *Sanders of the River* – for composing duties. The musical mix became even more complicated when, in April, after critical praise was showered on Miklós Rózsa's suitably Arabic-sounding score for *The Four Feathers*, Korda decided also to sound out his fellow Hungarian émigré.

The final upshot, after considerable rancour on many sides, was that Rózsa won the day as well as, it turned out finally, an Oscar nomination for his score. That was to be one of four nominations for the film, which, just under two years later at Los Angeles' Biltmore Hotel, won a trio of Academy Awards, the biggest haul of the night, for Vincent's art direction, Georges Périnal's colour cinematography and the special effects by Lawrence Butler (photographic) and Jack Whitney (sound).

Meanwhile, Berger insisted on trying to shoot his actors, including the one-time little elephant boy Sabu as the eponymous thief Abu, almost puppet-like in sync with music until Korda put his foot down, insisting that the music would be added afterwards in the usual way. 'Even without the pre-recorded music, Berger's vision of a minimalist, stylized Arabian Nights fantasy conflicted with Alex's more lavish concept of a Technicolor extravaganza. But Alex was unable to sack the director without having to pay an enormous sum in compensation. So instead he watched him closely, stepping [in] whenever a scene did not meet with his approval.'[19] Not, it should also be added, just 'minimalist' but ideally, Berger believed, monochrome.

So, hopelessly conflicted with Berger, Korda's way out of this creative and contractual impasse was to employ other directors on the periphery, as well as more directly undermining Berger by co-directing the actors himself at Denham. The other credited directors included two Americans; Tim Whelan, who shot some action material; William Cameron Menzies; and, perhaps most significantly, Michael Powell, who was about to make his own feature breakthrough later that same year with a Great War thriller, *The Spy in Black*, which also happened to star *The Thief*'s villainous vizier, Conrad Veidt.

Powell, together with Korda's great location cameraman, Osmond Borradaile, left for, first, Cornwall then Pembrokeshire where they filmed key scenes on some beautiful rocky beaches between Sabu and Rex Ingram as the giant genie. A third unit under Lawrence Butler was responsible for the flying horse sequences while Cameron Menzies also had an effects brief to capture the genie and the flying carpet. In fact, Powell's directing duties didn't end in Britain's far west as months later he found himself back in South Bucks, supervising three key scenes on sets erected along the banks of the Colne under Korda's very watchful and endlessly critical eye. A further complication was the very close involvement of Technicolor, more specifically, the formidable Natalie

Kalmus, wife of the man who had founded the company, and who closely supervised, with a suitable on-screen credit, all Technicolor's films between 1934 and 1949.

According to Crichton, who claimed he never had to deal directly with the pioneering company: 'Technicolor said the tricks that Alex used – flying carpets, horses galloping in the sky, all that sort of thing – were impossible and wiped their hands of it. Alex had a very good special effects man [Lawrence Butler] and he solved the problem for them. But according to Technicolor, the picture was "impossible".'[20]

It was work as usual on Sunday 3 September, when cast and crew, including Hornbeck and Crichton, overwhelmed as ever with footage, gathered in the studio's coal bunker to listen to Chamberlain's famous wireless broadcast as the first air-raid warning of World War II sounded. Almost immediately after, on the orders of Churchill, suddenly out of the wilderness as the newly appointed First Lord of the Admiralty, Korda and Denham were switched to propaganda film-making chores.

As for the still unfinished *Thief*, it was relocated to the American West for final locations in the Grand Canyon and the Painted Desert (doubling for originally intended exteriors in Arabia and Egypt) directed by an uncredited Zoli, and some pick-up shots with the main actors on a Hollywood sound stage. As Sabu had inconveniently grown some inches during the film's extended production, some of his scenes had to be reshot. However, said Crichton, '99% of the film was completed in this country'.[21]

Premiered in the States – also in Georgia where *Gone With the Wind* had been launched earlier the same year – then boosted by reviews like *Variety*'s 'one of the most colourful, lavish and eye-appealing spectacles ever screened'[22] and from the *New York Times*: 'No motion picture to date had been so richly and eloquently hued, nor has any picture yet been so perfectly suited to it,'[23] helped underpin what Korda had most craved, a huge international hit, which was consolidated yet further by its Oscar triumph the following February.

The nationwide UK reaction was no less ecstatic. Typical was the review in the *Liverpool Evening Express*, which may well have been spotted by Crichton's parents still living in Wallasey just across the Mersey: 'For sheer ravishing beauty I cannot think of any that comes up to some of the scenes in *The Thief of Bagdad* ... It is not a case of there being one or two outstanding sets. Korda seems to have been determined to make every single scene the equal of all those before and after. In plain words, all are equally lovely.'

Of the five main Korda films with which Crichton was involved between 1933 and 1940, perhaps only *The Thief* – to a lesser extent

Henry VIII – comes closest to what might be called enduring, maybe even timeless, in terms of its skill and artistry. It helps that the subject matter is pure fantasy therefore not hamstrung by a specific period like *Sanders* and *Elephant Boy*, which are, despite some fine documentary realism, also rather hobbled by their rather uncomfortable imperialism. Despite innovative sets and some trail-blazing special effects, *Things to Come* is undone by the histrionics of the actors before, perhaps fatally, suffering from, as Michael Korda puts it, 'Wells' own failings. It takes itself too seriously and concentrated on a problem that was more Wellsian than human.'[24]

The reviews of *The Thief* concentrated principally, if not unsurprisingly, on the film's peerless colour and sheer spectacle. But boasting unfussily seamless transitions between landscapes, sets, effects and dialogue-spouting actors, it is all-too easy to overlook the editing that in an admittedly auspicious year for the Oscar category – *The Grapes of Wrath*, *Rebecca* and *The Long Voyage Home*, among the elegant contenders – was shamefully cold-shouldered altogether.

Crichton's last gasp of Korda and Denham, and his first in what would be, over the next few years, a series of ever closer encounters with his industry's involvement in the war effort, got underway in February 1940 with one of its milder propaganda comedy efforts. Directed by Ian Dalrymple, *Old Bill and Son* (1941), was inspired by a popular comic-strip character created by Bruce Bairnsfather. With the simplest of plots, walrus moustachioed Great War veteran Old Bill (Morland Graham), envious of his son (John Mills) enlisting in the army, talks his way into the Pioneer Corps then follows the boy to France, assisting in the capture of a Nazi platoon. The film opened in London as France fell – 'so did the film,' Dalrymple told Karol Kulik. Blending some interesting contemporary footage with its rather jolly tale of cockney father-and-son and their cross-Channel feuding, *Old Bill and Son*, despite its great age, remains a breezy and even mildly anarchic, if unjustly neglected, early entry in the unfolding propaganda film war.

Boasting some of Alex's top creative people – such as Périnal and Vincent Korda – the film may have been unique among the Korda output, certainly in the Denham years, being, to all intents and purposes, Korda-less. He was otherwise much occupied in Hollywood and with more prestigious products, specifically, the flag-waving *That Hamilton Woman* (1941), with the newly married Olivier and Leigh, as Nelson and Lady Emma, proving that then as now, in the early years of the war, Britain ruled the waves.

Crichton, soon to graduate to an altogether different kind of film 'family' at Ealing Studios (Figure 2.1), would have had the kind of film

Figure 2.1 Ealing Studios

education at Denham under Korda that not only set him up at thirty as one of the country's leading editors but that also, having experienced even second-hand, every kind of film-making conundrum, must have proved a useful preparation for his eventual switch to directing just four years on.

Verdicts on Korda himself have varied wildly. Christopher Sykes, friend and biographer of Evelyn Waugh who, unlike his fellow literary pal Graham Greene, had a brief, lucrative but ultimately abortive working flirtation with Korda, wrote testily of his 'huge hollow reputation'. For Laurence Oliver, however, Korda was 'the most brilliant of all Hungarian imports'.

At first hand, Crichton witnessed across eight years the fascinating contradictions that were Korda at work, brilliantly summed up by Karol Kulik:

> Korda's belief in films that 'grow' derived from a more serious problem, which may have been one of his major weaknesses as a film producer. Once a scene was filmed, once Alex saw the rushes, he could usually grasp what was right or wrong with the sequence, but he had difficulty in visualising a scene – from the printed page, sketch or model – before it was shot.

If we accept this idea of a deficiency in Korda's visual imagination, then we can better understand certain quirks in his production methods, such as his lack of concern about whether scripts were finished before shooting began and the huge number of retakes that accompanied almost every Korda production.
Since Alex's critical faculties operated best during the final stage of filming, everyone connected with the film had to remain flexible, ready to re-build, re-write, or re-shoot at a moment's notice, throughout and often beyond the production schedule. It was a lot to demand of film crews, players and directors.[25]

And of the cutting room stalwarts, one should probably add.

Looking back years later on this formative period in his career, and from that initial break handed to him in Oxford by Zoltan Korda, Crichton reflected:

> Because I worked for Zoli, it followed that I also worked for Alex. I dearly loved them both, and Vincent as well. I worked on around five of Alex's main pictures, but when Denham was being built and pictures were being made everywhere, I worked on several others, which were disastrous. Then there was the time when Alex was rushing about trying to find the money to keep the studio going rather than making pictures himself.

As for Crichton's own final verdict on his first boss? 'I think Alex really should have stayed a director.'[26]

Notes

1 Nick Cooper, *Things to Come Viewing Notes* (Network, 2007), p. 11.
2 *Ibid.*
3 Brian McFarlane, *An Autobiography of British Cinema* (Methuen, 1997), p. 152.
4 Cooper, *Things to Come Viewing Notes*, p. 14.
5 BEHP.
6 Michael Korda, *Charmed Lives: A Family Romance* (Random House, 1979), p. 12.
7 *Ibid.*
8 Karol Kulik, *Alexander Korda: The Man Who Could Work Miracles* (Virgin Books, 1990), p. 188.
9 Patricia Warren, *British Film Studios* (Batsford, 2001), p. 28.
10 BEHP.
11 Graham Greene, *The Pleasure Dome* (Secker & Warburg, 1972), p. 144.
12 Graham Greene, *Ways of Escape* (Penguin, 1980), p. 50.
13 BEHP.

14 Greene, *The Pleasure Dome*, p. 262.
15 Basil Dean, *Mind's Eye* (London: Hutchinson, 1973), p. 250.
16 Kulik, *Alexander Korda*, p. 125.
17 *The Times*, 19 September 1938.
18 Charles Drazin, *Korda: Britain's Movie Mogul* (I.B. Tauris, 2011), p. 207.
19 *Ibid.*, p. 208.
20 *BEHP*.
21 *Ibid.*
22 *Variety*, 31 December 1999.
23 *New York Times*, 6 December 1940.
24 Korda, *Charmed Lives*, p. 122.
25 Kulik, *Alexander Korda*, p. 225.
26 *BEHP*.

The forties: Enter Ealing, 1940–45   3

As bombs began to rain down on Britain in 1940, Pearl, who was getting increasingly nervous in the village, and three-year-old David 'evacuated' to the Mathiesons at the Little House ('it wasn't little', recalls David) in Higher Denham where, during the air raids, David and fellow toddler Muirne, Muir and Hermione's daughter, slept together under the dining room table. On one occasion, a parachute mine, which the Luftwaffe intended for the studios nearby, landed instead in the Mathiesons' garden but, thankfully, did not explode.

Crichton had, around this time, been taken under the wing of yet another exotic émigré, the Brazilian film-maker, Alberto Cavalcanti, who after involvement in the French avant-garde during the twenties followed by much distinguished documentary work in Britain for the GPO Film Unit (later, the Crown Film Unit) under John Grierson during the thirties, became an associate producer and director at Ealing just as the West London studios were properly revving up for the war effort under Michael Balcon, who had left MGM in 1938 to take over the facility. Crichton's mind was equally, perhaps understandably, on matters other than just film-making in these turbulent times, as he expressed in a suitably stiff-upper-lip letter to his father in Wallasey:

> The Home Guard gives me considerable comfort these days because I cannot help feeling a little conscience-stricken at not having to put up with the rigours of the regular army. But at least we are improving and smartening ourselves up and growing better armed and efficient week by week. If the time ever does come we will be able to do something really useful.

He then asked his father to pass on 'our love to everyone in the north', before concluding:

> We don't like Germans and we don't like war and we don't like Italians but we do like being BRITISH, and I don't think there are many who

would get out of it if they could. In later years we will think it is a lot of rubbish but just at the moment I think everybody has grown terribly proud. Do you know the nicknames I have earned in the film business – 'John Quality' and 'True Blue'. Also many people among them Donald Calthorpe [he meant the character actor Donald Calthrop] have been convinced I am a parson's son. Prosy idiot I must be!

After he finished work at Denham on *Old Bill and Son*, Crichton, barely thirty, fully expected to be called up for the army when out of the blue he was contacted by Cavalcanti, whom he had never met, and asked if he'd join him at Ealing to cut a film he was directing called *Young Veteran*. This was to be the first in what would be a series of short documentaries – eventually some thirty in all – from a new Ealing Shorts Unit, also headed up by Cavalcanti, universally known as 'Cav'.

Just as Crichton's previous film had been inspired by a comic-strip character, so *Young Veteran* (1940) also took its cue from a popular cartoon, in this instance, Robert St John Cooper's series for the *Daily Express* about 'Young Bert', a callow British soldier, who memorably told his mother to hang out her washing on the Siegfried Line. Written by 'Michael Frank', later revealed to be a pseudonym of fellow Beaverbook journalists, Michael Foot (later leader of the Labour Party) and Frank Owen, the twenty-three-minute film shows a 'young Bert' and other recruits like him at the outset of World War II being trained, equipped and despatched for service at the front. In parallel, there's footage of the Home Guard being similarly put through their paces.

Explained Crichton:

> These so-called documentaries which Cav made weren't really documentaries at all. He would assemble masses of material from many sources – newsreels, libraries, etc ... and then completely re-edit them to put over a point, which had never been intended by the originators of the material. *Young Veteran*, for example, was about 'the boys' returning from the disaster of Dunkirk and rebuilding a new and formidable Army. Somehow or other, Cav managed to use shots of French troops skiing in the Alps to put over his point. Another lesson for me: film is a highly malleable medium.[1]

For Crichton, Cavalcanti's approach wasn't too dissimilar from the way Bill Hornbeck worked at Denham, adding: 'Somehow or other he managed to find beautiful images to illustrate what he was getting at.'[2] According to Katy McGahan in *BFI Screenonline*: 'Charles Crichton's expert weaving of library footage with freshly shot sequences guides us through the achievements and setbacks of the early phases of the war. Showing the low points, such as the chaotic evacuation of Dunkirk, alongside the high points gives the film a real dramatic charge.'[3]

Contemporary reaction was also extremely positive – 'if this is a typical example, Cavalcanti's unit is assured of a distinguished future', reported the *Documentary News Letter*, for example. Mark Duguid and Katy McGahan's fascinating essay, 'From Tinsel to Realism and Back Again' in *Ealing Revisited*, offered:

> In lesser hands, *Young Veteran* might have merely applauded military successes as a means of maintaining public confidence in the defence of Britain, but Cavalcanti's intercutting of the successes and failures of Britain's military missions maximises the dramatic effect of his library (and some freshly shot) footage, while the decision to focus on the experiences of one young recruit, Bert, enhances its emotional impact, expressed in the poignant closing comments: 'We went to France young soldiers and came back veterans.'[4]

Cavalcanti and Crichton were again jointly to the fore on *Yellow Caesar*, whose very title brooked no equivocation. It was a twenty-four-minute character assassination of Benito Mussolini, from his days as a rabble-rousing trade unionist to his ascendancy as Europe's first fascist dictator, as traced by the Foot/Owen writing/narration tandem, using everything from Italian newsreels and some reconstruction to short comic sketches. As the review in *The Times* put it: a 'restless jumble of styles that more than makes up in punch what it occasionally loses in coherence'.[5] That *Times* review was typical. 'Not a well-constructed film and certainly not a subtle one, but it hits extremely hard in its own hearty way and there is certainly very little of Mussolini left at the end of its 20 minutes,' noted Mark Duguid.[6]

Crichton then edited three more Cavalcanti-produced shorts – *Guests of Honour*, directed by Ray Pitt, about those forces from occupied Europe who were resisting from London; *Greek Testament*, by Charles Hasse, reconstructing the true story of Petty Officer Leonides who escaped to England to join the Greek Navy; and *Find, Fix and Strike*, a training film for Fleet Air Arm recruits. This last marked the directing debut of Crichton's former assistant, Compton Bennett, another London Films 'graduate', which, as will shortly be explained, would be the eventual catalyst for Crichton's own switch to directing.

He was, meanwhile, to be found musing on the nature of propaganda, among other things in a long, hand-written, letter to his father dated 1 April 1941:

> The fog of war is hanging rather heavily over the film business. The powers that be are examining carefully the claims of each of the 1,000 odd surviving technicians to remain in their jobs. As I am fairly young I suppose the chances of my going into the army are again quite considerable.

But I would like to get my next job done before they take me. This job is to direct the 2nd unit (a sort of 2nd XV) on a big picture we hope to make here called 'Melbourne Johns'. It is the story of a bloke who rushed over to France and rescued a great deal of valuable machinery before the advancing Germans. I am not sure it is first-rate propaganda because although it is meant to portray the British character during its most crucial test, the background will of necessity be an unstoppable advance of ferocious Jerries.

I think people are ready for a more active type of propaganda. They may be tired of hearing what we can do in adversity and want to see what we can do with our successes. I have always felt, incidentally, that the value of all this propaganda business is a bit overrated. It can never take the place of success. Germany's propaganda has brought results only because German armies have produced results.

Now that we have such considerable victories to our credit maybe we can spread around the news by print, radio and film. But nobody can make victories out of defeats, not even the Italians, no matter how they talk and blather. The propaganda film is simply a way of spreading information, steadying people's nerves and raising their courage. If it can achieve these ends to any degree at all, it is well worth preserving the industry.

Two months later, Crichton wrote again to his father. After describing quite graphically a nearby bombing raid, he then revealed: 'I'm rather bored at the studio at the moment as I have had a picture which had gone wrong to doctor and I am a little tired of it and just not as full of enthusiasm as I ought to be. I hope to be finished with it soon and maybe then I will be able to get on with preparatory work for the "Melbourne Johns" picture.'

The 'Melbourne Johns picture', in which, as it turned out, Crichton would take no part, was one of Ealing's first realist wartime features, inspired by the true story of the eponymous Welsh works manager who went to France shortly after the outbreak of war to try and retrieve – successfully as it turned out – some crucial machinery before it fell into the hands of the advancing Germans. Retitled *The Foreman Went to France*, it was directed by Charles Frend, who, before taking on *The Foreman*, was embroiled at the helm of *The Big Blockade*, his Ealing debut. This rather odd drama documentary, depicting the work of the Ministry of Economic Warfare (MEW) was the film Crichton had described as 'gone wrong'.

In a further letter to his father, he went into more detail:

> I am still laboriously trying to get 'Blockade' finished, trying to satisfy the whims of the MEW waiting for our commentator who had a nasty accident the day before he was to record, trying to get a bit of co-operation from the other departments of the studio – a difficult job nowadays when we are so badly understaffed.

I have had one little triumph with the picture. There is a big air raid at the end, all done in model shots. The model king – a cameraman of considerable ability named [Roy] Kellino – was not being very successful. So I was sent along to keep a sort of tactful eye on him, which I did, I think, with a very large degree of success. Anyway it was suggested that I should cease doing my present work and become another model king – a suggestion, which I turned down because it would of course be a dead end.

Later in the letter, Crichton told his father – presumably following up from something he already hinted at in an earlier missive home:

> Anyway I am much more interested in doing the Press picture. I feel a bit disconsolate about it at times as I am afraid after all these long delays it may never come off. But in the meantime we have got a first-rate scenarist working on it and it promises to be quite interesting.
>
> The form it has finally taken is as follows. First we decided that it should be treated through the eyes of an American. Then we decided that the opening scene should be a number of pressmen discussing what would happen to the Press in the event of war. They think it may go Totalitarian. We show what did happen to the Press in Germany, Italy and France and then we take four cases in England where the Press, not being bound by a tight censorship, exerts a healthy influence in the course of the war, broadening out at the end of wider issues.
>
> I am personally very pleased about this treatment because it will be so much more exhilarating than a petty little picture as originally conceived about how brave men turn out a newspaper in the middle of a blitz. I think the only goal we would have reached had we tried such a treatment would have been to make people wonder why lives should be risked in a needless cause.

The same letter also once again – 'I do feel a bit of a rotter at times' – exposed Crichton's continuing concern, mild guilt even, about not being more directly involved in the war especially when, perhaps making it more personal and poignant, his father was a Great War army veteran and had been wounded, too. The fact is, Crichton was now, whether he liked it or not, officially 'Reserved Occupation' because of his work on Ealing's propaganda films, therefore officially excused boots, as the army slang had it.

Getting *Blockade* right was also, it seems, taking a considerable toll on the two Charles' own friendship. Said Crichton:

> Charlie [Frend] was a good pal of mine, but on this picture we had terrible rows and were on the verge of being deadly enemies – until the pub opened across the road. The Red Lion was a spot where we all gathered in the evening and discussed the day's work, each other's scripts, rough

cuts, future projects and so on. Many problems were sorted out over a pint of beer or a tot of whisky.⁷

No wonder it was often referred to as a 'spiritual home', with the emphasis on spirits.

The Red Lion was nicknamed Stage Six because periodically it was probably just as busy as the official five stages at the studios just across the road, where Frend and Crichton together with Basil Dearden, Robert Hamer – these four were born within a year or two of each other – Harry Watt and, a little later, Alexander Mackendrick would became the core of the directing team mustered by 'Cav' and Michael Balcon in the early years of the war. As Charles Barr points out, these six men alone would direct no fewer than 60 per cent of Ealing's films during Balcon's twenty years with Ealing, between 1938 and 1958.⁸

So much has already been written elsewhere about Ealing and its enduring contribution to British and world cinema, some of which, by necessity, must inevitably be repeated here as Crichton's career continued to bloom in this unique creative environment, which originally opened for business in 1902 and today can claim to be the oldest continuously working studio facility for film production in the world.

When the studios were sold to the BBC in the mid-fifties, Balcon, the son of Latvian immigrants, wrote the following inscription on a plaque at Ealing: 'Here during a quarter of a century many films were made projecting Britain and the British character.' He would later enlarge on that in a 1986 BBC documentary:

> I think we all came here convinced that films made in this country should be really from the roots, right down in the soil, should be absolutely indigenous British. That was the real idea behind it. It sounds chauvinistic but is not intended to be because I do happen to think that the only sort of nationalism that's worth a damn is cultural nationalism. I don't suppose we said those words to each other but I think that was possibly the idea.⁹

In the case of *The Big Blockade*, its British 'character', as such, was beginning to get a bit compromised by politics as production ground on with yet another delay, this time caused by the Nazi invasion of Russia in June 1941. Apparently this now required the inclusion of a freshly written character – a Soviet commissar, played by Michael Redgrave – to reflect a suitably updated record of official allies versus the Axis. Despite Redgrave's late addition to an already starry cast that included Leslie Banks, John Mills, Bernard Miles and Michael Wilding along with a preening Robert Morley as a hissable Nazi villain, the film, despite the prolonged efforts in the cutting room of Crichton and his assistant Compton Bennett, was a failure. As Balcon himself later conceded: '*Blockade* is a dull word and the subject rather too abstract to be dramatic or exciting.'¹⁰

Although Crichton claimed 'in those days it never crossed my mind that I might direct' – a little oddly in view of the fact he had hinted at the possibility in some of his letters – the idea suddenly took on a much sharper focus when he discovered that Compton Bennett had 'been elevated to that noble position'¹¹ after being assigned to *Find, Fix and Strike*. 'So what about me?' he asked Balcon one day. 'Why not? All right, go off and do something', came the reply.

But before that 'something', there was a kind of promotion in store for Crichton when found himself appointed as associate producer on Harry Watt's *Nine Men*, among the first of the studio's more uncompromisingly focused features about men at war. It should be pointed out here that 'associate producer', a major designation on the studio's films, was Ealing's shorthand for 'producer', these days probably more akin to the position of 'line producer' managing day-to-day physical aspects of that film's production. Meanwhile, Balcon, together with his trusty lieutenant Hal Mason, oversaw all production at the studio.

Crichton later cheerfully denied having any such ongoing producer role on *Nine Men*: 'I didn't really produce it. I was credited, but all I managed to do was wangle the rights to the story from the poor author for an incredibly small amount of money, and he offered to bash me up when he found the picture was so successful. I wasn't really creative on that picture at any level.'¹² Despite his protestations, he did, when quizzed in 1988 by fellow industry veteran Sidney Cole (who was supervising editor on *Nine Men*) for the invaluable *British Entertainment History Project* archive, admit to being involved in the cutting room and, yes, he might have done a bit of second-unit work on the film. But, added Crichton, 'In the sense of working on the script or helping Harry Watt in any kind of way, I don't think I helped very much.'¹³

The 'poor author' in question was Gerald Kersh, best known for his 1938 London-set gangster novel, *Night and the City*, which was twice filmed, in 1950 and 1992. In 1941, Kersh had written an account of recruit training in the Guards called *They Died with Their Boots Clean*, and when the War Office approached Balcon about the possibility of an army training film, Kersh was sought for a suitable synopsis based on his book. When the project was assigned to Harry Watt, who, like Cavalcanti, had arrived at Ealing via the Crown Film Unit, he had rather different ideas about the right way to approach the material.

According to Paul Mackenzie: 'Watt ditched most of what Kersh had written in favour of a reworked version of the 1937 Soviet film *The Thirteen* (situated during the Russian Civil War) reset in the Western Desert. As reworked by Watt, the idea was to show how individual soldiers, drawn from a variety of class and regional backgrounds, operate as a fighting unit.'[14]

Originally titled *Umpity Poo*, a corruption of the French phrase '*un petit peu*' (a little bit extra), *The Nine* cast included experienced actors like Jack Lambert, as the battle-hardened sergeant, and Frederick Piper, along with newcomers such as Gordon Jackson just out of his teenage years, and Bill Blewitt (a one-time Cornish postman who had been 'discovered' by Watt for a GPO Unit documentary in 1937) in his first credited feature role.

Framed mostly as a flashback from action a year earlier in Libya, its miniscule budget (just £20,000, equivalent to a little over £300,000 in today's money) required considerable film-making ingenuity, which was mostly achieved on a dune-studded beach at Margam near Port Talbot in South Wales, where the eponymous troops are marooned, with limited ammo and in the face of an imminent Italian onslaught.

'Mr Harry Watt's direction triumphantly avoids both facetiousness and melodrama,' purred the *Times* reviewer, adding, 'it tells a heroic story without ever faltering into heroics'.[15] Edgar Anstey wrote in the *Spectator*: 'It is as though a front-line glimpse from a newsreel had been expanded and given unity.'

Crichton reflected, modestly:

> The only thing I ever did to help him [Watt] was after he rang me up at about half past nine at night, said he was in terrible trouble and could I catch a train immediately and come down to Wales. I replied, 'But Harry, it's only twenty minutes before the last train goes.' He said, 'You must come, you must come.' So I put my clothes on over my pyjamas and rushed out and managed to catch the train from Paddington – one of these terrible night trains which was absolutely crammed with people, no seats or anything. I sat in the bog all the way, the only place I could find a seat. It was a nightmare journey. I get down to the location about 9 o'clock in the morning, walk across the sand towards Harry, who looks at me in amazement and says, 'What the fucking hell are you doing here?' He'd forgotten all about asking me.[16]

Nine Men was a vivid example of the effect wrought on Ealing's early wartime features by Cavalcanti's and Watt's documentary background. As Charles Barr wrote in 'Projecting Britain and the British Character' for *Screen* in 1974, a 'first sketch', as he'd describe it, for his acclaimed book on Ealing Studios published three years later, 'There was no special political or aesthetic rigour in the documentary tradition. Perhaps the main influence was in the areas of: location shooting, editing technique, sober narratives.'[17]

Released in February 1943 after victory in the desert was assured, *Nine Men* proved not just a hit with audiences but was a palpable triumph of technical skill allied to economy of budget and, at just sixty-eight minutes, also of running time; just a minute longer than Crichton's directing debut the following year.

For Those in Peril (1944)

In between cautionary titles such as Thorold Dickinson's *Next of Kin* (1942) – 'careless talk costs lives' – and Cavalcanti's *Went The Day Well?* – 'Your neighbour could be your enemy' – films, while unashamedly scare-mongering and that also happened to be two of Ealing's most creatively satisfying, the studios continued to do their more stolid propaganda bit, as with *Nine Men* and the army, for all the various branches of the armed forces as well as some other crucial emergency services.

After co-directing a pair of Will Hay comedies, Basil Dearden, who unlike Frend and Crichton, both graduates of the cutting room, had enjoyed instead a theatre background, made his solo debut with *The Bells Go Down* (1943) about the Auxiliary Fire Service and its courageous crews tackling the Blitz in London. Balcon was then approached to make a film about the Air Sea Rescue Service, and with the blessing and then active cooperation of the Air Ministry and the Admiralty he assigned Crichton to direct. There are four writers on *For Those in Peril*. The first, credited with simply 'By', is Richard Hillary, the twenty-one-year-old Battle of Britain fighter ace, who after being shot down by the Luftwaffe in August 1940 became an acclaimed author while recovering from horrendous injuries. *The Last Enemy* was his bestselling 1942 memoir, but the *Peril* script was most likely inspired by his vivid recall of being rescued by a lifeboat from the North Sea after bailing out of his flaming Spitfire (Figure 3.1). A night-training flying accident over Scotland finally claimed his life in January 1943 several months before the film started shooting.

Then, as well as Harry Watt, there was J.O.C. 'Captain' Orton, one-time head of the story department at Gaumont British under Balcon, principally writing comedies for the likes of Jack Hulbert, Arthur Askey and Will Hay. Finally, T.E.B. 'Tibby' Clarke, whose importance to Ealing's enduring legacy was probably more significant than any other screenwriter, especially in terms of his collaboration across no fewer than seven films (out of a total of thirteen for the studio) with Crichton, three years his junior (Figure 3.2). Only the hard-drinking Angus MacPhail and John Dighton were more prolific

Figure 3.1 David Farrar (left) and Ralph Michael in *For Those in Peril*

than Clarke in the Ealing years with twenty-three and seventeen credits, respectively.

Clarke, a die-hard devotee of the Turf, worked in advertising and journalism before becoming a novelist, and on the day Hitler invaded Poland signed on as a war reserve constable in London. After three and a half years in the police and ready to resume his career as a freelance writer, Clarke, an old friend of Monja 'Danny' Danischewsky, Ealing's director of publicity, was, at thirty-six, summoned to the studios where he was hired as a writer, on trial at first, for the princely sum of £15 a week. After working on an abortive project with Robert Hamer, another former editor and another of Ealing's new talent pool, Clarke next found himself on back-to-back projects: a ghost story, *The Halfway House*, directed by Basil Dearden, and then, in his own words, 'a "doctoring" assignment' on *Peril*.

> He [Crichton] was not satisfied with the script as it stood and I cannot recall that my contribution to it amounted to much, but it nevertheless provided my first full screenplay credit. This film was released before *Halfway House* [according to the records it actually arrived in cinemas a month after], and the first line of mine that I ever heard from the screen – an experience comparable to receiving the proofs of one's first book – was spoken by John Slater.[18]

THE FORTIES: ENTER EALING, 1940–45 **45**

Figure 3.2 Crichton (left) with T.E.B. Clarke

Slater plays Air Craftsman Wilkie, one of Flight Lieutenant Murray's (David Farrar) regular Air Rescue Service launch crew in Kent, who doubles as wise-cracking chef and gunner. As befits its sixty-seven-minute running time, the tale is very simply told. The action begins on 23 August 1940 at the height of the Battle of Britain as we see a Royal Air Force (RAF) pilot bailing out of his stricken fighter before parachuting into the Channel. Despite an attempted search and rescue, we learn it failed.

This particular dateline is significant. Not only was Richard Hillary shot down just ten days later but it also brought into sharper focus the likely plight at the time of downed British airmen during the Battle of Britain, who had, records stated, just a 20 per cent chance of being returned to their squadrons after ditching in the Channel or the North Sea. In all, over two hundred pilots and aircrew were lost to the sea during the battle.[19] A few months later, in February 1941, the Directorate of Air Sea Rescue was created with the motto, 'The sea shall not have them'.

Cut to 2 February 1944, when Pilot Officer Rawlings (Ralph Michael), bitter because he has been grounded for medical reasons, arrives at the South Coast port to work with Murray on launch 183, nicknamed 'Sally'. Rawlings's personal plight is exacerbated when during an encounter at the pub with a friendly RAF crew, led by Squadron Leader Leverett (Robert Wyndham), the Air Sea Rescue chaps are referred to as 'wingless wonders'. Rawlings soon gets a mild taste of authentic sea salt on an otherwise incident-free sortie, during which he receives a minor dressing down by Murray for his sarcasm, followed very soon by the real thing, as 183 and her high-speed sister vessel 134 are despatched when a Boston bomber ditches not far off the French coast with three of its crew, including none other than Squadron Leader Leverett, left bobbing about in a dinghy, fog-bound in heavily mined waters and an armed German trawler within spitting distance.

The film, produced by Balcon's older brother S.C. 'Shan' Balcon, marked the first feature credit for another man who would become one of Crichton's regulars: cinematographer Douglas Slocombe, arguably the doyen, certainly the longest lived – he died in 2016 aged 103 – of all British cameramen (Figure 3.3). He and Crichton made eleven films together. Slocombe's initial background as a photojournalist for *Life* magazine and *Paris-Match* evolved into his transition to newsreel cameraman who was present in Danzig just before the invasion of Poland by the Nazis.

And it was that familiarity with gleaming monochrome reality that adds immeasurably to an otherwise fairly predictable, triumph-over-adversity tale leavened by plenty of deadpan humour, an unselfconscious mingling of the service classes and some striking set pieces, notably a stunning sequence involving a Supermarine Walrus amphibious aircraft that comes explosively to grief on its attempted rescue mission. As well as Slocombe, there were three other key cameramen on the project: Ernest Palmer, who photographed interiors, and Roy Kellino – 'the model king' from *The Big Blockade* – who together with Lionel Banes supervised the special effects.

Slocombe's impressive exteriors range from glimmering early morning vistas of a peaceful Newhaven and attack aircraft to close-ups of the launches at speed tearing across the waves. His keen desire for authenticity did on occasion concern Crichton:

THE FORTIES: ENTER EALING, 1940–45

Figure 3.3 Crichton (left) with Douglas Slocombe

The big danger was Dougie. One day we went out and arranged all sorts of things like Spitfires diving at us and actually firing at us; it was an extremely rough day and all ships were confined to port except the film unit because they were mad and expendable anyway. So we were tossing about in the Channel and these Spitfires were coming and we were trying to get the boats with machine gun bullets hitting the water and so on. And Dougie was in the wheelhouse saying, 'Can't you shoot a bit closer?'[20]

Crichton, whose second son, Nicholas, was born during the film's editing, also admitted that it was 'hugely exciting' tearing around the Channel in high-speed motor boats that had been made available during July and August of 1943. The main problem was, he suggested, 'just hanging on to the boat. We were warned beforehand that if a crash call came, they'd take no notice of us if anybody needed help; and we got a crash call once and from ambling along at five knots, accelerated to something like 45 knots in no time at all. How we didn't go overboard I don't know. Mind you, we rather enjoyed our predicament.'[21]

The propaganda is quite lightly propagated. We somehow know that in the final reel the baton is likely to be passed from the senior officer to his once disgruntled junior who is now a true believer: 'Tricky first show,' Murray tells, breathing his last on the floor of the wheelhouse, adding, kindly, 'You'll do'. Back at base, a fresh batch of RAF types populate the Mermaid Inn. Now it is no longer talk of 'wingless wonders' but, as one of the airmen declares, admiringly: 'You'd have to press-gang me before I join that lot – too dangerous!'

The reviews were very positive, from 'admirable and exciting' in the *Liverpool Daily Post*, to *The Times* describing it as 'another example of the success of British studios in mingling the facts of documentary with the excitements of a fictional story'. It concluded: 'There is some lovely photography of the sea, the sky, and the English coastline, and Mr David Farrar, as an officer who is killed, gives a performance which should lead to the immediate offer of a Hollywood contract.'[22]

As for Farrar himself, talking to Brian McFarlane in 1990, he recalled a

> great film … I had a fine part as the tough skipper of the launch and we shot this in the Channel under combat conditions. Charlie Crichton was something of a sailor and used to like watching us go green in a rough sea. Unhappily it turned out that the film was not booked to go into any West End cinemas. Perhaps it was because of its awkward length, too short for a West End first feature, though it was booked throughout the provinces. I felt I'd given my best film performance to date, but there were no cables from Hollywood! Perhaps if it had been padded by a further thirty minutes and had some feminine interest introduced, it might have been a success at the box office as well as with the critics.[23]

So much for the predictions from *The Times*.

Painted Boats (1945)

'It is hard to believe,' Crichton later reflected,

> that a picture which was largely about the history of the English canal system could, in the time of war, have in any way encouraged the people of Britain. But the war was clearly coming to an end and we wanted people to believe, as we believed, that when peace did come it wouldn't be like 1918, with the soldiers all coming back and no work for them. We were trying to say there was a future.[24]

THE FORTIES: ENTER EALING, 1940-45   49

Or, as Dr Keith Johnston, lecturer in film and television studies at the University of East Anglia, put it:

> Although produced during wartime, and very much linked to wider propagandistic aims to remind audiences what Britain was fighting for (the film is, in many ways, a love letter to British history, industry and a particular way of life), its choice of an instructional documentary approach can feel more like a return to the 1930s documentary movement than a look forward to the documentary aesthetic-informed dramas that Ealing were becoming known for.[25]

However viewed, this sixty-three-minute drama documentary, the last of Ealing's small films – henceforward all the studios' output would be full feature length – is an authentic oddity, odder still when you consider it was being made in June 1944 when, barely sixty miles away, Nazi V1 rockets – the so-called 'doodlebugs' – were raining down on London. Compared with that, and his previous film experience battling the ocean waves on *Peril*, *Painted Boats* was, understandably for Crichton, a 'much more docile, peaceful experience'.[26]

The 'drama' element of this hyphenate, or 'story-documentary' as one critic dubbed it, is simplicity itself – bordering on the simplistic – centring around two narrowboat families: the Smiths, who still rely on traditional horsepower, while the more progressive Stoners depend on diesel. As well as their canal lives, the families are also linked by the romantic attachment of Stoner son, Ted (Robert Griffith, the stolid coxswain from *Peril*), to the Smiths' daughter, Mary (Jenny Laird). Cast as Mary's father was the irrepressible Bill Blewitt, the one-time Mousehole postie, in his final film role (Figure 3.4).

'He was a natural actor,' said Crichton.

> He enjoyed his drink, was a rogue and a lovely person to talk to and be with. He would sit in the pub at the side of the canal and tell a fascinated audience long stories about his early days when he was a boy on the canal, ever since, supposedly, he'd first opened his eyes to see his mother straining at the tiller of the barge. Well, he'd never seen a canal before, but everyone believed him.[27]

The opening credits are intriguing. Laird, an established stage actor and already veteran of more than a dozen films, featured above the title, surely a rarity in those days. *The Girl of the Canal* also happened to be the US retitling for *Painted Boats*. Lower down in the roll call was one Billy Russell, the production manager, or, according to a report in the *Northamptonshire Mercury and Record*, 'assistant director', responsible for recruiting much local talent to the film, including some scene-stealing

Figure 3.4 Bill Blewitt and May Hallatt (centre) in *Painted Boats*

children and a dog call Gyp. He was also, it seems, the same Billy Russell, who with his trademark pipe and droopy moustache, had been a considerable music hall star in the twenties and thirties before combining the job of film backroom boy with occasional acting role right up to his final movie performance in 1971's *A Clockwork Orange*.

'Written for the screen' was, rather grandly, accorded to New Zealand-born scenarist Stephen Black, who had shared a writing credit on *The Bells Go Down*. His duties, and those of the rather more mysterious 'story contribution' for 'Micky McCarthy' (later, writer-director Michael McCarthy) were presumably confined solely to the dramatic punctuations in between predominantly documentary footage for which the commentary and some poetry was provided by Irish poet Louis MacNeice and narrated by James McKechnie. Linking and, happily, making visual sense of this at times rather awkward blend of fact and fiction was quite stunning cinematography by Douglas Slocombe, earning his first solo feature credit of what would amount to more than seventy-five across almost five decades.

'This is England,' proclaims the narration, portentously, over sweeping aerial shots of countryside, a country of farmers and factory workers, of ups and downs, of noise and stillness, a man-made landscape where the Romans made their roads straight and the English made their roads crooked. A criss-cross of human communications; some of those are by water, waterways, canals, the Cut. Life on the Cut is the life of nomads with a boat instead of a tent, moving through life at five miles an hour. Living with their own kind, marrying their own kind. Through nearly two hundred years their temple has hardly changed.

We are then introduced to the Stoners, on their narrowboat *Golden Boy*, and the Smiths aboard *Sunny Valley*, and to their respective, equally narrow, lifestyles. 'It's a life but it's not a picnic,' intones the narrator. You'd hardly think there was a war on apart from a brief mention of Ted awaiting 'call up'.

With regular prompts provided by the commentary on everything from schooling and literacy – or lack of it – to the back-breaking practice of 'legging' (walking horse-drawn boats horizontally through long, dark, tunnels) Crichton handles the human factor confidently with his mixture of trained and non-professional actors. When, for example, Harry Fowler (as Alf Stoner), a youthfully ubiquitous cockney fixture in films at the time, skips school, he's admonished colourfully by Ted, his older brother, with, 'Don't be such a mug. If you don't learn your lessons like, I'll shove your teeth down your bleeding throat.' Then, there's this exchange between traditionalist Pa Smith and his complaining missus (May Hallatt), after negotiating a tunnel. 'God made horses but he didn't make no ruddy motor engines,' he wheezes, ominously. 'And who made my varicose veins I'd like to know,' she furiously retorts, 'them blasted tunnels if you ask me.' That 'blasted' tunnel sequence is vividly underscored by a soundtrack of rhythmic prose poetry by MacNeice in the style of some earlier documentaries.

After the Smiths are ordered to motorise *Sunny Valley*, almost literally over Pa's dead body, the dramatic interludes impinge rather less while the history and current status of the canals move rather more centre stage, notably when 'the war' finally gets its proper recognition about two-thirds of the way in to the film. 'Their work', the canal workers', that is, the narration dutifully reminds us, 'is part of *our* war effort'. We finally learn that Ted has joined up unbeknown to Mary and Ma, who together with young Alf, and with romance on hold, have managed to negotiate *Sunny Valley* all the way from the Midlands to Limehouse Basin and out into the Thames.

Although there were brief inserts of industrial landscapes, a Cheshire boat lift and a Welsh aqueduct, not to mention the Cut at Limehouse, the bulk of location filming occurred over a twenty-mile stretch of the Grand

Union Canal between Stoke Bruerne (where a Canal Museum, with a preserved upper-section of *Sunny Valley*, still resides) and Braunstone in Northamptonshire including the Bilsworth Tunnel, at almost three kilometres, the third longest canal tunnel in Britain.

The local paper was, not surprisingly, wildly excited at the presence of film-making in the vicinity especially with the recruitment of locals as active extras: 'Stoke Bruerne was chosen because it is an ideal setting of sylvan beauty, road winding up the hill over the bridge by the lock, a tavern on the lock-side, and the picturesque village itself all combining to give just the right atmosphere for a film of simple charm,'[28] the *Record* simpered in the manner of a press release. Its excitement about matters celluloid on those same golden-hued summer days of June then reached virtual fever pitch when the *Record* suddenly discovered that director Anthony Asquith and playwright Terence Rattigan were staying at a hotel in the county town, while 'prospecting' for a new film: 'Full details of the new film ... are not yet released but it is understood that the picture will have an Anglo-American flavour ... shots are to be taken at an aerodrome in the district.' Sadly, the bubble burst when Rattigan explained that although 'we would [have] liked it to have been Northampton ... we want a place with a smaller, more intimate atmosphere'. Their film, which settled instead for locations in North Yorkshire, turned out, of course, to be *The Way to the Stars*, voted in 1945 by one national newspaper's readers the most popular film of the war years.

Asquith/Rattigan's brilliant and moving RAF homage was released in June. Four months later, In October 1945, and already looking a little dog-eared as propaganda with the war now over by two months, *Painted Boats* went out at the bottom half of a double-feature headed by *Ten Little Niggers*, a smooth Hollywood adaptation (more sensitively titled *And Then There Were None* in the States) of the Agatha Christie thriller, directed, ironically, by Crichton's hero, René Clair, albeit far removed from the 'soufflé-like' quality of the film-maker's earlier French films.

Painted Boats' occasionally uneasy brew of drama and documentary attempted with the tricky combination of trained and non-professional performers was called out by some of the reviewers. The *Liverpool Daily Post* noted, for example:

> The semi-documentary film is a tricky thing and Mr Charles Crichton would have done better to have made his *Painted Boats* a straight account of life on the canals. The film has many lovely studies of Midland reaches, authentic boater families, and towpath pubs. But it also has a hero and heroine who derive more from dramatic art than the 'Cut' and so much time is given to canal bank love scenes, full of painstakingly dropped H's that there is none left to show us how a lock is worked, or to relate the slow-moving cargoes to the general transport picture.[29]

The *Scotsman*, however, declared that the film 'has so many virtues that it may well be forgiven its few shortcomings ... Charles Crichton and his cameraman bring to the screen the gentle sylvan beauty of the English countryside. Here is more than a hint of the pictorial wealth which the British cinema has so long neglected.'[30] The critic was, though, rather less convinced by the intrusion of 'an experiment in expressionistic verse commentary over the tunnel sequence', recalling W.H. Auden's contributions to *Coal Face* (1935) and *Night Mail* (1936). '[It's] treated half-heartedly and misfires,'[31] the critic concluded, tersely.

For *The Times*, 'although the commentary is occasionally inclined to the pretentious, the film without over-glorifying the picturesque anachronism of a bargee's way of life and place in industry absorbs into itself some of the quiet loveliness of the English countryside in war-time'.[32] It also praised the performances of Laird – 'just erring on the right side of cleanliness' – and Hallatt – 'a figure as uncompromising as she is inarticulate' – who would be memorably reunited two years later in Powell and Pressburger's' *Black Narcissus* (1947).

For Dr Johnston, it is the focus on those two women at the climax that

> sets up the most interesting part of the film, as Ted is called up (off-screen, we only hear about this via his brother Alfie Stoner) and the Smith women decide to stay onboard and crew it themselves. It is a very wartime-based message, given the crucial role women played in keeping British industry going, but it is also striking to see a film that ends not in marriage, but in female solidarity and action.[33]

Dr Johnston's observation is a useful reminder that among its other virtues, *Painted Boats* is among just a very small handful of British films – *The Gentle Sex* and *Millions Like Us* from 1943 clearly qualify – to place women (albeit somewhat belatedly in Crichton's case) firmly (in *Painted Boats*' case literally), at the helm in the 'war effort'.

Dead of Night (1945)

Crichton's comic contribution to what is generally regarded as an iconic entry in the Ealing canon can be viewed either in isolation, as a complete misstep or, perhaps rather more charitably, as an early hint of the tone that would eventually best characterise the studios', as well as the film-maker's own, most lasting legacy to British cinema. The film itself hardly needs any introduction; the second, and most distinguished, in a sort of unofficial trilogy of the supernatural – book-ended by *The Halfway House* (1944) and *Train of Events* (1949), the last more just odd than actually spooky. As what he first perceives as déjà vu, a nervous architect arrives at an isolated farmhouse where he meets a group of disparate characters all then linked by their own unfolding tales of the weird, premonition, the paranormal and, in probably the portmanteau production's most celebrated segment, sheer horror.

The anthology originated with producer-editor Sidney Cole and director Charles Frend who thought it could be derived from some of M.R. James's ghost stories. Then, said Cole, 'We decided the stories weren't as visual as we had thought when viewed in film terms. Everybody got interested in the idea and we had very interesting script discussions; it finally evolved into what it is and involved practically the entire studio – except, oddly enough, Charles Frend, who was by then involved in making another subject.'[34] The murderous last, directed by Cavalcanti, his penultimate work for Ealing, concerned a ventriloquist possessed by his dummy, Hugo. However, the second of the five episodes about the domestic chaos wrought by an antique haunted mirror – which marked the first directing credit for Robert Hamer – is considered by many to have trumped even Cavalcanti's for effective chills.

Crichton was responsible for the film's fourth segment, inspired very, very loosely by H.G. Wells's popular *The Story of the Inexperienced Ghost*, first published in 1902. 'Tibby' Clarke was long past his three-month trial at Ealing when he asked Balcon why he hadn't yet been asked to work on a comedy. He was initially given short shrift. Then realising, rightly or wrongly, the film required some drollery to lighten the darkness of the subject matter, the producers put Clarke to work, which, he later wrote, 'qualified me to join in the lap of honour after the triumph of that ghost film'.[35] After their engaging double-act as Charters and Caldicott, a pair of cricket-obsessed 'silly ass' Englishmen in Hitchcock's *The Lady Vanishes* (1938), Basil Radford and Naunton Wayne repeated the same Launder and Gilliatt formula thrice in quick succession – in *Night Train to Munich* (1940), *Crooks Tour* (1943) and *Millions Like Us* (1943) – before being resurrected in remarkably similar guise as Parratt and Potter for *Dead of Night* (1945) (Figure 3.5). This time round, it was golf instead of cricket as the presiding passion, more pertinently as practitioners rather than as just passive fans. 'Golfing Story', as the sequence was styled – but of which there's no hint in the Wells original – tells of Parratt (Radford) and Potter (Wayne), best friends off, but deadly adversaries on the golf course, a clash further inflamed when they become love rivals for Mary (Peggy Bryan), prompting a challenge of eighteen holes of match play for her hand. Thanks to some sneaky cheating, Parratt wins the day by a single shot at which, much to his surprise, Potter walks calmly into a course-side lake and drowns himself. Cue a series of comic hauntings climaxing with a bizarre and rather risqué role reversal on Parratt's wedding night.

THE FORTIES: ENTER EALING, 1940–45   55

Figure 3.5 Basil Radford (left) and Naunton Wayne in *Dead of Night*

After a pair of propaganda-prompted films that relied rather more on the settings and atmosphere than actual performance, Crichton was here confronted for the first time with seasoned professionals and, although decorated with some smart effects and a dialogue-driven comic scenario, he was, he admitted, 'scared stiff' of Radford and Wayne,

> even though they were the most helpful of gentlemen. My first day's work was appallingly bad. I was trying to slow up Basil's performance, trying to make him express every single thought, which might lie behind each line of dialogue, hitting it on the head with a hammer. I was looking at it more from an editor's point of view, really. Basil very politely said, 'I don't think it will work that way. I will try, but it won't be funny.' He was dead right. The rushes were awful. We reshot the scene Basil's way and it was very funny indeed. I'd learned another lesson: cast with care and then trust the instincts of your artistes.[36]

Crichton's sequence was the first of the anthology to be filmed. Aside from interiors at the studios, the locations included Stoke Poges golf course and the village and church of picturesque Turville in Buckinghamshire, which, three years earlier, had been used rather differently as the site for a Nazi incursion in *Went the Day Well?*

What then was to be made of this comic intrusion, and generally of a film, which has now achieved the kind of stature that it is included in reverential terms in every important anthology of horror cinema? In the autumn of 1945, reviews were decidedly mixed. *The Times* suggested 'four directors and five or six stories are rather too much for one film', and as for the Golfing Story, it 'has the effect of a guffaw at a séance'.[37] By contrast, the *Belfast News-Letter* extolled: 'Four directors have co-operated in blending as one a series of bizarre tales of the supernatural, and the imaginative power and sensitivity of the editing gives the production an intelligent force reminiscent of the German films in their silent heyday', adding of Crichton's bit in relation to the eerie whole, 'a delightful contrast is the lively fun provided by ... a golfing story of the *Topper* type.' The *Monthly Film Bulletin* also noted of the latter, 'excellent comic relief'.

The *News Chronicle*'s Richard Winnington, one of the more thoughtful reviewers of the day if, later, one of Ealing's harsher critics, was invited to contribute a 'critic's prologue' for the inaugural edition in 1946 of the *Penguin Film Review*, published to coincide with the fiftieth anniversary of cinema. After casting a beady eye over half a century of film, he then focused on the past twelve months, concluding that in *Dead of Night* along with five other films, including *Brief Encounter* and *The Way to the Stars*, 'you sense the magic possibilities of the British cinema, fragile, encompassed, hardly daring to breathe'.[38] That sense of awe continued to reside in latter days with the late, lamented Philip French, a sort of heir to Winnington with similar brilliance as a film commentator and critic. Writing in the *Observer* on 16 February 2014, French noted: '*Dead of Night* has haunted me since I first saw it just after my 12th birthday, and with each viewing something new is revealed in the stories. I now value each story, both for itself and for its contribution to the cumulative impact.'

But it was in an entirely different vein that the venerable James Agate, a contemporary of, though by 1945 far longer in the tooth than, Winnington, set about the film, which he called 'a mess' of which the messiest is

> a spoof episode about two golfers, one of whom lies about his score. Whereupon the friend who is cheated walks into a pond and drowns himself in order that his ghost may haunt the cheater. Which he does

only to discover that he has forgotten how to dematerialise. All this, as played by Basil Radford as the cheater and Naunton Wayne as the cheated, is extremely funny but makes nonsense of the film whose tension it breaks with Abbott-and-Costello-like nonsensicality. The explanation that it is a story invented to calm the nerves of the house party occurs too late; the mischief is done.

After paying brief respect to the dummy episode, Agate then decried it for its faulty construction. 'This, however,' roars Agate, back on the golfers' case,

> is a minor fault in comparison with the major blunder of the golf foolery. It will not avail to Mr Balcon to say that the audience laughed. Of course it laughed ... if Mr Balcon was merely out to rake in the shekels I have no doubt that he has tremendously succeeded. If he was out to make a first-class film, I have equally little doubt that he has failed ... was there nobody at Ealing Studios to tell Mr Balcon to cut his golfers and put them in another film? That since one laugh will ruin a ghost story, his golf episode puts this film into a bunker from which it never recovers.[39]

When *Dead of Night* was released in the States only nine months after the UK, the film ran just seventy-seven minutes, mysteriously shorn of twenty-six minutes from the British version. So any reaction to *Variety*'s review that each episode 'is equally good' should probably be tempered by the fact that the 'Golfing Story' along with Cavalcanti's 'Christmas Party' story near the beginning of the film had been entirely slashed, allegedly for reasons of length.

In the case of Crichton's contribution, it would be nice to think that it was not so much the duration as the tale's shamelessly amoral pay-off that so offended America's post-war new puritanism that the editing scissors were swiftly sought. In any event, Crichton's fifteen-minute comic cut clearly did him no harm at all as his stature was boosted at Ealing, and it also must have helped play a major part in earning him a crack at a new studio project on which historians have regularly conferred the title 'first of the Ealing comedies'.

Notes

1 Brian McFarlane, *An Autobiography of British Cinema* (Methuen, 1997), p. 152.
2 *BEHP*.
3 See www.screenonline.org.uk/film/id/1423850/index.html (accessed 16 January 2021).
4 Mark Duguid and Katy McGahan, 'From Tinsel to Realism and Back Again' in Mark Duguid, Lee Freeman, Keith M. Johnston and Melanie Williams (eds) *Ealing Revisited* (BFI, 2012), p. 63.

5 *The Times*, 28 February 1941.
6 *BFI Screenonline*, www.screenonline.org.uk/film/id/1423861/index.html (accessed 16 January 2021).
7 McFarlane, *An Autobiography of British Cinema*, p. 152.
8 Charles Barr, *Ealing Studios* (Studio Vista, 1977), p. 39.
9 *Made in Ealing*, BBC Omnibus, 1986.
10 S.P. Mackenzie, *British War Films 1939–1945* (Hambledon & London, 2001), p. 47.
11 McFarlane, *An Autobiography of British Cinema*, p. 152.
12 BEHP.
13 *Ibid*.
14 Mackenzie, *British War Films*, p. 106.
15 *The Times*, 27 January 1941.
16 BEHP.
17 Charles Barr, 'Projecting Britain and the British Character'. *Screen* 15, no. 1 (1974), p. 97.
18 T.E.B. Clarke, *This Is Where I Came In* (Michael Joseph, 1974), p. 147.
19 Jon Sutherland and Diane Canwell, *The RAF Air Sea Rescue Service 1918–1986* (Pen & Sword, 2010).
20 BEHP.
21 *Ibid*.
22 *The Times*, 3 July 1944.
23 McFarlane, *An Autobiography of British Cinema*, pp. 183–4.
24 BEHP.
25 *The Great Ealing Film Challenge 81*, http://keithmjohnston.blogspot.com/2012/06/great-ealing-film-challenge-81-painted.html (accessed 16 January 2021).
26 BEHP.
27 *Ibid*.; McFarlane, *An Autobiography of British Cinema*, pp. 152–3.
28 *Northamptonshire Mercury and Record*, 9 June 1944.
29 *Liverpool Daily Post*, 28 September 1945.
30 *The Scotsman*, 10 June 1945.
31 *Ibid*.
32 *The Times*, 1 October 1945.
33 *The Great Ealing Film Challenge 81*.
34 McFarlane, *An Autobiography of British Cinema*, p. 135.
35 Clarke, *This Is Where I Came In*, p. 155.
36 BEHP; McFarlane, *An Autobiography of British Cinema*, p. 153.
37 *The Times*, 6 September 1945.
38 Richard Winnington, *Film Criticism and Caricatures 1943–1953* (Elek Books, 1975), p. 167.
39 *The Tatler*, 12 September 1945.

The forties: 1946-49   4

A little over a month after the release of *Dead of Night*, Ealing's twentieth feature film since the arrival at the studios of a new generation of talent cultivated principally by Cavalcanti, there was, according to the minutes of a round-table company meeting held on 31 October 1945, a distinct 'spirit of rebellion' festering in London W5. The smoke-filled gathering, attended by most of the key in-house personnel, including Crichton, listened attentively as Balcon 'pointed out that if any of the persons concerned felt frustrated despite their contractual arrangements, he'd be pleased to let them go at any time they felt there were better chances elsewhere. Mr Balcon said he was willing to sub-let, but he was bound to say that no applications had been received for their services.'[1]

The tone of this firm rebuke, paternalistic and patronising in about equal measure, must have felt very familiar to a workforce comprised, in no small measure, of former public school boys, most of whom then went on to Oxbridge. It is no coincidence that Ealing was quickly characterised by the sobriquet, 'Mr Balcon's Academy for Young Gentlemen'. If Balcon's censure did not exactly stop the creatives in their tracks it did probably serve to remind them forcefully that just a couple of months after the official end of World War II, and as a new austerity began to bite, Ealing was actually a comparatively peaceful and pleasant place to be berthed, indeed a sort of sanctuary from the often more cut-throat realities of everyday film-making outside the walls of W5.

As Crichton would later admit: 'The great thing was we had creative security, [and] an enormous excitement about being part of a going concern. There was enough anguish about and misery; budgets were too low, didn't earn enough money, some of our ideas got stamped on, but all the burden of setting up a picture was taken from our shoulders and we were relaxed.'[2] 'Ealing was a snug nursery where one was surrounded by talented playmates and supervised by a tolerant headmaster. Well, he was not *all* that tolerant. We were each expected to make one picture a year, or else! Outside, it was very much colder, more daunting.'³ Such so-called rebellious feelings that had first stirred then, in most cases, as quickly subsided, probably related in the main to financial worth. It claimed Cavalcanti, who quit Ealing in 1946 in, reportedly, a dispute over money. There may also have been some truth in suggestions that Balcon, possessed of a puritanical streak that made him recoil at any suggestion of on-screen sex or even, Crichton told the *Independent* in 1993, the word 'lavatory', disapproved of 'Cav's' homosexuality. But in those first five or so years of Ealing's output, and in its continuing ethic, Cavalcanti's influence cannot be underestimated. Said Crichton: 'I think he was the really creative thing about Ealing. He always was talking about the necessity for truth, and he didn't mean you couldn't make a comedy, but he was always looking for sincerity. The word is too small, "sincerity", but we always knew what he meant.'⁴

Several months before his round-table ultimatum, Balcon had, in one of the film industry's trade papers, spelled out, in no uncertain terms, a kind of mission statement for Ealing's future film-making policy, as detailed by Charles Barr in his justly lauded *Ealing Studios* history, first published in 1977.

> Every shade of opinion should be represented, and the scope of the films should go far beyond the purview of the Government documentary. Fiction films which portray contemporary life in Britain in different sections of our society, films with an outdoor background of the British scene, screen adaptation of our literary classics, films reflecting the post-war aspirations not of governments or parties, but of individuals.⁵

But Balcon's other main tenet, as outlined in Basil Wright's book, *The Long View*, that 'British production would remain economically viable only if costs were kept low enough to be recovered from the home market alone'⁶ seemed, sooner or later be bound to clash – and so it would turn out – with the increasingly ambitious, mid-Atlantic, aspirations of the Rank Organisation, of which Ealing had effectively become a satellite from 1944.

'In looking at Ealing's post-war films,' Barr observed, 'we get the impression of an animal emerging from its burrow, blinking in the sunlight, making a few excursions without ever cutting itself off from its base, then scuttling back into the familiar warm atmosphere of home.'⁷

Hue and Cry (1947)

It was Henry Cornelius, known to his colleagues as 'Corny', who came up with the 'embryo of an intriguing idea' for *Hue and Cry* before getting 'Tibby' Clarke to 'nurture' it into a fifteen-page outline. This proved a sufficient hook for Crichton to realise the potential for what would become a full-length and, as it transpired, trail-blazing Ealing comedy, quirkily paving the way, it has been suggested, for more famous studio titles from the end of the decade. South African-born Cornelius and Crichton, three years his senior, were, in many ways, kindred spirits. They had both served editing apprenticeships with Korda at Denham and had, subsequently, been introduced, separately, to Ealing by Cavalcanti. Crichton must also have been impressed by the fact that French-speaking 'Corny' had been personally selected by his hero, René Clair, to be an English-speaking assistant editor on *The Ghost Goes West*. Their working relationship was cemented when 'Corny' served as Crichton's producer on *Painted Boats*.

'Tibby' Clarke later offered a vivid outline of 'Corny's' original idea:

> He had in mind a picture based on what might be called the freemasonry among boys, all of them participants in that life of semi-fantasy exclusive to boyhood which can be so satisfying in the brief time it lasts. 'I want to aim,' he said, 'at some sort of situation that only boys are competent to handle. I'm completely vague about what it could be, except I think it should have a snowball effect – one boy getting his three or four pals interested, they in turn roping in other boys at the places where they work, until eventually we have a tremendous chase or round-up with boys from all over London taking part. I'd like our final sequence to give the impression that for one glorious hour boys have taken over the city.'[8]

After a week trying to seek inspiration but getting nowhere – 'a few years later I would probably have had to admit defeat'[9] – Clarke, possibly influenced by Erich Kastner's 1929 children's classic, *Emil and the Detectives*, suddenly spotted a lad on the streets nose-deep in a popular comic of the penny dreadful or, as one critic had it, 'penny blood', variety, and a plot then quickly coalesced in his mind. What if the tale being unfolded week by week in the comic contained coded messages to a band of criminals giving details about the next job? Who then would be most likely to decipher the code? Why, probably kids.

Simple as that, really. What these bare bones can't possibly convey is how the brilliance and humour of Clarke's script with input from Crichton and Cornelius, allied to the ingenuity of the director, his crew, actors and, in no small measure, a superb, witty, score by French composer Georges Auric – yet another René Clair connection – helped transform an embryo of an idea into a rollicking entertainment that, despite its obviously immediate post-war London setting, seems remarkably fresh, exhilarating and even still mildly anarchic more than seventy years later.

The fun starts from the very outset with kids roughhousing against the background of a large wall graffitied with the film's credits. 'Wot no producer?' proclaims one before revealing 'Michael Balcon' in the next scrawl. The action begins, and ends just over eighty minutes later, with a church choir of surplice-wearing youths. At the outset, wee, angelic-looking Alec (Glaswegian Douglas Barr, fifteen at the time but looking about ten) has his score taken from him during 'Oh, for the Wings of a Dove' from a fierce looking choir master to reveal a comic, the *Trump*, carefully folded inside. It is the *Trump* and the adventures of fictional detective Selwyn Pike, which so engross Alec's gang, the Blood and Thunder Boys, led by resourceful Joe Kirby (Harry Fowler, still barely in his teens) and also conceals the truth behind some ingenious local skulduggery led by a mysterious Mr Big (Figure 4.1).

The script has, as ever, to be the starting point and its blend of visual and verbal touches delight throughout, from an inventive use of inserts like comic speech bubbles to a speak-your-weight machine activated accidentally then mangled terminally during a department store incursion. Most of the best lines are reserved for Alastair Sim in a tiny cameo as Felix Wilkinson, the reclusive creator of Pike's exploits blissfully unaware that his creation is actually being misused

Figure 4.1 Harry Fowler (centre) with Joan Dowling (left), Douglas Barr and Stanley Escane in *Hue and Cry*

for nefarious purposes. It turns out he never actually reads the stories that he authors so when Joe and Alec confront him with their theory, his first, agonised reaction is: 'Here's a split infinitive, and all under my name!'

While it really wasn't too much of a stretch for Sim with his trademark blend of the amiably seedy and slightly sinister, it was certainly a bold move to cast Jack Warner as Nightingale, who unbeknown to Joe until it is almost too late, is the cackling brains behind the unfolding villainy. Already a much loved star of music hall and radio comedy, Warner clearly relished being the baddie for a change, despite initially anyway, Balcon's misgivings. 'I don't think it's quite you,' he told Warner, preferring the actor to stick to the kind of chirpily genial non-commissioned officer character he'd played in his first Ealing film, *The Captive Heart* (1946), a prisoner of war (POW) drama, a year earlier.

Warner, however, was adamant he wanted to try and play different types but Balcon persisted that he simply wasn't sinister enough for the role. Warner continued to argue with him until it was agreed he should at least be tested for Nightingale, the black marketeer: 'I put on a moustache ... donned a mackintosh with the collar upturned, tipped my hat at an angle and stuck a cigarette in the corner of my mouth. I then stepped through a doorway in half-light. I got the part!'[10] He was also a kind of mentor to Harry Fowler, who at eighteen, a former news vendor and an authentic cockney veteran of nearly a dozen films, had been temporarily released from the RAF to appear in *Hue and Cry*. Warner gave him this advice: 'Never turn anything down, because every time you appear on that screen, it's an advert; to be a character actor at eighteen is worth being; stars come and go but as a character actor you'll work until you're ninety.'[11]

But more even than the ingenious plot or the colourful performances, it is *Hue and Cry*'s naturalistic settings, far removed from the usual, stodgy, set-bound artifice of so many films of the period, that help mark it out as an authentic classic of British cinema – 'not just a piece of fiction, but also a historic record of the times'[12] as its cinematographer Douglas Slocombe would correctly observe. The Blood and Thunder Boys' playgrounds were the authentic bombed-out London ruins of the day, the majority in the film sited just to the east of Southwark Bridge. Most notable was a crumbled swathe between Cannon Street station and the river, which doubled as fictional 'Ballard's Wharf', where 'Corny's' dream of rushing hordes of kids descending finally on the band of unsuspecting criminals was climactically realised.

Balcon's concerns about Warner had also applied to the film itself. Despite getting his blessing on the strength of the story outline along with the enthusiasm for it generated by Cornelius and Crichton, 'It was impressed on us,' wrote Clarke, 'that our comedy was obviously going to be unconventional and thus a risky venture which meant it *must* be made on a low budget.'[3] That suggested not a penny more than the already penny-pinching £80,000 that traditionally graced Ealing's film budgets of the forties.

As well as the anonymous-looking bombsites, rather more recognisable locations included Holborn, the old Covent Garden, the Duke of York Memorial off the Mall, St Paul's Cathedral, the Pool of London and Wapping pier head. One of the most striking settings was a derelict building over ten storeys high near Charing Cross Station, scene of a chase and (mildly) violent face-off between Fowler and Warner, who had been made by Crichton to 'perfect an awful laugh'[4] that echoes round the ruin as the apparently mismatched pair close in on each other. Recalled Warner: 'I had to sprint through this depressing ruin with its broken steps and rotten floors until, eventually ... pushed through a hole in the floor. I was supposed to fall eight storeys to my death. In fact, I fell backwards from the eighth to the seventh floor and into a stretched tarpaulin.'[5] Not dead, of course, it wasn't that sort of film, badly winded instead and sat on by Fowler until the police arrived.

'In Mr Charles Crichton,' *The Times* declared, 'the English film has a new director – there are very few of them – with something to say and knows precisely how to say it,' before lavishing unrestrained praise on the film itself – 'scene after scene is brilliantly composed, with the dialogue always giving bite to what is merely conventional in the situations,' then concluded, 'throughout the film the boys, led by Harry Fowler, remain delightfully unselfconscious, absorbed in an adventure we can all share and understand.'[6]

The critical accolades for Crichton and the film were pretty much universal at a time when immediate post-war austerity not to mention foul winter weather required some leavening of the general gloom that *Hue and Cry* supplied in the form of laughter. 'It had so joyous a welcome that it became an instant hit,' Clarke would reflect, also noting how the director had 'handled the blend of contrasting talents with admirable patience and much skill'.[7]

That 'blend' of the professional – predominantly male but memorably complemented by two female actors, seventeen-year-old Joan Dowling (who eventually married Fowler before committing suicide aged twenty-six), in her first film role playing a key Blood and Thunder gang member, and Valerie White as a hard-bitten blonde 'moll' – was supplemented raucously by hundreds of young recruits from the labour exchange while an all-in wrestling consortium provided the bulk of criminal muscle; a heady mix indeed confronting a film-maker on his first full-length feature.

Crichton was asked years later whether it had been an 'enjoyable' film to make: 'Making any picture is rather a masochistic experience, but, yes, I suppose it was,'[18] he replied. He also conceded that it was in the truest sense, despite being singled out so glowingly by the *Times* reviewer, a team effort citing especially the efforts of Cornelius, Slocombe and the main camera operator, Jeff Seaholme. Cornelius's contribution in particular shouldn't be underestimated. This was emphasised by Harry Fowler who said: 'Charlie was, foremost, a good technical director. Corny was great with the kids. Very sympatico. He had a lot to do with directing *Hue and Cry*. He was never off the set.'[19] Crichton, a modest man, would probably have concurred. He certainly gave full credit to 'Corny' for supervising one of the final sequence's most memorably droll images, of kids, maybe up to fifty of them, pouring out of a taxi to join in the fray.

> I was on the bombsite at the time shooting other stuff and then I saw him doing this shot. I had always envisaged that the taxi would stop at a place where we could conceal a whole lot of boys. We would open one door and boys would pour out and [then] be re-fed into the cab. [Anyway] the taxi came didn't stop at a pre-prepared position; he [Corny] had just crammed about 50 boys into one taxi, to hell with what they thought about it.[20]

Perhaps one of the more surprising legacies of *Hue and Cry* was that it would still take another two years for the tireless Cornelius to get his own feature-directing break at Ealing – with *Passport to Pimlico* (1949).

Of working with children, Crichton wrote in the *Penguin Film Review* that year, of their 'ability to create out of an imagination unfettered by too much dull experience, and ... to believe with a solid, concrete conviction'. All, he added, 'very useful when it comes to making a film'.[21] While admitting that *Hue and Cry*, on the back of his *Dead of Night* segment, helped establish him at the studios as a comedy director, he resisted the idea, indeed the historical notion, that the film was somehow a sort of template for 'Ealing comedies':

> I think it broke away from traditional film comedy, which relied heavily on dialogue and slapstick. But if *Hue and Cry* had not been made, Robert Hamer would still have given us *Kind Hearts and Coronets* and Sandy Mackendrick would have made *The Man in the White Suit* and *The Ladykillers*. *Kind Hearts* and *The Ladykillers* were black comedies. *The Man in the White Suit* had a serious theme behind it. I do not think *Hue and Cry* was the first of a genre.[22]

66 CHARLES CRICHTON

For a film so well received at the time, some kind of retrospective viewpoint is always salutary. My own positive assessment of *Hue and Cry* from a distance of nearly three-quarters of a century is, for example, in marked contrast to, say, the rather less admiring judgement of, for example, Charles Barr who seems to suggest, among other things, that the success of the film was much more just an accident of good timing.

He wrote:

> It offered a relief from various solemnities bound up with the experience of war; it gave expression to the energies of children (who were necessarily somewhat submerged beneath the earnest endeavours of the war-winning pictured); it made novel use of locations such as the London bomb site where much of the action takes place. At the same time, it risked no offence or aesthetic challenge to its audience. Despite some inflated claims that were made for it (not by Ealing), it overlaps not at all with the location aesthetic of the Italian neo-realist film-makers of the same period, being staged and acted in a perfectly conventional 'studio' manner, much of it within the studio walls. Nor is there anything very anarchic about its content: the children create their own sense of community in a responsible cause.[23]

Barr then goes on to reprimand the film for its 'lack of spontaneity – in acting, response to locations, and "directorial" touch',[24] all of which seem strangely to contradict almost everything that we have just witnessed across eighty-two gleefully freewheeling minutes of indigenous cinema; 'English to the backbone', as the *Monthly Film Bulletin* applauded.

Against the Wind (1948)

In the years 1955 to 1958, what you might call a suitably discreet distance from the end of World War II, there were more than twenty British films alone dealing with all aspects of the conflict: from the Battle of the Atlantic, the North Africa campaign and the Far East theatre, to the plight of POWs and the secret work of undercover operatives. In 1955 and 1956, *The Dam Busters* and *Reach for the Sky* – coincidentally, or perhaps not, both biopic tributes to different aspects of RAF heroics – were, respectively, the top UK box office attraction of that year, while David Lean's *The Bridge on the River Kwai* (1957) trumped the lot as the British cinema's biggest international success of the whole decade.

Reflecting on the popularity of war film genre in his essay, 'British Film in the 1950s' for *BFI Screenonline*, Professor Neil Sinyard notes:

Critics were sometimes dismayed by this trend, seeing it as a nostalgic wallow in former national greatness during a time of uncertainty about Britain's international role. More recently, however, such films have been seen as part of a distinctive genre – the British equivalent of the American Western – that offers illuminating observations on British values, emotions and notions of heroism and masculinity.[25]

Sinyard then goes on to observe that even within my designated time-scale, there were also 'some fascinating deviations' to the 'traditional formula of stiff-upper-lip heroics and deference to authority',[26] citing, for example, *A Town like Alice* (1956), *The One that Got Away* (1957) and *Ice Cold in Alex* (1958), all of which also happened to be extremely audience friendly at a time when the Cold War had probably, and quite understandably, supplanted World War II as a no-go area for mainstream film-making subject matter.

Against the Wind was, significantly, Ealing's *only* war film between *The Captive Heart* and, seven years later, *The Cruel Sea*, which, in 1953, turned out to be that year's top UK moneymaker. The war's end together with the rather cold-blooded ousting of Churchill as prime minister seemed also to proclaim a different mindset for cinemagoing audiences, one that would, for instance, so enthusiastically greet *Hue and Cry*. Lee Freeman writes in his essay, 'Mild Revolution?' in *Ealing Revisited*: 'Balcon explained that during the war Ealing had been mainly content to "put films to work in the national interest in wartime" but the coming of peace meant that thoughts were turning to readjustment as Ealing began to ask questions about what form post-war society should take.'[27] That Ealing produced comparatively few war films after 1945, was, added Andrew Roberts in his 'People's War' essay for *Ealing Revisited*, also 'partly due to increasing friction between Balcon and John Davis of the Rank Organisation'.[28]

Against that backcloth, and with 'Tibby' Clarke's own much later assessment that his fourth screenplay for Crichton was 'a classic example of a mistimed film',[29] *Against the Wind*, despite being a resounding flop in its day, now deserves some sort of reassessment. In his memoir, Clarke, makes, a little oddly, no mention of J. Elder Wills who not only received a 'based on a story by' credit but also served as the film's art director. An industry veteran from the silent days, Wills, a one-time scenic artist, also directed a dozen films during the thirties before joining the army. During the war, he led a special section designing unorthodox devices, such as booby-trapped rats and exploding pens, mainly for use by agents of the Special Operations Executive.

Devising his screenplay from elements of Wills's own wartime experiences, Clarke felt that enough time had passed since the actual events to try and create an exciting tale about the exploits of a disparate band of British-trained saboteurs dropped into occupied Belgium that was essentially realistic, occasionally absurd, sometimes even tragic. Neither overly romanticised nor merely 'heartening propaganda'.[30] During research-gathering recces in Belgium, often talking face to face with men and women who had enabled the resistance, Clarke and Crichton were confronted with an abundance of material, some of which was deemed frankly 'too fantastic for fiction'[31]; in the event, there was sufficient material in the resulting screenplay, also inspired by other source material, to suggest already more than enough 'stranger than ...' There were, it should perhaps be noted too, an 'adaptation' credit for Michael Pertwee, and 'additional dialogue' credit for Irish writer Paul Vincent Carroll.

The film's title is taken from some lines in canto IV from *Childe Harold's Pilgrimage* (1818), Byron's long, semi-autobiographical narrative in verse, published in four parts across six years either side of the Battle of Waterloo, and recounts, appropriately enough, a journey across a Europe torn by conflict and violence.

'Yet, Freedom! Yet thy banner torn but flying, streams like the thunder storm against the wind; Thy trumpet voice, though broken now and dying; The loudest still the tempest leaves behind.' Earlier in the same poem, Byron more specifically evokes Belgium's capital city where 'bright the lamps shone o'er fair women and brave men; a thousand hearts beat happily', before concluding the stanza darkly, 'But hush! Hark! A deep sound strikes like a rising knell!'

Somewhere in London, 'a few years ago', spymaster Ackerman (James Robertson Justice, in his fourth Ealing role in as many years) gathers together in rooms within a tatty Jurassic-themed museum a motley group of would-be saboteurs for imminent war work. These include a French-Canadian priest Father Philip (Robert Beatty), Emil (John Slater) who requires plastic surgery so he won't be recognised in his native Belgium, Max (Jack Warner), a chirpy cockney despite his multinational origins, Johnny (Gordon Jackson), a very youthful-looking Scots explosives expert, and Michèle (Simone Signoret), a bitter expat whose ex-lover has turned quisling (Figure 4.2).

Part of the film's enduring fascination is quite simply to do with the casting, notably Warner and Signoret, and their subsequent interaction as the band is required to parachute into Belgium in order to try and rescue another of their number, code named 'Andrew' (Peter Illing), who has been captured and imprisoned in the city after attempting to destroy a prime Allied target, the Brussels Records Office.

THE FORTIES: 1946–49 **69**

Figure 4.2 Simone Signoret and Jack Warner in *Against the Wind*

'One of the main characters,' Crichton explained,

> was a double agent, a traitor, but a man of great charm. Who better to play this, we thought, than Jack Warner? He accepted the role, then suddenly, one week before shooting, he foresaw danger and wanted to withdraw, but it was too late. He played the villain and the result was disastrous; the audience would not believe that their beloved Jack was a two-faced sewer rat; it destroyed their belief. In *Hue and Cry*, his villainy was a joke, the picture was pure fantasy so Jack could do what he liked.[32]

At the time it was, as Crichton suggested and Clarke also, separately, concurred, an audacious if ultimately misguided piece of casting. After his jovial knavery in *Hue and Cry*, Warner had in the same year inaugurated (in *Holiday Camp*) an altogether more wholesome character Joe Huggett, lovable patriarch of a close-knit fictional family that would return regularly on film and then in a long-running radio series. Later, Warner's image is perhaps even more indelibly that of Britain's favourite TV policeman, PC George 'Evenin' all' Dixon, miraculously resurrected after being shot dead in Ealing's *The Blue Lamp* (1950). All of which makes Warner's gleefully amoral Max Cronk seem even more chilling when re-viewed today.

In his autobiography, Warner made no specific reference to his unorthodox casting and its alleged factor in the film's box office failure, preferring instead to concentrate on the physical requirements of the role including some hair-raising preparation at the RAF's Upper Heyford Parachute Training School in Oxfordshire, which, for him, easily eclipsed his near fatal, single-storey plunge in *Hue and Cry*.

Signoret, who would later come to epitomise, in British films at least, like *Room at the Top* (1959) and *Term of Trial* (1962), a mature kind of world-weary continental exoticism, was still in the first flowering of her career when, at twenty-six, she was imaginatively cast in her first English-language role as Michèle. Crichton and Sidney Cole, who at the time was dividing his associate producer duties between *Against the Wind* and Ealing's rather more prestigious production, *Scott of the Antarctic*, went to Paris together to check out Signoret for the role. They were due to meet her in the bar of the five-star George V Hotel just off the Champs-Élysées. Cole recalled: 'Simone wasn't known in England at all at that time. The door opened and she came towards the table, but as far as I was concerned, by the time she was halfway to the table she got the job. Then she sat down and spoke in very good English, in fact, I think she'd been to school in England for a while. She had an extraordinary aura about her.'[33]

Crichton agreed:

> Simone was wonderful in it, and so was Gordon Jackson. She was then at the top of her form and very beautiful; Gordon was an innocent twenty-year-old. We were preparing to shoot a love scene between the two of them, when Simone came to me in an unusually worried state of mind. 'So we kiss,' she said, 'and what will Gordon's reaction be? How will he respond? ... All right, leave it to me.' I left it to her. We shot the scene and Gordon's reaction was ecstatic. Afterwards he came to me, eyes bulging from his head: 'Charlie, why didn't you warn me? I went to kiss her and before I knew it, her tongue was halfway down my throat!'[34]

We learn of Warner's impending treachery just after it is too late to abort the rescue mission before the group land in Belgium. The question is whether a message can be got to Michéle, the group's wireless operator, before Warner realises he's been exposed. In a superbly staged scene, Warner is whistling while shaving at a mirror while Signoret, elsewhere in the room, is making routine contact with London. 'How are the folks back home?' Warner asks. 'One minute while I get this decoded,' she replies. As Warner continues to shave, Signoret's expression slowly changes when the decoding becomes clear. Quietly she reaches into her wireless case, removes a pistol, turns round and points the weapon at Warner whose back is still turned to her. She calls out his name, he turns and she fires, hardly changing expression, not just once but, as he collapses to the floor, five more times. The noise has attracted the attention of the farmer in whose house they are billeted. He begins to pull off Warner's boots.

Both shocking and coolly brutal, the scene is uncannily reminiscent of a crucial sequence five years earlier in Cavalcanti's *Went the Day Well?* when the well-mannered vicar's daughter (Valerie Taylor) shoots dead the silver-tongued village squire (Leslie Banks) who we, the audience, already know is the local community's leading fifth columnist. It is tempting to speculate that this was Crichton, the protégé, according a sort of homage to 'Cav', his mentor.

But as if to underline what must have contributed to the negative reaction at the time to the scene, Professor Robert Murphy notes: 'There is no catharsis. Our balance of sympathies have turned against Cronk but not to the extent that we enjoy seeing him shot in cold blood.'[35] The sense of downbeat continues, as Murphy also points out, with another telling Brussels sequence, which Clarke loosely based on a war story told him by another of his pals. In this, Johnny, having developed toothache, is spirited to a dentist by Michèle who waits for him at a safe distance outside the building. He re-emerges still dazed by the anaesthetic only to step out into the road and almost into the path of a Belgian police vehicle, which grinds to a halt. Answering barked questions, Johnny's halting French is entirely unconvincing and he's inevitably taken into custody much to the horror of Michèle from afar who then turns and walks away.

Johnny's plight would recall starkly another memorable war cinema moment with the same actor when, as fleeing 'Macdonald, "Intelligence"' in *The Great Escape* (1963), Gordon Jackson is scooped up by the Gestapo after famously failing the simple language test he had earlier tried to instil in his fellow POWs.

While revealing the happier conclusion to this dilemma, Professor Murphy makes a point that would also have probably contributed to the film's rejection by a war-weary nation: 'The subsequent successful mission and the uniting of Johnny and Michele create an optimistic strand, but this is a far more harrowing film than the Resistance films made during the war.'[36]

Once on location, Crichton discovered a startling contrast between the rather dreary, cold and desolate Paris he'd witnessed when casting Signoret, and Brussels, which was 'absolutely brimming with food and light'.[37] Filming took place in various parts of the capital, more than 150 kilometres away in the Ardennes, and at Bouillon in the south of the country near the French border. Co-star Robert Beatty recalled Crichton spending whatever downtime he had river fishing out in the country. It was not always sweetness and light as Cole briefly discovered. He told Robin Buss of the *Independent* on 24 July 1993:

> Sometimes the best way of getting to know someone is to have a tremendous row with them. I did with Charles [while] we were shooting on location in the Ardennes. I can't remember what it was about. After dinner, I was in Charles's room and the discussion got a bit heated. I went out and slammed the door behind me, at which point Charles's washbasin fell off the wall. We were very good friends from then on.

Exteriors were also shot at the Prison de Saint-Gilles, about four kilometres from the city centre, where resistance fighters had been held during the war. It should also be mentioned that, after four successive films in collaboration with Douglas Slocombe (away shooting Ealing's first colour feature, *Saraband for Dead Lovers* (1948)), Crichton was paired this time round with Lionel Banes, making a fine feature debut for Ealing after working mostly as an operator and on second units at the studios.

However, when, more than forty years later, Crichton was questioned about *Against the Wind*, he would claim he had not ever really want to make the film: 'It wasn't very long after the war, and I thought anything which glorified war in any way was a pity to do.'[38] It is worth noting that in the same year, David Lean announced then-abandoned plans to follow *Oliver Twist* with an adaptation of H.E. Bates's *Fair Stood the Wind for France*, about a downed bomber crew trying to make it home from occupied Europe.

Crichton's own reservations were, perhaps inevitably, given the climate at the time, echoed by a number of the critics. After invoking the lines from Byron, *The Times* wrote:

> There are moments when one wonders whether the accent is not most appropriately on the word 'yet'. Is there to be yet another film on the fight for freedom in occupied countries? Certainly it is a splendid subject, a subject that a good writer might use 100 years hence. But it is not a subject, which any longer justifies, by its mere splendour of achievement, the tame recitation of battles long ago. And in this film even the excitement that the mere mention of the theme still engendered is unaccountably absent. Perhaps the explanation is that the people who made it were themselves asking whether the subject was sufficiently up to date.[39]

Reg Whitley, the headline-provoking critic of the *Daily Mirror*, warmed to the same argument, but with a twist. Whitley, who earlier the same year had ripped into *Brighton Rock* as 'false, nasty, cheap sensationalism ... in all sincerity, I say we should produce no more like it', asked, portentously, 'is it too early to show war films again? This question is worrying British producers quite a lot at the moment, with the "ayes" and "noes" about equal.' He then answers his own question by stating: 'Personally I think there is a market now for the adventurous type of war yarn especially if the grim side is played down.'[40]

The *Tatler* riffed on a similar theme: 'Whether we are ready for a new cycle of Resistance pictures, I doubt,' before adding, 'this pleasantly acted, erratic little study of an Anglo-Belgian sabotage unit is saved, however, from total redundancy by its leaven of documentary, but Crichton's difficulty seems to be to blend his facts smoothly with his fiction. A number of things happen which are probably perfectly true to fact, but paradoxically fail to be credible in terms of fiction.' The critic then noted some of the film's more dramatic sequences, including the Signoret–Warner showdown, before chiding, 'such touches may be real. They are not realistic, because Mr Crichton has failed to mould them into the pattern of documentary, or into the shape of drama.' The review's conclusion that 'Resistance recollected in peace is at least one stage ahead of the Resistance imagined in safety in Hollywood' was hardly a cause for celebration.[41]

Countering all this was Leonard Mosley from the *Daily Express* who had been chief war correspondent of the *Sunday Times*. Attesting to the film's accuracy, he wrote, under the headline, 'It's Real Enough to Be Good', about some of his own close encounters with Special Operations Executive agents. Of the film itself? 'There have been other films about them [agents]. But Balcon's is to me the first that is not only tensely exciting but seems to be absolutely authentic ... Their adventures have about them the speed, movement, and spectacular pictorial effect of a first-class cowboy film, yet retain their reality throughout.'[42]

Internationally, reviews were equally mixed. *Variety* suggested, 'although the film is well made, it can't hope to do more than average business here, and will only suit for duals [double features] in America'. It did however note Crichton's direction as 'firm. He did a good job particularly in the unexciting moments.'[43] And perhaps it was a mark of just how far his directorial career had come in comparatively such a short time that the *Sydney Morning Herald* felt it could already note a kind of Crichton touch: 'Probably only a Crichton would think of having his secret London headquarters in a museum of stuffed dinosaurs.'[44]

Another Shore (1948)

Crichton might not have wanted to make *Against the Wind*, but he should surely have rejected even the very idea of *Another Shore* from the very outset. Can it be just coincidence that in Crichton's two most comprehensive whole-career interviews – in 1988 and 1992 – there's not a single, solitary reference to the director's sixth feature? While almost all of Crichton's early Ealing work bears repeat viewing – whether for its engaging material or its documentary-style realism – it is difficult to find any similar saving grace for this painfully misjudged slice of Irish whimsy. Not even 'mistimed' can, on this occasion, really be used as an excuse.

The source material, rather promising at first glance, was Kenneth Reddin's 1945 novel of the same name about a young Dubliner who dreams of exchanging his dull job in the city's Customs and Excise Department for the exotic, beachcombing lifestyle of a South Seas island. Not just some imagined isle but, most specifically, volcanic Raratonga, the largest of fifteen Cook Islands in the Central South Pacific. Reddin, who as a young man had been interned after the Easter Rising of 1916, wrote books and plays while doubling up as a district court judge. A friend of James Joyce's, Reddin's best-selling third novel was adapted for Ealing by Walter Meade who, in the same year, also shared a co-writing credit on *Scott of the Antarctic* with *Another Shore*'s bookish associate producer, Ivor Montagu.

An outspoken communist who had worked closely with Hitchcock in the thirties, Montagu might have seemed an odd fit with the seemingly more conventional Crichton ('True Blue', as he himself said he'd been described by colleagues, but actually was not in reality), but their joint love of films – Montagu, a friend of Eisenstein among others, had, after all, been one of the founders of the Film Society in London, which Crichton frequented – probably helped draw these two apparent opposites together.

Another key name at the film's pre-production stage was Alexander 'Sandy' Mackendrick who joined Ealing's film fold in 1946. American-born but Scottish-bred, he started out in Glasgow as a commercial illustrator and animator before moving to London where he worked as an art director at a large advertising agency. His first Ealing screen credit, jointly with John Dighton, one of the studio's most prolific writers, was on Basil Dearden's *Saraband for Dead Lovers*. With his background in illustration, Mackendrick provided a detailed storyboard for the colourful seventeenth-century period romp. He was then asked to do the same for *Another Shore*. According to Philip Kemp in his biography of Mackendrick,

Crichton found the technique no less restrictive than Basil had done: 'Of course, I'm not blaming Sandy for the picture not being very good. But I don't like the precision of everything being drawn out beforehand. The unit looks, and everybody looks, and they try to do it like that. You're putting yourself in a terrible corset. He did all these beautiful drawings, but the picture just didn't work that way.' The storyboard, Mackendrick realized, would work properly only when the director devised it himself and so could feel free to deviate from it with 'no contradiction between planning and spontaneity'.[45]

Whatever the merits or otherwise of preliminary storyboarding, the film's more fundamental problem was neatly summed up in the *Times* review, which was published about three weeks before its release just before Christmas. 'Both plot and mood waver and are inconstant and it is unlikely that any two people will think precisely the same way about *Another Shore*. To some it will seem an intolerable hotch-potch of bogus Irish whimsicalities; for others it will have charm, naivety, and freshness.'[46]

This, ultimately fatal, ambivalence of tone is quite literally spelled out in the opening image where a hand appears on-screen scrawling the word 'comedy' before scoring it out, replacing it instead with 'tragedy', then just as swiftly deleting it for the final proclamation, 'A Tragi-Comedy of Dublin Life'. After some typically shimmering Slocombe images of a bustling city and its morning workers, we learn that eighteen months earlier, Gulliver Shiels (Reddin's middle name) had quit his job at Customs and Excise to try and fulfil the dream of a future life on Raratonga. So every day, apart from Sunday, he sits in St Stephen's Green, Dublin's picturesque central park, armed with smelling salts hoping that his heroic intervention in the sudden collapse of a passing citizen will receive just reward that can help financially towards his South Seas goal of two hundred guineas.

As if this scenario wasn't already dubious enough, it deteriorates yet further after Gulliver (Robert Beatty) (Figure 4.3) reads of regular traffic accidents in Grafton St, the city's main thoroughfare, so decides to switch his 'pitch' to the steps of the Bank of Ireland instead, which will give him the best vantage point. Weeks later, during which time he has been told to 'move on' by police and public alike, Gulliver has also made the acquaintance of Alastair (Stanley Holloway) a rich, irascible, drunk, and his long-suffering chauffeur. Then, while daydreaming on the beach – filmed at Greystones south of Dublin – in the imagined guise of a semi-naked islander by a palm tree spearing fish – in reality, fully clothed with water lapping round his ankles – a beautiful, very posh Anglo-Irish blonde, Jennifer (Moira Lister) first accosts before unaccountably falling almost instantly for him.

Figure 4.3 Robert Beatty (left) with Crichton on the set of *Another Shore*

The battle is soon joined for our anti-hero's heart and soul. After being extricated from a non-fatal car crash, will Alastair, an old Tahiti hand it transpires, lure Gulliver away with him to the Pacific for reasons not entirely unconnected with a faithless, money-grabbing wife? Or will Jennifer, who appears to be conducting a one-way love affair with Gulliver, make a married wage slave of him?

The bones of the plot are rather painfully recounted to suggest that, with the right kind of script and a rather better chosen cast, there was the stuff here not so much of 'tragi-comedy' as a potentially sparkling black comedy, the kind of thing that Ealing, would, just a year on, execute so sublimely with Robert Hamer's *Kind Hearts and Coronets* (1949). However, fans of the book would have been horrified or, just possibly, mildly relieved when they saw Meade's adaptation. For after being comparatively faithful to at least the spirit of Reddin's narrative for more than 90 per cent of his slim volume, the film version takes a massively sanitised turn at the resolution, substituting a conveniently romantic outcome for Jennifer and Gulliver instead of the author's own bloody climax involving two deaths – not, as it happens, either of the 'happy couple' – and a final line that has distinct echoes of Graham Greene's bleak pay-off in *Brighton Rock*.

As well as the script and its tired Irish tropes, the film's main problems start, and mostly end, with the cast and their characterisations. After his fine, muscular, performance in *Against the Wind*, Beatty, a Canadian who would regularly deputise as the token Yank in British films for the next couple of decades or so, is as inadequate as his accent, despite being apparently coached by an Irish actor chum for an earlier Belfast-based role in Carol Reed's superb *Odd Man Out* (1947). Crichton must take some blame for this particular piece of casting as he had suggested to Beatty that he should try his hand at comedy, 'something I'd never dreamed of doing,' the actor told newspapers at the time, 'and something in the nature of an experiment. I didn't find it easy', he added, presciently.

For a character described even by his would-be inamorata as a 'lazy, work-shy oaf', Gulliver requires at least a sort of amiable insouciance to somehow make more palatable his otherwise feckless, not to say shameless, modus operandi. As portrayed by Beatty, he is both bland and utterly charmless. Which in turn somehow makes complete nonsense of Jennifer's infatuation. Introduced into the plot much earlier in the film than in the book, Alastair and his persistent drunk act too quickly become wearing, something out of which not even Stanley Holloway, who would become one of the key figures during Ealing's pomp, could create comedy gold.

The actual filming proved to be an endless object of fascinated attention both to the Dublin populace and in the Irish press. 'Quidnunc', the pseudonymous author of the regular 'An Irishman's Diary' in the *Irish Times*, charted his efforts to insert himself as an extra in *Another Shore* without offering much useful information about the film itself apart from periodic disruption due to interested onlookers. One particular public intervention 'reported by film director Charles Crichton just back from Dublin' was passed on gleefully by Northern Ireland's *Larne Times*. A hidden camera was filming as actress Muriel Aked, playing the 'little old lady', had to make her way perilously through dense traffic at College Green. 'Suddenly an equally small, equally old, woman pushed through the crowd and rushed to Miss Aked's assistance, glaring at the watchers and upbraiding them for their lack of chivalry. The scene was ruined.'

The warning from *The Times* about the film's uncertain tone was clearly heeded by some of the critics. 'Having long severed all contact with reality in the first five minutes, [*Another Shore*] goes on to be lyrical and poetic in the ether between whimsy and downright absurdity', noted the *West London Observer*, concluding, in addition to crediting wrongly 'Moira Shearer' rather than Moira Lister, 'what a waste of talent!'

For an Irish reaction, the *Catholic Standard* refused even to equivocate. Under the headline 'Another Bore', the weekly growled, 'One had the feeling that at any moment Charles Crichton would say "I can't continue" and the film would end. But no, the thing continues to the bitter end ... the final effect is one of dreadful tedium.' 'Another good idea gone wrong,' wrote the *Sketch*.

And yet, in the strict interests of balance, perhaps it is only fair to return to *The Times* and disclose its own final, slightly unforeseen, verdict on the film: 'If a casting vote is demanded it goes unhesitatingly to those in favour of the film. The rut in which film storied and sentiments run is getting deathly deep, and *Another Shore*, in spite of its many imperfections, jolts free of it.'[47] Balcon, however, did not seem to share those concluding sentiments about *Another Shore* because it would finally end up on release as the bottom half of a double bill, paired with a reissue of Harry Watt's 1946 rambunctious Australian 'western', *The Overlanders*.

***

Crichton might not have fully appreciated Mackendrick's contribution to *Another Shore*, but he would, however, be instrumental in helping to ensure that *Whisky Galore* (1949), Mackendrick's directing debut, would turn out to be one of Ealing's most successful – arguably the most successful – global productions. It proved to be the studio's first US box office hit, and in France, for instance, where the film was retitled *Whisky a Go-Go*, spawned a nightclub and a new popular phrase.

Balcon assigned Monja Danischewsky to make his producer debut on the adaptation of Compton Mackenzie's 1947 novel. 'Danny', in turn, asked his boss if Mackendrick could make the film. 'The blind leading the blind', as 'Danny' would later describe it, a factor that Balcon would not, unsurprisingly, countenance at first. The comic wartime story of a small whisky-starved Hebridean island suddenly awash with fifty thousand cases of scotch after a freighter runs aground featured many hands, maybe as many as seven, in its eventual screenplay although the author and Angus MacPhail remained the only two actually credited.

As all the studio's directors were occupied with other projects at the time, 'Danny' offered the project to Ronald Neame who had been an Ealing cinematographer before teaming up with David Lean as, first, a cameraman then as a producer. Neame turned it down so 'Danny' finally managed to persuade Balcon to give Mackendrick his break. After an extended shoot, mostly due to rain and gales, on the island of Barra in the Outer Hebrides, standing in as the story's Todday, the film returned to the mainland with production finally completed after more than a hundred days, twice the length of the original schedule, and, at over £100,000, at least double the initial budget. The story then goes that Balcon, having viewed the assembled footage cut together by an inexperienced editor Joseph Sterling, panicked and decided that the film should be edited down to an hour and released as a B-feature.

According to Philip Kemp:

> Disaster was averted by Charles Crichton, who protested that the material itself was fine and simply needed good editing. 'So Micky Balcon said, "All right, go into the cutting room and see what you can do with it." So I did that, and every time I said to Sandy, "Well, I think this sequence should go like this and this and this," he said, "Well, of course, that's the way I intended it."'[48]

The glorious sequence, for instance, in which the islanders have swiftly to find every conceivable hiding place for the contraband, even beneath a baby in its cot, is attributed to Crichton's editing skills.

Along with Sidney Cole and Peter Tanner, he worked on the film uncredited for several weeks and also shot some pick-ups at the studios, while Mackendrick undertook tank work at Pinewood and some missing exteriors including a climactic chase. Crichton, who admitted he would like to have directed the film having read the script, said: 'The final result was the brilliant picture which Sandy and Danischewsky had envisaged in the first place.'[49] 'All I did was put the confidence back in the film,' he told *Distilling Whisky Galore*, a Channel 4 documentary, in 1991.

***

Train of Events (1949)

Contrary to received wisdom at the time and, subsequently, among a number of critics and commentators, Ealing's third and final portmanteau film actually proves to be a rather pleasant surprise with its mixture, admittedly uneven at times, of documentary realism, a little 'noir', much melodrama and some sophisticated comedy. Unlike the admittedly superior *Dead of Night* in which the various episodes are self-contained, albeit linked to its central chilling theme, the four different tales in *Train Events* dovetail throughout the film, briefly bookended with the (brief) before and chaotic after of a spectacular passenger rail crash on the London to Liverpool line.

Three of Ealing's faithful were assigned to the project: Basil Dearden was responsible for two of the tales involving, respectively, a German POW on the run with his adoring war-orphaned English girlfriend, and a young actor driven to kill his faithless estranged wife; Sidney Cole, in his only feature-directing assignment, handled the engine-driver's story; Crichton, predictably, was entrusted with the comedy about a romantic triangle. Who will survive the train crash?

Crichton's segment begins in a television studio for a slot called 'On the Mat' in which a smug, self-satisfied composer-conductor Raymond Hillary (John Clements) is confronted with a pair of young musicians who have been asked to discuss and possibly debunk his latest work 'The Legend of Lancelot', which has, we are told, provoked a 'storm' of controversy. She, a wide-eyed fan, can barely get a word out: 'I nearly died,' she gasps adoringly. He, clearly an aspiring critic, begins promisingly, 'Technically, I consider it to be a tour de force ...' Pause for effect, as Hillary savours the compliment, before the young man continues, pompously, 'But morally I consider it to be completely indefensible ... Your Lancelot instead of pursuing the Holy Grail spends 933 bars on an act of erotic bifurcation.' In layman's terms, this introduction to Crichton's 'Composer's Story' is basically to blaze the trail for a sketch on whether a man can ever love two women at the same time.

In Hillary's case, the two women, also both separately watching the broadcast, are his wife Stella (Valerie Hobson) and his latest protégée, Irina, a young Russian concert pianist. In a rather delightful virtuosic twist, Irina Baronova was cast as the soloist. Baronova was, of course, better known as a dancer, one of Balanchine's famed trio of formerly teenage 'Baby Ballerinas' with the Ballet Russe de Monte Carlo during the thirties.

Crichton's principal memory of the film revolved around the rehearsal period:

> We had John Clements, a stage actor, Irina Baronova, who was a ballerina, and Valerie Hobson who was a cinema actress. One of the difficulties a director always has is trying to get everybody's performance to gel at the same time. So here we were with these three people from different walks of life. Clements' performance improved all the way through rehearsals and it [also] improved on the floor. The ballerina's performance was stuck; she got it as far as she was going to go. She never changed. Valerie Hobson got worse and worse and worse the more we rehearsed because she was a film artist and used to doing it instantly.[50]

Crichton's memory really doesn't do justice to Hobson who, frankly, steals the show with some deliciously catty one-liners – 'I adore television – all those squiggly lines' – and a string of musical innuendoes, and also, incidentally, is not on the train as it conveniently extinguishes some of the more criminally culpable cast in the process. She is, however, present in one of the film's final sequences where, at a concert hall in Liverpool, Irina, with a large bandage above one eye, is thumping away at a piano concerto (by the film's composer Leslie Bridgewater, who also wrote the incidental score for *Against the Wind*) under the watchful gaze of Hillary, whose arm is in a sling. Then his gaze begins to fall on the pretty harpist ...

This denouement is more than reminiscent of the final scene in *Hue and Cry* when the choir is reassembled in church, the boys still bearing the scars of their climactic bundle with the baddies on the bomb site. In his memoirs, 'Tibby' Clarke, credited along with Dearden, Ronald Millar and Angus MacPhail as one of four writers on the film, merely mentions 'creating one of the episodes'[51] but in the absence of any other concrete evidence one might have reasonably assumed that because of his previous connection with Crichton, the 'composer's story' was his.

Happily, although buried deep down in the *Kensington Post* review of 16 September, we discover that Millar (later Sir Ronald Millar who became a distinguished playwright) was actually responsible for an episode that was easily the most regarded of the four in a generally mixed reception overall for the film. The *Post* called the episode 'the best of the bunch' while the *Tatler* declared it 'the real hit of the film'.

The Times, however, rather weakened its damning overall assessment by declaring the train in question to be 'the 3.15 for Liverpool ... from platform 13 at Euston' when, as we all know, it was the 3.45! 'More train, less events' was one recurring epithet, and whatever else, the film still remains a 'glorious visual feast for steam rail enthusiasts.'[52]

***

In its February 1949 issue, *Lilliput*, an elegant, small-format British monthly boasting humour, short stories, the arts, cartoons and photographs, devoted ten pages to the British film industry. This followed in the wake of, by any standards, a very decent year for quality domestic production with films like *The Fallen Idol*, *Hamlet*, *Oliver Twist*, *The Red Shoes*, *Scott of the Antarctic* and *The Winslow Boy*. Centrepiece of the focus, subtitled 'British Film Directors', was an array of eight atmospheric black and white photographs by Bill Brandt featuring whom, one presumed, *Lilliput* deemed the industry's top film-makers of the day: David Lean and Carol Reed, unarguably; Ronald Neame, producer-director and/or cinematographer; Anthony Asquith, at forty-eight, oldest of the home-grown talent; the Boulting Brothers, at thirty-five, the youngest on show; then, more surprisingly, no fewer than three directors from Ealing Studios – Cavalcanti, Robert Hamer and, despite successive box office busts with *Against the Wind* and *Another Shore* (*Train of Events* was yet to be released), Crichton.

Each film-maker was also accorded a caption. In theirs, Reed and Neame received unqualified praise while the others all merited, in between plaudits, just a whiff of censure. Crichton, pictured, pipe firmly clamped in mouth at his home, Mull Cottage, in Denham before a rather messy fireplace, earned 'has yet to find the film to give his theories full scope ... Wants to film original stories of real people observed in their authentic settings and circumstances. Is Ealing's most untemperamental director.'[53]

Bookending the photographs was a typically combative article by the ubiquitous Richard Winnington, the so-called 'stormy petrel of British film critics' (who might well also have provided the captions). His piece was entitled 'Nervy Birds in a Gilded Cage' and must have given the magazine's film-maker honourees some serious food for thought. In the first half of the article, Winnington paints a sardonic portrait of different director types, their antecedents, aims and ambitions. For the final two-thirds, his assessment is coloured by what he clearly perceives as the malevolent thrall cast over the indigenous industry by the shadow of the increasingly powerful J. Arthur Rank and his ever-expanding organisation.

'What Mr Rank's patronage has done to British directors can be seen in their films and studied in their faces,' writes Winnington.

> They have been vaingloriously led to the false assumption that to direct a film is to create, or they have succumbed to the delusion that the way of any artist can be easy on other terms than those of his own uncompromising standards. The weakness (seemingly national) of British directors is that they don't burn to get something out of themselves through the cinema but can get prettily worked up over any book, play, or (more infrequently) script that is generally suitable to their styles and tastes and not likely to cause more than a token battle with the sponsors on account, perhaps, of a vague sociological or arty flavour. British directors can not evade their sense of responsibility for the colourlessness of British pictures even though they are in general fatted victims of the industry ... But for all that I have said he is still with his inflated ego, his need for flattery and reassurance, his failures and timorousness, the main honest element in an industry not conspicuous for the possession of that quality.[54]

As Crichton's career progressed much more fruitfully on into the fifties, he would, with varying degrees of success, fulfil at least some of the ambitions claimed on his behalf in *Lilliput*.

Notes

1 *Made in Ealing*, BBC Omnibus, 1986.
2 *Ealing Comedies*, Tuesday Documentary, BBC, 1970.
3 Brian McFarlane, *An Autobiography of British Cinema* (Methuen, 1997), p. 153.
4 *BEHP*.
5 Charles Barr, *Ealing Studios* (Studio Vista, 1977), p. 61.
6 Basil Wright, *The Long View* (Paladin, 1976), p. 308.
7 Barr, *Ealing Studios*, p. 63.
8 T.E.B. Clarke, *This Is Where I Came In* (Michael Joseph, 1974), p. 155.
9 *Ibid.*, pp. 155–6.
10 Jack Warner, *Jack of All Trades* (W.H. Allen, 1975), p. 111.
11 McFarlane, *An Autobiography of British Cinema*, p. 196.
12 Robert Sellers, *The Secret Life of Ealing Studios* (Aurum Press, 2015), p. 91.
13 Clarke, *This Is Where I Came In*, p. 156.
14 Warner, *Jack of All Trades*, p. 112.
15 *Ibid.*
16 *The Times*, 24 February 1947.
17 Clarke, *This Is Where I Came In*, p. 156.
18 *BEHP*.
19 *Ibid.*
20 *Ibid.*
21 Charles Crichton, 'Children and Fantasy', *Penguin Film Review*, September 1948.
22 McFarlane, *An Autobiography of British Cinema*, p. 153.
23 Barr, *Ealing Studios*, p. 95.
24 *Ibid.*
25 Neil Sinyard, 'British Film of the 1950s', *BFI Screenonline*, www.screenonline.org.uk/film/id/1147086/index.html (accessed 16 January 2021).
26 *Ibid.*
27 Lee Freeman, 'Mild Revolution?' in Mark Duguid, Lee Freeman, Keith M. Johnston and Melanie Williams (eds) *Ealing Revisited* (BFI, 2012), p. 77.
28 Andrew Roberts, 'People's War' in Mark Duguid, Lee Freeman, Keith M. Johnston and Melanie Williams (eds) *Ealing Revisited* (BFI, 2012), p. 56.
29 Clarke, *This Is Where I Came In*, p. 157.
30 *Ibid.*
31 *Ibid.*
32 McFarlane, *An Autobiography of British Cinema*, p. 154.
33 *BEHP*.
34 McFarlane, *An Autobiography of British Cinema*, p. 154.
35 Robert Murphy, *British Cinema and the Second World War* (Continuum, 2000), p. 113.
36 *Ibid.*, p. 114.
37 *BEHP*.
38 *Ibid.*
39 *The Times*, 16 February 1948.
40 *Daily Mirror*, 13 February 1948.
41 *The Tatler*, 26 February 1948.
42 *Daily Express*, 16 February 1948.
43 *Variety*, 12 February 1948.
44 *Sydney Morning Herald*, 12 March 1950.
45 Philip Kemp, *Lethal Innocence: The Cinema of Alexander Mackendrick* (Methuen, 1991), p. 22.
46 *The Times*, 29 November 1948.

47 *Ibid.*
48 Kemp, *Lethal Innocence*, p. 26.
49 McFarlane, *An Autobiography of British Cinema*, p. 153.
50 *BEHP.*
51 Clarke, *This Is Where I Came In*, p. 162.
52 *The Times*, 22 August, 1949.
53 *Lilliput*, February 1949, p. 60.
54 *Ibid.*, p. 68.

The fifties: 1950-54

By the turn of the fifties, the studio's legacy had been assured after a momentous decade-ending year. Following Crichton's potent marker with *Hue and Cry* two years earlier, three films in particular – Cornelius's *Passport to Pimlico*, Mackendrick's *Whisky Galore* and Hamer's *Kind Hearts and Coronets* – all released in quick succession during 1949 ensured the label 'Ealing comedies' became not just common currency, but also, simultaneously, a term of audience expectation and affection. George Perry in his studio memoir, *Forever Ealing*, suggests that this fresh line of comedies 'in some ways developed from the war films of the early forties for many of them adopted the theme of the small group pitted against and eventually triumphing over the superior odds of a more powerful opponent. The quality shown to win is team spirit, the idiosyncrasies of character blended and harnessed for the good of the group.'[1] For peacetime, the formula would be redefined more specifically as the triumph of the community spirit over bureaucracy.

Dance Hall (1950)

Although Crichton had made a minor comic contribution to Ealing's prolific output during 1949 with his playful segment in *Train of Events*, he would have to wait another couple of years before complementing the brand with, first, *The Lavender Hill Mob*, then *The Titfield Thunderbolt*. Instead he was, as he saw it, now lumbered with a project that, at the outset anyway, he certainly did not want to make. According to Philip Kemp, 'Balcon always maintained that no Ealing director "was ever forced to make a film he didn't wasn't to make." Crichton agrees, but adds that Balcon would sometimes exert oblique pressure, "especially if you had another project he knew you wanted to make. He'd hint that if you wouldn't mind just doing *this* for him first."'[2] Crichton, however, admitted, 'Once we had got the research started behind the project, I found myself deeply involved – with the people who went to dance halls once a week, the different types of bands, a world which has now disappeared.'[3]

It was perhaps fitting that after the odd period piece like Frend's *The Loves of Joanna Godden* (1947), *Dance Hall*, Ealing's first film to focus specifically on women and their contemporary problems – in this case, four young factory workers who regularly dance the night away at the local palais – should at least have a female screenwriter albeit sharing credit with two male contributors. It is, however, telling that Diana Morgan, a Cambridge graduate, would prove to be the only major female creative ever to penetrate the studios' predominant patriarchy. With a background as an actress and playwright, Morgan, the same age as Crichton, had worked, credited and uncredited, on half a dozen Ealing films before being assigned to *Dance Hall* alongside the film's associate producer, E.V.H. 'Ted' Emmett, best known as a commentator, and Alexander Mackendrick.

The story follows Eve (Natasha Parry), Mary (Jane Hylton), Carole (Diana Dors) and Georgie (Petula Clark) whose spare time is a mixture of romantic entanglements and serious dance competition in and out of the 'Chiswick Palais' (actually the Hammersmith Palais) where the big band music of Ted Heath and Geraldo reigns (Figure 5.1). Of the four, Clark, at seventeen, was the youngest of the quartet but, in terms of previous screen time, probably the most experienced having been before the cameras as a singer and actress since 1944. For this film she was paired with Douglas Barr (as Peter), the same, though now rather taller, actor who had played the angelic-looking little choirboy-cum-Blood and Thunder gang member Alec in *Hue and Cry*. Together they have their eyes firmly set on the grand dance finals, which climax the film.

But, as Clark, in her late eighties at the time of writing and, seventy years after *Dance Hall*, still a singing and acting star, told me, she had been hoping, possibly praying, that her partner would have been played by Anthony Newley, with whom she had co-starred in *Vice-Versa* (1948) and on whom, she confessed, she 'had a bit of a crush'. Her role required getting dance lessons every day and she became so proficient that the school in Kensington entered her for competition and she earned a silver medal. But all that dimmed when she learned that Newley was not, after all, going to play Peter. Newley had, instead, been called up for national service. Clark's hopes of 'being kissed by him' in the film were finally dashed.

Apart from Newley, Clark retained two other abiding memories of making the film. The first was the live music of the Heath and Geraldo

Figure 5.1 (Left to right) Jane Hylton, Petula Clark, Diana Dors and Natasha Parry in *Dance Hall*

bands: 'I had worked with them before in my other career, so that was great fun.' The other was the director. 'I liked Charlie a lot; he had just the right touch with actors, and was charming and funny.' She contrasted him favourably with Michael Powell [who directed her in *I Know Where I'm Going* (1945)] 'who wasn't the same,' she suggested darkly.[4] Powell did indeed have a reputation for often being cruel to actors and crew alike.

The least experienced of the four – Dors, Hylton and Clark were all *Huggett* film regulars – was nineteen-year-old Parry who prior to *Dance Hall* had only enjoyed a spit-and-cough part in *Golden Arrow* (1949), a sort of *Train of Events* style international comedy directed by her stepfather, Gordon Parry. Parry's storyline as Eve is by far and away the most interesting and, on occasion, most complex of the four girls. Like the others she works in a nearby factory toiling away in steam and heat to an accompaniment of radio music. Doing quite what we, and especially Petula Clark as she admitted to me, never really discover. Work over, it is back to a tenement flat to get ready for the Palais where she meets up with her fiancé, later her husband, Phil (Donald Houston), who prefers motorbikes to Terpsichore.

Their already (mildly) conflicted relationship is exacerbated by the intervention of a fast-talking American, literally a smart Alec (Bonar Colleano), who dances enthusiastically, drives a sports car and seems to have cornered the black market in kippers. Also, even more unhelpfully, he fancies Eve. This now has the makings of a potentially stormy triangle. From a circus family, Colleano, at twenty-five, had, in some of his dozen British films to date including *The Way to the Stars* (1945) and *A Matter of Life and Death* (1946), pretty much cornered the market in fast-talking Yanks – at least the ones Robert Beatty was not playing – of the kind that personified the American GI, beloved and hated in about equal measure, who had proliferated in Britain during the war. So to give *Dance Hall* and its mixture of transatlantic musical stylings a useful and authentically Americanised feel, Colleano's casting seemed suitably apt.

That, however, was no consolation to Dermot Walsh, also twenty-five, another quite exotic-looking, dark-haired matinee idol type – Irish rather than American – who thought *he* had landed the role of Alec. But as he told Brian McFarlane:

> I was to play a character who had to dominate the first three scenes in the movie; the scene was a dance hall full of people, and this spivvy character had to come in and dominate all these other young people.
> Crichton set up the first shot of the dance floor, then he panned on to the crowd standing around watching the dancers. They had chosen very good extras – tall, good-looking people – and you see these people all smiling and beating time; then you see this little figure trying to push his way through them to come to the front, which was me! The next scene they shot was a three-hander and I had to dominate that as well. So Charlie put me downstage left in a chair, in profile. Now of course you can't dominate from downstage left. There was a third scene, which was equally inept from the point of view of presenting me as a dominant character, so I was taken off the movie. They replaced me with Bonar Colleano and reshot it, making it possible for him to dominate in ways that hadn't been available to me. So I did feel very cross about that. In effect, you see, they'd ruined my career in first features.[5]

Although Walsh continued to perform, albeit fitfully, on film for the next thirty years, it would, as he noted bitterly, be mostly B-movie fare. There is no official explanation for the replacement except to suggest that as Colleano had such a high profile at the time and also bearing in mind Rank's mid-Atlantic aspirations, his casting as Alec was quite simply a hard-headed business decision.

Although the film is rightly championed for Ealing's rare distaff perspective, both Dors's and Hylton's roles remain, for the most part, disappointingly peripheral. The brassy Dors is the (too occasional) comic relief while the more homely Hylton seems to exist merely to help Phil (whom she loves) back on track after his relationship with Eve appears to have gone terminally pear-shaped. There is even a brief moment in Eve and Phil's turbulent tie when the worst is suggested.

This hint of self-harm apparently set off a serious row between two of the writers, Morgan and Mackendrick. Morgan recalled:

> We had Donald Houston standing on the roof [of the palais], gazing down thinking of suicide I kept asking how the audience would know. Sandy said, 'Oh, everyone knows.' This went on all morning, all through lunch, and all afternoon. At half past five, Sandy burst out laughing and said, 'The bitch is right, you don't know!' So we went over to the Red Lion where we all drank too much.[6]

After the success of *Whisky Galore*, Mackendrick might have reasonably felt entitled to the immediate award of a new directing project. What he got before regaining the helm nearly eighteen months on with *The Man in The White Suit* was what he considered 'demotion', contributing instead dialogue for *Dance Hall* then *The Blue Lamp*. This may have explained why, Morgan told Philip Kemp, Mackendrick was 'tirelessly argumentative' during the production. On *Dance Hall*, he also got to direct some second unit stuff, 'all the material where the bands are playing, close-ups of the trumpeters and drummers and things like that. Very good experience, and I enjoyed it thoroughly'. Crichton recalls him being 'very particular about what I wanted, and I couldn't be precise – and he tried to nail me down, the bastard! But they were very simple shots, and he took just what was wanted, and that's all there was to it'.[7] This may have been some kind of compensation for Crichton's intervention in *Whisky Galore*.

Diana Morgan may have provided Ealing's only ever female perspective, but at heart she was pretty much considered just one of the chaps, as also evidenced by her own recollections of hanging out with the likes of Hamer and Crichton over long lunches, playing intellectual word games. Of Crichton, she remarked: 'He was bliss, lovely to work with, a lovely, funny man and very understanding. The dance hall wasn't really a different world to me, because my husband [Robert McDermot] was with the BBC and he was on what was called the "Slush Committee", which meant we had to go to a lot of dance halls and take notes on people like Geraldo.'[8]

Meanwhile, back at the film, just when it also seems that Petula Clark has been relegated to the sidelines after flitting in and out of the early action, her character Georgie returns to share centre stage with Eve for the final quarter of the film. If this were Hollywood, she and Peter would have won the dance final against all the odds. But kitted out in a lush palais frock lent to her by the hall's oily manager (Sydney Tafler) instead of the dress made for her by her adoring mum, Georgie and Peter are not even placed. But like the eventual outcome for Eve and Phil, following a punch-up with Alec in the palais car park, love, not dance trophies or a motormouth Yank, triumphs.

When Crichton watched the film again years later, he said he was surprised by its rather enduring fascination as, if nothing else, a fairly accurate historical record of a long-gone phenomenon. The exuberant socio-economic backcloth to *Dance Hall* is explained by Dr Claire Langhammer of the University of Sussex:

> Throughout the film dancing is embedded in everyday and community life. The dance hall itself provides a forum within which contemporaneous themes are addressed: Americanisation, consumerism and relationships between men and women are amongst the most notable. The dance hall also acts as an arena within which young women's postwar dreams can be voiced and pursued. Seen through the eyes of the film's key protagonists, the Palais de Danse has significance beyond its primary function. The importance of dance hall culture to the lives of many millions of people right across the middle years of the 20th century has long been clear, not least because memories of the dance hall loom so large in oral and life histories that reflect on the period.[9]

It is that disconnect between the film's documentary-like realism and its quality as purely film entertainment that finally divided critics then as now. What, though, still unites reviewers up to seventy years apart was rather neatly summed up by *The Times* in 1950: 'The trouble with the film is that the characters do not match the authenticity of the background, and the working girls, who are the heroines, are too clearly girls who work in the studio and nowhere else.'[10] The contrast is made even starker by the casting of the actors playing older generation, especially some of the girls' parents, like Fred Johnson, Dandy Nichols and the ubiquitous Gladys Henson, who much more convincingly resonate Bow Bells.

The *West London Observer*, in whose parish the dance action was focused, was unequivocal: 'How anyone could have written a reasonably good story around these silly characters is beyond me; someone has tried and failed. The dialogue is terrible. The acting is undistinguished and the whole thing bored me to distraction.'

THE FIFTIES: 1950–54 **91**

Contrast that with Roger Philip Mellor's modern appraisal in *BFI Screenonline*:

> Editing and photography are first rate, from the opening sound edit (soft dance music to deafening machine noise), with a tracking shot set up in a real factory introducing the girls. The car park scenes are dramatically lit and edited, and when Eve climbs to the roof and a train speeds by below, we fear tragedy is looming. And locating personal tragedy in a carnival setting clearly references the French classic of poetic realism, *Les Enfants du Paradis* (1945).[11]

Mellor's positive references to both the film's 'noise' and its allusion to Marcel Carné's 1945 classic are, separately, contradicted in 1950.

The *Daily Herald* fumed: 'Never in my puff before did I sit through such a noisy film. Factory machines roar, whistles blow, trumpets blast, drums roll, everybody shouts and even the cutting is rowdy. Charles Crichton has picked up an abominable habit somewhere of changing scene by noise.' Freda Bruce Lockhart wrote, rather more thoughtfully, in the *Tatler*:

> This not one of Ealing's prouder products ... the private lives of the dance hall patrons, not very interesting in themselves seem to call either for more subjective sympathy (in the Italian style) or for more objective candour (*à la Française*). Director Charles Crichton cannot compensate for lack of a point of view by cutting, which it would be more apt to call slashing.[12]

What could be described as some sort of meeting of minds between the intervening years can at least be detected in the respective verdicts of Derek Winnert, who wrote in 2014 of *Dance Hall*'s 'honest attempt to paint a down-to-earth and truthful portrait of Britain in its tatty era of post-war austerity',[13] while the *Daily Express* of the day concluded, 'The story is trite but atmosphere authentic. I could almost smell the cheap scent and perspiration.' In the end, it might have all boiled down simply to a matter of timing. After a series of hit comedies a year earlier, all of which genuinely provided light relief from the current gloom, an Ealing template had, helpfully or not, been established, which probably accounts for the 'judgement' from *The Times* that *Dance Hall* does not quite live up to the high standards set by Ealing Studios. In retrospect, *Dance Hall* was not, observes Roger Philip Mellor, 'a great success, perhaps because the world depicted (factory work, tenement flats, the suburban Palais dance hall) was too familiar to much of the urban audience',[14] the emphasis being firmly on 'too'.

After three successive box office duds, not counting *Train of Events*, Crichton began, perhaps understandably, to fret that his career was 'sliding'. Even as he brooded on this, matters were, happily, already in train to develop a new project, which, as he would admit much later, 'rescued me'.[15]

The Lavender Hill Mob (1951)

About ten years after the release of *The Lavender Hill Mob*, Crichton was to be found reflecting very specifically on the film and its success to, mostly, senior Wallasey school boys and girls at a meeting of the Merseyside Film Institute Society, Britain's oldest film society, in its regular venue, the Bluecoat, a three hundred-year-old, Grade 1 listed building in Liverpool's city centre. Although hard to pin down the exact date of the encounter, just across the river from Crichton's birthplace, it is likely to have been late 1961 or early 1962 since the film-maker rather intriguingly invokes the latest works by Fellini (*La Dolce Vita*) and Antonioni (*La Notte*) – both of which would seem, on the face of it, a million miles removed from the traditional Ealing output – during his lecture.

Crichton guided the students through the various stages of the film-making process and its key personnel using, in quite broad strokes, *The Lavender Hill Mob* as his principal case study. So how did the film actually come about?

> One of his [from 1948, Sir Michael Balcon] staff writers, T.E.B. Clarke, had been writing on a serious crime story, but somehow he couldn't take it seriously, and one day he came into [Balcon's] office and asked permission to go off for a while and turn it into a comedy. The result was the first draft of *The Lavender Hill Mob*, the story of a mild, underpaid bank clerk who had dreamed for years of robbing the Bank of England, and one day got his chance. I was asked to direct and Michael Truman to produce.[16]

Crichton's convenient nutshell for his film had, it transpired, an altogether more fascinating genesis according to 'Tibby' Clarke. He had been originally assigned to work with fellow writer John Eldridge, a former documentarian, on a serious crime drama, a sort of sequel to *The Blue Lamp*, called *Pool of London*.

> His [Eldridge's] provisional villain was a Bank of England employee who was secretly planning a bullion robbery. 'Because of his job he should be able to steal the gold without much difficulty,' John said. 'His big problem will be how to smuggle it out of the country. Have you got

any ideas about that?' We discussed it for a while without getting anywhere. Then I confessed I was rather worried about that villain of his. 'I think there's a danger that he may emerge as a comedy character,' I said.[17]

Eldridge, it seems, was finally convinced and so decided to dispense with his 'rascally bank official' opting instead for a different kind of 'heavy'. Back at home, Clarke was searching through some drawers and came across a gold-coloured Eiffel Tower he'd once been given as a souvenir from Paris – now a script rather different from the one envisaged for *Pool of London* began to form in his mind and, two hours later, he claimed, a new five hundred-word outline emerged. The next morning he cornered Balcon as the boss was getting out of his car. 'How's the river story going?' Balcon asked Clarke. 'Bit of a development. Can we lose the river?' he replied, before beginning to explain to Balcon his new comedy ideas for 'the river story'.

Balcon was initially outraged before being placated by Clarke who suggested that there was no reason why two entirely different films couldn't still be made. After reading, and falling for, Clarke's outline, Balcon concurred, adding, 'Show it to Charlie Crichton, and see how he likes it.'[18] Amusingly, *Pool of London* (1951), directed by Basil Dearden and with a rare leading role for a black actor (Earl Cameron), ended up being filmed simultaneously with *The Lavender Hill Mob*; they actually clashed on location when a chase in the latter went past a camera being used for the former. Crichton, about to be reunited with Clarke for the sixth time, 'liked it'[19] and the pair were joined on the project by Michael Truman, who had been an editor on seven Ealing productions, making his producer debut.

So, as Crichton explained to the students:

> From that moment the three of us, Truman, Clarke and myself, were closely involved working on the script. I didn't mean to imply in any way that Truman and myself did more than bully, harass and possibly stimulate Clarke. The script is, of course, his work, but I mean that in the film world there's nearly always a considerable overlapping of functions. For me, anyway, it is essential that I work with the writer on my scripts. In that way I grow up with the story, subconsciously. I probably help to shape it towards that kind of thing that I can do on the floor.[20]

The final story concerned two fundamentally honest middle-aged men – one, Holland, a meek long-time Bank of England official; the other, Pendlebury, a manufacturer of holiday souvenirs, or 'gewgaws', joining forces for an ambitious heist of £1m worth of gold bars from

Holland's place of business. The bars would then be melted down, reshaped into mini Eiffel Towers and shipped under the noses of the police and customs to France for eventual collection and dispersal by the duo and their two authentically crooked minor associates, Wood and Fisher. The robbery goes fine until, at the Eiffel Tower itself, a box of the actual gold towers is mistakenly opened instead of cheap gewgaw lookalikes, with six being sold to a group of visiting English schoolgirls. Now the Mob must retrieve the treasure before its gilt secret is revealed.

Truman, in particular, was responsible for mooting a serious change of direction from the story in Clarke's original script, which, said Crichton,

> followed the adventures of these gewgaws as they passed into different hands. Michael pointed out that the audience would not care less about the Eiffel Towers or about any new characters who became involved with them. They would want to know what happened to the architects of this imaginative crime. So the three of us sat down and hammered out a new storyline, with Tibby, of course, doing most of the hammering.[21]

Some crucial facts about the Bank of England and its bullion business were obtained by Clarke from the horse's mouth as it were after enquiring directly of the old lady 'for information required on means of stealing gold bullion'. Once the bank had ascertained this was for a film, advice was guilelessly forthcoming with the useful hint that for any possibility of a successful robbery, the heist itself would have to take place between the refinery and the bank. The parts were falling into place as, instead of a sequel to *The Blue Lamp* as Clarke had originally started out, the way he and the others were now developing the script and especially the role of the police force in the unfolding comedy, this was beginning to shape instead more like a good-natured parody of Ealing's successful police procedural.

Naturally, casting was key, though in retrospect it is difficult to imagine any better star pairing than Alec Guinness, as 'Dutch' Holland, and Stanley Holloway as 'Al' Pendlebury, with their satirical echoes of notorious gangsters, respectively, Schultz and Capone (Figure 5.2). 'We were,' Crichton admitted, 'very lucky with casting. Their styles were completely different but they made a perfect duet.'[22] Holloway thought that he and Guinness made a good team because, as he explained, 'When he is playing comedy I think he is at his best when he has another comic personality to play against, to set off his own performance. On his own – and I stress I mean in comedy, not necessarily serious roles – he needs to disguise to help him.'[23]

Guinness, after eight roles in *Kind Hearts and Coronets*, and Holloway, the chief protagonist of Clarke's *Passport to Pimlico*, were surely Ealing's

THE FIFTIES: 1950–54

Figure 5.2 Pendlebury (Stanley Holloway) and Holland (Alec Guinness) embrace in *The Lavender Hill Mob*

biggest names of the day and their combination, at £6,000 each (just under £200,000 in 2020 money) in *Mob* proved a partnership made in film heaven. Guinness, in particular, worked closely with Clarke and Co. 'making suggestions that would never otherwise have occurred to us'[24] about his character. These included the addition of some tummy padding and a lazy 'r' speech defect. Anyway, whatever he, make-up and wardrobe finally came up with, Guinness, only thirty-seven at the time, might easily have passed as sixty-year-old Holloway's middle-aged contemporary. It would be their only film together, but as a result of their instant rapport, Guinness invited Holloway to play first gravedigger in his ill-fated production of *Hamlet*, which opened just a month before *Mob* premiered in London.

Just eighty-two minutes, and like the best films leaving you wanting much more, it is simply packed with wonderfully witty dialogue, some colourfully off-kilter characters and a string of memorable scenes, of which the so-called 'Seduction Sequence' was easily Crichton's favourite.

For his Merseyside Film Institute Society lecture, Crichton wanted to use the sequence, in which Guinness snares Holloway into becoming his partner in crime, to illustrate the overlapping functions of some of the creatives by explaining each of their separate roles within it. He cited, in particular, Michael Truman, Alec Guinness and Douglas Slocombe, as well as 'my intention in shooting it'.[25] Unfortunately, the actual lecture content of this 'seduction' was spoken, not, sadly, written out in Crichton's notes. All 'Tibby' Clarke could confirm in his memoir was that it 'had to be written and rewritten eleven times before it satisfied all concerned'.[26] As for the film's climax, a spectacular car chase around various London streets involving a stolen police car, collisions, tangled radio aerials and a Welsh constable on a running board lustily singing 'Old McDonald had a farm', Clarke was slightly more forthcoming. 'In my time as a war reserve policeman I was on telephone duty one night when I received a report of a stolen car with a number that seemed oddly familiar, then I delightedly realized what was not being given out – that it was in fact our own duty officer's car. As soon as I made Alec and Stanley steal a police car, our final sequence promptly clicked.'[27]

In another of Clarke's subtly comic exchanges, which is all about reading between the lines, Holland, who has planned the robbery down to the minutest detail, is suddenly summoned to his boring boss Turner's (Ronald Adam) office to hear, to his horror, that he has been granted a 'promotion' to a different department.

> Holland: I'm too old to change my views now, sir.
> Turner: Nonsense. You're never too old to better oneself. Think of what you can do with an extra fifteen shillings a week.
> Holland: But, sir, I like the bullion office. It holds all I ever wished for.
> Turner: The trouble with you, Holland, if I may speak frankly, is that you do not have enough ambition. When a good opportunity comes along, grab it with both hands. May not occur again.
> Holland: Very good, sir, I'll follow your advice.

Then, of course, there was Paris, and the Eiffel Tower – available to the unit for two to three hours a day at £30 a session – where Guinness and Holloway must try and retrieve their golden gewgaws before the schoolgirls make it to Blighty and possibly into the long arm of the local law. The duo's pursuit required them to descend the Tower not conveniently by lift but via the dizzyingly circular, perilous-looking staircase on its exterior. Guinness recalled:

The director ... said, 'Alec, there is a trap door over there – where it says Workmen Only – I'd like you to run to it, open it, and start running down the spiral staircase. Stanley will follow.' So I did as asked. A very dizzying sight to the ground greeted me. But I completed half a spiral before I noticed that three feet in front of me the steps suddenly ceased – broken off. I sat down promptly where I was and cautiously started to shift myself back to the top, warning Stanley to get out of the way. 'What the hell are you doing?' the director yelled.

'Down! Further down!' 'Further down is eternity,' I called back. Stanley and I regained the panoramic view of Paris pale and shaking. No one had checked up on the staircase and no one apologized; that wasn't Ealing policy.[28]

Guinness's near dice with death seemed, however, to have been forgotten when he told Brian McFarlane in 1989: '*The Lavender Hill Mob* is a very good-natured film with a well-told story. Charlie Crichton had a very good eye for cutting and a feeling for getting away from drab reality into the world of fantasy.'[29] Guinness added that unlike with Hamer and Mackendrick, 'I never got to know Crichton well'.[30] The bulk of the descent was actually filmed back at Ealing, where they had built a replica of the winding staircase with laminated wood stairs rising to the full eighty feet of the studio and a camera lift that was able to follow the two men's descent without missing a trick.

Making up the mob were Sidney James, five years before he became Tony Hancock's regular sidekick, and Alfie Bass, on his fourth Ealing assignment, who also, thanks to some crafty scheduling, managed to score a role in *Pool of London*. After the female focus of *Dance Hall*, it was very much back to Ealing's more familiar male dominance this time round, although two of the women's roles were, for very different reasons, especially eye-catching.

In the film's very first scene set in an exclusive Rio de Janeiro club where Guinness is about to unfold in flashback details of the famous heist to a fellow diner (who turns out at the end to have more than a passing interest in the crime), a twenty-one-year-old Audrey Hepburn, as the exotic Chiquita, stops by the table where she is given some money by Guinness for 'a birthday present'. Her single line before disappearing altogether is 'How sweet of you!' This was to be Hepburn's third successive spit-and-cough film role before, a year later, moving up to 'major supporting' (in *Secret People*) then, twelve months after that, an Oscar-winning best actress for *Roman Holiday*.

At the other end of the age spectrum and afforded rather more screen time was seventy-year-old Edie Martin as Miss Evesham, proprietor of the Balmoral Hotel in Lavender Hill, South London, where Holland and Pendlebury first meet then begin to hatch their get rich plot. Tiny but firm, she runs an orderly establishment, unaware she's housing would-be felons. 'You naughty men,' is about as fierce as she gets berating the two men after they return home drunk after celebrating the success of the robbery. She might have been the template for Mrs Wilberforce in *The Ladykillers* four years on, and indeed also appeared in that film – in an uncredited role.

'Tibby' Clarke might reasonably have been a little blasé after completing his eleventh screenplay, in whole or part, for Ealing over the past seven years, but when he sat through the first screening of *The Lavender Hill Mob* it was, he confessed, 'with enraptured astonishment ... for I saw that Charles Crichton had this time made a better film than the one projected months ago in my own mental viewing theatre'.[31] A decade after, Crichton, ever modest, played down his contribution by declaring to the students, 'I didn't really choose *The Lavender Hill Mob* – it was handed to me on a platter!'[32]

Clarke's surprise and delight with the finished film was echoed throughout the critical community home and abroad as the film earned the kind of praise that must, for Crichton anyway, have helped soften some memories of the mauling he had received in some quarters after *Another Shore* and *Dance Hall*. Praise was principally reserved for Clarke and Guinness, but Crichton earned a decent share as well.

Beneath 'The Goodness of Guinness' headline – in the same vein as the oft-applied 'admirable Crichton' – the *Daily Mail*'s Fred Majdalany noted on 22 June 1951: 'In Clarke's previous films the idea has been the main strength. This time character has been added too. The result is a quite irresistible funny film – to date [halfway through 1951] the comedy of the year. Charles Crichton has squeezed the maximum effort out of every scene; the fun never lets up.' *The Times* was no less glowing, opining of Crichton:

> In his previous film *Hue and Cry* [conveniently ignoring the intervening three years of comparative duff] Mr Crichton showed great skill in the handling of crowd scenes and in the exploitation of character, and [with] *The Lavender Hill Mob* he has again used his talent to good effect ... there is also great fertility of invention in minor details and in the incidents of the chase which such a film as this demands and which is handled by Mr Crichton with all the skill he has shown in his previous comedies.[33]

The *Tatler* wrote: 'Charles Crichton has directed and his past experience of suspense and timing, with clear-cut photography, provides the right realistic base for the tower of fantasy and farce.' Alan Dent of the *Illustrated London News* praised the 'admirable' director as well as suggesting the two main characters might have come out of novels by Arnold Bennett and H.G. Wells, 'and how both those authors would have relished this film'. C.A. Lejeune in the *Sketch* marvelled at the way 'this wonderfully matched team of comedians storms its way through ... with all the colours flying; scoring an undisputed triumph for nonsense, skill, practice, observation and plain audacious fun'.

The plaudits were not just confined to the capital commentators. Outside London, the *Warwick and Warwickshire Advertiser* was typical: 'The strength of the *Lavender Hill Mob* is in the understanding of British characteristics and habits obviously possessed by director Charles Crichton', while the *Belfast News-Letter* suggested, 'no film for months has been better for space and sheer good fun ... its mixture of fantasy and realism, absurdity and logic, is blended with warm humanity and wit ... Directed by Charles Crichton ... the tale never loses its element of surprise.'

When it came to awards time, these were the days, in the UK anyway, before 'the little white envelope'. The fifth British Film Academy Awards, comprising just five categories of film and no mention of creatives, were announced in the press ahead of the actual presentation, on 8 May 1952. *The Lavender Hill Mob* was named best British film from a list of eight including fellow Ealing contender, *The Man in the White Suit*. Both were also recorded in the eighteen-strong line-up for best film from any source, from which Max Ophüls's *La Ronde* emerged the winner.

On 19 March 1953, almost eighteen months after its US release, the American industry's great and the good gathered at the RKO Pantages Theatre on Hollywood Boulevard for the Silver Anniversary edition – perhaps 'Golden' would have been more appropriate – of the Academy Awards, for which *The Lavender Hill Mob* had been nominated in two categories: actor – Guinness (in the first of six nominations across thirty-six years) and story and screenplay – Clarke. Complemented simultaneously by a companion show in New York, the Oscars were covered for the first time ever live on television and garnered the largest single audience in the States to date in TV's five-year commercial history.

This was also the year of films like *Moulin Rouge*, *High Noon*, *The Bad and The Beautiful*, *The Quiet Man* and *The Greatest Show on Earth*, so it came as no huge surprise when Gary Cooper's slow-talking Marshal Will Kane trumped Guinness in the performance stakes. As for writing, there were three categories; separate ones for story and screenplay then a combined category in which Clarke was pitted against the likes of Ruth Gordon and Garson Kanin (*Pat and Mike*), Terence Rattigan (*The Sound*

Barrier) and – this must have really tickled Clarke – John Steinbeck (*Viva Zapata!*). Despite the studio's writing nominations in succeeding years for both *The Cruel Sea* (1953, Eric Ambler) and *The Ladykillers* (1955, William Rose), Clarke's win that March evening in Los Angeles turned out to be Ealing's only ever Oscar win. Transatlantically, Crichton had to make do with just a nomination, and a gold medallion, from the Directors Guild of America.

American acclaim for the film, which would go on to gross over $500,000 (almost $5m in current money) at the US box office, had been first trumpeted towards the end of 1951 by the *New York Times* critic, Bosley Crowther, who opened up with

> that genius for civilized humor possessed by Britain's Ealing Studios, where they have tossed off such dexterous rib-ticklers as *Passport to Pimlico* [which Clarke had considered a superior screenplay to *Mob*] and *Kind Hearts and Coronets*, has been wound up again and set humming in a jolly trifle called *The Lavender Hill Mob* ...
> Jot it down as a picture that you will find it best to see at a moment when your mood is mellow and your sense of righteousness is slightly askew. For here again is a frolic that, like *Kind Hearts and Coronets*, indulges a serene and casual tolerance for undisguised lawlessness in man. And once again Alec Guinness, who played eight roles in *K. H. and C.* [*Kind Hearts and Coronets*], delivers himself of one character that is as wickedly droll as Halloween ... Charles Crichton has directed the whole thing with a touch of polite and gentle mockery applied to wholehearted farce.[34]

The popularity of Ealing comedies and, in particular, its latest success, naturally made it tough for rival British film companies attempting their own brand of indigenous whimsy. *Green Grow the Rushes* arrived in cinemas less than six months after the release of *The Lavender Hill Mob*. Partly set up by the technicians' union, the Association of Cinematograph Technicians (ACT), and backed by British Lion, it boasted some delightful rural settings, a strong cast, including Roger Livesey, Honor Blackman and Richard Burton, and in any other timescale might have proved a modest success. However, its tale of a shipwreck off the Kent Marshes, brandy smuggling and blinkered bureaucracy was for critics just too familiar and, worse still, derivative of everything from *Whisky Galore* to *Passport to Pimlico*. 'Written by a T.E.B Clarke ... and directed with the benevolent charm of a Charles Crichton ... this might well have become excellent satire with its debunking of officialdom.' Ealing was, for the time being, the gold standard.

Concluding his lecture in Liverpool in front of an audience probably more knowledgeable about contemporary British films like *The Day* the Earth Caught Fire, A Taste of Honey, Whistle Down the Wind or The Young Ones, Crichton explained that The Lavender Hill Mob was 'one of a series of successful comedies from Ealing – there were enough of them for people to talk about the "Ealing School."' But was there such a thing as an 'Ealing School?' he asked, rhetorically. If so, what was the common denominator? Personnel? Method of treatment? Put simply, for Crichton, it was 'affection'.³⁵

Forty-five years after making the film, Guinness reflected briefly and a little grudgingly on the film in a diary entry of 6 May 1996, included in his second volume of memoirs, My Name Escapes Me:

> The Lavender Hill Mob is being shown on TV this evening but I won't be watching it. (If only I had received £1 each time one of the Ealing comedies was shown I would be a rich man [conveniently ignoring his profit participation in 1977's Star Wars]. My contract didn't cover mechanical reproduction.) It was a good film, I think; well over forty years old now and mercifully it lasted only an hour and a half.³⁶

Hunted (1952)

Balcon's admonitory words in 1945 to his creatives about flying the Ealing nest, with that sardonic rider about the apparent lack of outside interest in their talents, surely rang rather differently seven years on, by which time all six directors of what Charles Barr calls 'The Team' had scored major box office hits. Five would continue to soldier on in W5 with varying degrees of success while Crichton became the first of the sextet to take a break from Balcon's bonds, albeit only temporarily, with a subject that could not have been further removed in content and tone from his 1951 comedy blockbuster. At a time when a strand of hard-boiled thrillers, dubbed 'film noir' in 1946 by French critic Nino Frank, were flourishing in Hollywood, Hunted turned out to be a much more modest, altogether gentler but yet still extremely stylish British complement to that influential American genre.

Dirk Bogarde, who had made his screen debut as an uncredited extra in Ealing's Come On George! in 1939, the second in a series of Formby comedies throughout the war, returned to the studio a decade later, by which time he was a fully paid-up Rank contract artiste, to make a much more startling impression as the young cop killer in The Blue Lamp. Two years after that, Bogarde was aching to get away from the kind of working-class, raincoat and cap roles, for which he felt he was being typecast by Rank, desperate instead to play officer-and-gentlemen parts to which he deemed himself much better suited. At this very early stage of what would eventually become a glittering career, Bogarde's choices were still dictated by the Rank Organisation, which is why he found himself cast as Chris Lloyd, another cor blimey killer in *Hunted*. Crichton recalled: 'At that particular time he was absolutely fed up with playing sneaky boys in mackintoshes. He didn't really want to do it, but he was contracted.'[37]

Crichton and writer Jack Whittingham were originally approached by producer Julian Wintle, whose company, Independent Artists, was one of the Rank satellites. He had a script written by Michael McCarthy, who had directed *Assassin for Hire*, a B-feature, for Wintle, in 1951. McCarthy was already known to Crichton because he had contributed to *Painted Boats* back in 1945. Balcon was willing to loan them out [Whittingham, with three Ealing screenplays already under his belt, was also a studio contractee] if they wanted.

Said Crichton, who got a raise of £500 above his normal Ealing salary: 'The picture was due to start in four weeks' time, and we were given one week to make up our mind. The script was terrible, but the idea behind it was possible.'[38] Less than a week later, Whittingham had come up with ideas about how to solve various script problems, and within three weeks, he and Crichton had devised a suitable shooting script for *Hunted*.

The story was simplicity itself. Chris Lloyd, a sailor home from the sea, discovers his wife has been unfaithful, kills the lover and then goes on the run with a small boy who had unwittingly stumbled on Lloyd and the body of the murder victim in some bombed-out London ruins. It turns out that the boy Robbie, a slight six-year-old, is trying to evade his abusive adoptive parents after a household accident. Rather than return home to face possibly painful retribution, he prefers instead to attach himself to Chris now in full flight from the police.

Rather less simple was the question of how would they manage to find a suitable child actor to play Robbie in such an adult-themed film thriller. Dozens of children – some eighty in all – had been tested for the demanding role without success, and Crichton had even started shooting when, in one of those serendipitous moments beloved of movie lore, the solution suddenly presented itself more than five hundred miles away in the small Aberdeenshire village of Monymusk. Jonathan Whiteley, known as Jon, son of the local headmaster, was taking part in a twenty-minute 'Children's Corner' BBC broadcast at the school. Not yet six, Jon recited Lear's 'The Owl and the Pussycat' in his gentle native lilt. Listening in was the Scots actor Moultrie Kelsall, an old friend of Crichton's, who had been one of the police officers in *The Lavender Hill Mob*. After contacting the broadcast's producer who confirmed that Jon

THE FIFTIES: 1950–54 **103**

Figure 5.3 Dirk Bogarde and Jon Whiteley in *Hunted*

seemed to be an outstanding talent, Kelsall sent an urgent message to Crichton. Following a hurried conference at Pinewood Studios, Jon was invited to come south for an audition (Figure 5.3).

Whiteley, long a distinguished art historian at Oxford's Ashmolean Museum who sadly died aged seventy-five during the writing of this book, told me:

> I remember my parents receiving a telegram asking me to come down to Pinewood for a screen test. Initially my parents were very, very reluctant, my mother particularly who was quite against it. She thought it

would interfere with my schooling. So my grandmother intervened. Her superstition was that 'if something comes uninvited, it's meant'.

The screen test comprised a scene taken from right at the beginning of the film when the boy is grabbed by Chris, with a stand-in for Bogarde, following their chance encounter after the murder in a bombed out cellar. 'That's all it was,' said Whiteley, 'then I went back to Scotland.'[39] Two days later, with the family's summer holiday in Dumfries postponed, Whiteley was on set in the fishing village of Portpatrick, Wigtownshire, on the Irish Sea coast, for the film's dramatic climax when Chris turns Sydney Carton – a role Bogarde would actually play for Rank in a 'Tibby' Clarke-scripted version of *A Tale of Two Cities* six years later – to save a sick Robbie while sacrificing his freedom at the same time. Whiteley also thought it is likely that the script was quickly tweaked to account for his Scottish accent as well as that of his adoptive parents.

After three weeks of locations in Scotland and the Potteries, the production moved back to Pinewood with several exteriors also in London, in particular at Albert Dock where Whiteley recalled he had a major run-in with Crichton:

> One of my clearest memories was getting a downright row from him for not being cooperative. I was in a sulk. I knew there was a ship coming in that morning and I wanted to go and watch it. He said 'No!' and I'm afraid I rather messed up things a bit. He took me aside and wiped the floor with me, and I felt quite ashamed. I saw his point very clearly.

That squabble aside, Whiteley said: 'I liked him very much. I thought of him as being a bit like a genial Edinburgh doctor with his pipe and a slightly gravelly voice which is common in Scotland.'[40]

Unlike some former child actors who much later charted disastrous fallout from their brief fame – notoriously, little Bobby Henrey who had been brilliantly coaxed by Carol Reed to a remarkably naturalistic performance in *The Fallen Idol* (1948) – Whiteley had nothing but happy memories of not just *Hunted* but all his subsequent four films before retirement on parents' orders at the grand old age of eleven. The 'adventure' of film-making continually fascinated Whiteley and was, I suspect, encouraged by Crichton, whose younger son was almost exactly the same age. He said: 'I used to look through the camera, and I also loved the sound of the arc lights switching on, and the idea you could build a set and through the camera it became a room or a Scottish barn.'[41]

But what of his, at first, rather reluctant co-star? Whether or not he began to realise all too quickly that the untrained little boy was proving to be a natural scene-stealer, Bogarde – disgruntled 'mackintosh boy' again notwithstanding – very quickly knuckled down to the job in hand and became not just a mentor but also a close friend to Whiteley. As Crichton told it, 'When Dirk started to work with Jon, something happened, and the result was two perfect performances, and, I think, a moving film.'[42] 'We were together for three months', said Bogarde. 'All that we did together was extemporary; we just invented it. We didn't have much rehearsal.'[43] Said Whiteley,

> I liked him very much and we got on wonderfully well; he was like an older brother. When the filming ended, he bought me quite a large Triang toy tractor. This was a consequence of his asking me what I wanted above all else as a present, and I said, 'a monkey – probably a chimp – from Harrods'. Much to my sorrow he said he'd have to ask my mother first, so that was the end of that, and I got the toy instead.[44]

It was not all sweetness and light. In an early scene, Bogarde has to drag the boy towards the sanctuary of a barge on the Thames, Bogarde shakes him roughly as he spits, 'Shuddup and let me think'. Whiteley, who had got used to the gentler Bogarde in their first weeks of shooting in Scotland, was suddenly non-plussed and thinking he had done something to upset his new hero burst into tears and it was several minutes before he could be pacified. When Bogarde explained it was all just a great game and this is what 'acting' meant, Whiteley responded accordingly.

Although away from his native Scotland for most of the filming, albeit in the company of his mother and two sisters, Whiteley clearly relished both the London locations and the studio work at Pinewood, where, for instance, with back projection, clever editing and judicious use of a stunt double, he had to jump off a railway bridge and into some rolling stock of a moving train following Bogarde's character (who thought he had finally managed to dump Robbie). 'I really loved that bit,' said Whiteley. 'Of course, the bridge was in the studio so it was only a drop of about three feet on to a mattress the other side. When I was back at school I used to boast to my friends about doing it.'[45]

For Crichton, the Scottish locations afforded him a chance to get back close to his roots, and, more importantly, some decent fishing, while London saw him revisiting elements of *Hue and Cry*, *Dance Hall* and *The Lavender Hill Mob*, especially with a capital landscape still dotted, if decreasingly, with bomb sites. He was also able to call again on the expertise of one Joey 'Sawn Off' Carr, a tiny, ex-flyweight boxer who, when he was not minding his fruit and vegetable stall in the East End, was able to provide child extras from his Bow backyard for film productions, like the forty or so he had rounded up for *Hue and Cry* back in 1947.

This time, Crichton required a dozen or so lads for a kickabout outside the tenement block – the same Ebury Buildings in Pimlico used as an exterior for the factory girls' flats in *Dance Hall* – where Chris's erring wife Magda (Elizabeth Sellars) lives. Keeping in the shadows outside, Chris tasks Robbie with getting into Magda's flat and stealing some cash. As Robbie makes his way across the courtyard, he gets briefly caught up in the game with Joey's troupe of lively youngsters playing football. Oddly, the *Daily Mirror*'s showbusiness writer Donald Zec noted, none of them asked for Bogarde's autograph.

Released in the same week as Cecil B. DeMille's circus spectacular *The Greatest Show on Earth*, which would go on to win – unaccountably, to many – the year's Oscar for Best Picture, *Hunted* gave some UK critics the perfect chance to contrast the comparatively penurious, determinedly low-key, home-grown thriller very favourably with its hugely expensive, star-laden and flashy Hollywood rival. About one thing, they were all united – in Whiteley, a star was born, and that Crichton had succeeded with, wrote the *Manchester Guardian* on 16 February 1952, the same kind of 'patience and observation' that David Lean and Carol Reed had demonstrated in extracting similarly remarkable performances by their young stars in *Great Expectations* (Anthony Wager) and *The Fallen Idol* (Bobby Henrey).

They were also bracketed by C.A. Lejeune in her *Observer* column on 17 February 1952: 'A delightful little boy has been handled by the director with uncommon tact and sensibility ... it is a brave film by people whose care to do better is plain and admirable to see.' There was a common thread in the *Evening Standard*'s verdict: 'The slow development of the affection and loyalty that springs up between these two hunted creatures is admirably achieved by C.C.'

The *Liverpool Echo* suggested, 'It is never easy to assess how much of a child's performance is due to his own intelligence and how much to the director's handling but Jon Whiteley's remarkable facility in registering tension, fear and awe is as an impressive example of child acting as I have seen for a long time.' And the *Belfast Telegraph* commented that 'it is difficult to decide where the talent of Jon ends and the genius of Charles Crichton begins'.

The critics' concentration on Whiteley and the extent or otherwise of Crichton's influence on his performance tends rather to overshadow the important contribution of Bogarde, of whom only some reviewers, after marvelling at the little boy, almost grudgingly conceded had delivered easily his best performance to date, easily eclipsing his shrill 'mackintosh boy' in *The Blue Lamp*, for instance. Bogarde's off-screen relationship with Whiteley must also have had much to do with the way Crichton was able to tease out both naturally and via sly editing the boy's range of open emotions, a fact conceded by Whiteley: 'My big broad grins were, for instance, mostly impromptu, and were left in; there were several shots of that kind not originally intended.'[46]

There was, of course, much more to work with in *Hunted* in terms of Chris's own character development and Bogarde rose to the challenge. One scene in particular is a standout. The odd couple have arrived at a guest house in the Midlands and Robbie, now at a very low ebb, cowers in a corner of the bedroom, before being slowly placated by Chris who proceeds gently to tell him a bedtime story that inexorably turns into a kind of moving confessional. 'What do you think girls marry sailors for?' Chris asks the uncomprehending Robbie. Whiteley still retained vivid memories of the film's premiere in London, an occasion, he said, rather overshadowed by the death of King George VI. He sat with his parents and recalls being 'very touched by the film. Yes, I might have cried.' He also remembered another, stranger, moment, probably some time later, when while watching Bogarde on live television, he heard the actor say he would like to adopt the boy. 'I was sitting with my mother and fortunately she had her back to the TV and didn't hear. She would have been furious.'[47]

The film was released in the States four months after the UK following an unhelpful retitling to *The Stranger In Between*, but despite this and the misleading award of the production to 'Michael Balcon' – perhaps Crichton, Ealing and *The Lavender Hill Mob* were still too fresh in the mind of reviewer Howard Thompson – the *New York Times* commended it:

> The fine pictorial impact of this production, which describes the cross-country flight of an escaped murderer and a small boy, must be attributed to the English knack of conjuring up a chase, drenching it in atmosphere and incident and, in general, keeping spectators' eyes riveted to the sprinters ... Director Charles Crichton in dead serious contrast to his droll guidance of *The Lavender Hill Mob* again has done a dandy job.[48]

In a less than vintage year for British cinema, the film performed respectably at the UK box office grossing today's equivalent of £3m. There was also some award recognition for Crichton, not, despite the notices, in Britain, but at the sixth annual Locarno International Film Festival in Switzerland, where he was awarded the Golden Leopard for Best Film.

As for a more glittering US appreciation of the film's worth, there was, albeit unwittingly, an element of prescience in the *Birmingham Daily Gazette*'s assertion that 'if there were Oscars for child actors, little Jon Whiteley would walk away with the 1952 award for his performance in *Hunted*'. Two years after *Hunted*, Whiteley and his seven-year-old *The Kidnappers* (1953) co-star and fellow Scot, Vincent Winter, became just the tenth and eleventh recipients of the Academy Juvenile Award, dubbed the 'Oscarette', since it was inaugurated in 1934 (and discontinued after 1960 when Hayley Mills, for *Pollyanna*, was the twelfth and very final honouree).

***

Soon after filming *Hunted*, Crichton found himself on the way back north of the border in the company of his old Ealing colleague, Sidney Cole. Their mission was to look into the possibility of bringing Eric Linklater's 1951 comic novel, *Laxdale Hall*, to the screen. Two of his earlier fictions, *Poet's Pub* and *Private Angelo*, had been turned into indifferent films in 1949 by other companies, but Balcon might have thought that *Laxdale Hall*'s Scottish tale of a close-knit community bucking bureaucracy could piggyback on the success of Ealing hits like *Whisky Galore* and *Passport to Pimlico*.

Linklater, a Welsh-born Scot, who had fought in the Great War before becoming a prolific writer of poetry, fiction and non-fiction, lived for years in the Orkneys before moving back to the mainland where he settled in Ross-shire. Crichton's and Cole's memories of their trip mostly centred around Crichton's water-drenched fishing expeditions with Linklater, principally to catch river salmon. Ealing decided to pass on the project, but soon after, another British production company, the state-subsidised Group 3, headed by the great documentarist John Grierson, with, ironically, Balcon as chairman, took it on as part of its mission to encourage new low-budget product by young British film-makers; for *Laxdale Hall*, it was none other than thirty-five-year-old John Eldridge, who already had form with Ealing (*Pool of London*) and would also later write two films for Crichton, *The Man in the Sky* (1957) and *The Boy Who Stole a Million* (1960).

Meanwhile Crichton, now back in W5, was about to embark on a new collaboration with 'Tibby' Clarke which in many ways was just another variation on the by now well-trod Ealing formula that had held good on everything from *Passport to Pimlico* to, well, *Whisky Galore* with one big innovation: it would be the first 'Ealing comedy' in colour.

The Titfield Thunderbolt (1953)

Britain in 1953 was socially and economically beginning to be a very different society compared with a nation coming out of war just a few years earlier, or, for that matter, even the one at the turn of the new decade. Labour, which had enjoyed a landslide victory in 1945, was now replaced by a Conservative government led again by Winston Churchill, who had been unceremoniously dumped by voters in the immediate onset of peace. The old king had died to be replaced by a twenty-six-year-old queen who was, many believed, ushering in a new Elizabethan age. Yet, in the year of the Coronation, which also marked the first major emergence of television in the UK, the old world as represented by 'Winnie' seemed almost at odds with a new beginning somehow personified by Elizabeth II.

Cinema audiences, which had so roundly rejected revisiting the war in films from the late forties like Ealing's *Against the Wind* while, at the same time fondly embracing the same studio's gently anarchic comedies, were also changing in their tastes. Kitchen-sink realism was just a handful of years away as were, with the odd exception (Launder and Gilliatt's *St Trinian's* cycle), two major new strands of big-screen British comedy as explored separately by the *Carry On* farces and the Boulting Brothers' satires. Cinema historians will often earmark *The Titfield Thunderbolt* as the beginning of the end of a classic comedy cycle whose final, exceptional, hurrah was 1955's *The Ladykillers*. Not, for some, just a cycle, but for Ealing itself. 'In retrospect', a 1986 BBC Omnibus documentary intoned, '*The Titfield Thunderbolt* seems like the beginning of the end of Ealing, the retreat from a confusingly different Britain into safe fantasy world.'[49]

Ironic then that the same studio's *The Cruel Sea* would, as noted in the previous chapter, prove to be the country's top moneymaker of 1953. Just as it took American cinemagoers several years before they felt ready to embrace the realities of the Vietnam War in films from the late seventies like, say, *The Deer Hunter* and *Apocalypse Now*, so it was here with World War II eventually revisited spectacularly with *The Cruel Sea* and for several more years after that.

At first glance, the notion of the main *Lavender Hill Mob* creative team – Crichton, Truman, Clarke and Slocombe – reuniting for a new Ealing comedy in 'glorious Technicolor' must have seemed irresistible. Certainly it was embarked on with the best of intentions, beginning with Clarke following a visit in North Wales to his old friend, the writer Richard Hughes, whose best-known novel, *A High Wind in*

Jamaica, published in 1929, was turned into a post-Ealing film in 1965 by Alexander Mackendrick. Hughes introduced him to the delights of the Talyllyn narrow gauge railway operated since 1951, in pre-Beeching days, by amateurs, and that was the spark. The first preserved railway in the world ran, and still runs, from the edge of Snowdonia National Park to Abergynolwyn seven miles away.

For his screenplay, Clarke chose instead a quintessentially English rural setting for his fictional branch line between the village of Titfield – apparently an amalgam of Limpsfield and Titsey near his own Surrey home – and the nearby town of Mallingford. When nationalised British Railways posts notice of closure, some, but not all, of the local inhabitants are devastated, notably the young squire Gordon Chesterford (John Gregson, in his sixth Ealing film), whose great grandfather built the line, and the vicar Sam Weech (George Relph, father of Ealing art director, later prolific producer Michael Relph), a railway nut, who are determined to keep the line open and given a month's grace by the Ministry of Transport to prove themselves worthy. There is extra pressure from the ambitious local bus company who would be only too delighted to see the line shut down.

Into this bucolic melange are added, on the rail team, a rich drunk Mr Valentine (Stanley Holloway), who is persuaded to fund the new enterprise only when he learns that on a train, the bar can be open at any time; Dan (Hugh Griffith), a retired engineman who lives in an ex-railway carriage, and a couple of token female characters – by now Ealing had pretty much reverted to the usual male focus – comely Joan (Gabrielle Brune) and spirited little old lady Emily (Edie Martin). In the four-wheel corner are the bus people with the addition of volatile tractor driver Hawkins (Sidney James). Remaining fussily neutral is town clerk Blakeworth (Naunton Wayne) who simply needs to commute as quickly and efficiently as possible. In other words, the transport rivals are essentially fighting for his favour.

When the forces of good, as we're meant to perceive them, rally at the start of the film to save the railway, the vicar declares it to be 'God's work', and Clarke, who said he had also heard that clerics seem to have a special affinity for steam – the Reverend Awdry's railway book series starring Thomas the Tank Engine was in full cry by this time – underlines this by also adding a coal-shovelling Bishop (Godfrey Tearle) on to the footplate for the Thunderbolt's crucial climactic run against the clock (Figure 5.4).

Clarke may have been generalising about men of the cloth but he was much more specific, at least with its origin, about the amiable Valentine, played by Holloway as a kind of tweedy cross between sozzled Alastair in

Figure 5.4 Godfrey Tearle and George Relph in *The Titfield Thunderbolt*

Another Shore and solid Pendlebury in *The Lavender Hill Mob*. Contrary to his usual practice when inventing characters, Valentine was actually based on an old boy Clarke used to encounter occasionally at a seaside hotel. However, when his pals took him to see the finished film, hoping to get his, hopefully amused, reaction to Holloway's performance, he stormed out of the cinema after the opening credits, 'snorting indignantly,' wrote Clarke, '"You never told me the film was in colour."'[50]

Although the eponymous village derived its name from the Home Counties, Crichton, Truman and Slocombe – reunited with the director for the eighth time – had to take their cameras much further afield to find suitably rustic locations and, even more importantly, a functional branch line to double for Clarke's creation. Like the Talyllyn line, which first inspired the writer, the Camerton branch of the Bristol and North Somerset railway had also closed in 1951, though, in this case, it was the film-makers rather than some nerdy local amateurs who needed to operate it again. Using principally the Limpley Stoke to Hallatrow section of the branch line – about four miles or so from Bath – Crichton turned Monkton Combe Halt – now disappeared beneath the playing fields of the local public school – into Titfield station while Mallingford station's stand-in was the still very much bustling Bristol Temple Meads.

The Thunderbolt itself does not make an appearance in the film until about two-thirds of the way through, and only after the enthusiasts' original loco has been sabotaged and its stolen replacement – actually a wooden mock-up mounted on a lorry chassis – accidentally wrecked by drunken Dan and Valentine after careering across the countryside. The nineteenth-century Thunderbolt was actually the 114-year-old *Lion*, once of the Liverpool and Manchester Railway, lent to the production by the Liverpool Engineering Society. For the scenes where it is purloined from a local museum, for the film's purposes, the Imperial Institute (now Imperial College) by the Royal Albert Hall, a studio-built replica was used. Model or not, concertgoers leaving the Albert Hall one night in August 1952 must have been a little surprised to see dozens of extras manhandling what appeared to be a full-size engine down the steps of the neighbouring building.

While filming in and around the West Country, the provincial press, which proliferated in those days, paid close attention to the production. So we learn from the *Hampshire Telegraph*, for instance, that during their downtime, Stanley Holloway, Naunton Wayne and Hugh Griffith play skittles at the 'local', while Sidney James and Crichton 'make for the nearest river for fishing'. The *Wiltshire Times & Trowbridge Advertiser* reported the visit of a five-strong team from the film, including John Gregson, Crichton, Truman, Slocombe and Paul Beeson, the second-unit cameraman, to the RAF station 'Astra' cinema, in nearby Melksham, to answer questions from a hall packed with airmen about the current production and film in general. Asked 'how material was gathered for the production of a film', Crichton answered, blandly, that 'the obstacles faced were mainly financial as a picture had to be kept within a certain budget'. For this particular audience, however, Gregson was quite literally the star of the show simply because his latest film, *Angels One Five*, in which he played a courageous Battle of Britain pilot, was on general release (Figure 5.5).

While filming *The Titfield Thunderbolt*, Crichton did bump up, albeit quite amiably, against the ever loyal Slocombe, who had decided he wanted to shoot his own 'making of ... "on a little 16 mm camera at the same time": Every time I said "Dougie, I think this is the best set up for what we've got to shoot," he'd say, "No," and talk me out of it. When I saw the film he had made, he'd used every set up that I wanted.'[51]

THE FIFTIES: 1950–54 **113**

Figure 5.5 Flanked by Michael Truman (left) and Crichton (right), Sir Michael Balcon (centre) visits the set of *The Titfield Thunderbolt*

Slocombe, who had shot *Saraband for Dead Lovers*, Ealing's colour debut five years earlier, certainly had a most beguiling country canvas on which to paint Crichton's first foray into Technicolor, under the ever-watchful eye of the remarkable Joan Bridge, who worked on more than forty films as a 'colour consultant' before later becoming an Oscar-winning costume designer. Crichton told Brian McFarlane: 'I don't think colour necessarily adds a great deal to most films, but *The Titfield Thunderbolt* just required it, to do justice to the ancient and gaily painted engine and the rural scenery. If the picture was not entirely satisfying, at least his [Slocombe's] work gave one something lyrical to look at.'[52] Crichton went on to admit: 'I don't think it's a very good film, [but] there are lots of things in it that I like.'[53]

With *The Lavender Hill Mob*, having sustained, maybe in global terms even slightly raised, the high bar set by Ealing's trio of 1949 comedies, then considerably cemented his own directorial reputation with *Hunted*, Crichton must have been considerably dismayed by much of the response to *The Titfield Thunderbolt*, which went on to enjoy only a modest box office success. Critics at the time generally conceded that, like the *Monthly Film Bulletin* wrote, the premise was 'ingenious and anarchically attractive' before delivering this typical hammer blow, 'here the invention is unfortunately below par. The script itself is disconcertingly short on wit ... and Crichton's handling fails to supply the charm that could still have been the film's justification.' In the States, where the film opened six months after the UK, the *New York Times* was similarly damning: 'Director Charles Crichton must take the burden of the blame. The idea and the country air confused him. That sometimes happens to grown-up men who play with trains.'[54]

There were, of course, some pockets of praise amid the carping. 'Nonsense, then', said the *Western Mail*, 'but in the hands of Messrs Clarke and Crichton, clever nonsense. Ealing has come in for some criticism for thus letting its hair down until it drapes itself around its feet. I say – good luck to *The Titfield Thunderbolt*. May its railway lines never grow rusty.' At the other end of the country, the *Sunderland Daily Echo* was also quite thoughtful: 'A searching examination of the treatment may well reveal weaknesses which spring from the farcical approach, but the delightful thing about the whole film is the way human traits have been accentuated to make each character a rounded and credible individual.'

Ealing's historians have tended to veer towards the harsh in their assessments of the film, and it is difficult not to disagree with elements of their respective observations and objections. For *BFI Screenonline*, Mark Duguid concludes cruelly if wittily:

> With its images of steam trains, country squires, warm beer and village-green cricket, the film seems now like a party political broadcast for the Conservative Party under John Major. Perhaps the then Prime Minister even had the film in mind when, in the mid-1990s, his government rushed through the deeply unpopular re-privatisation of British Rail, the disastrous results of which mean that Britain's trains, like Titfield's, run slowly.[55]

While acknowledging its 'wonderful colour', Tim O'Sullivan in his 'That Ealing Feeling' essay for *Ealing Revisited*, decries the film's 'steam-driven, creaking, leaking and variable whimsy'.[56] As it happens, not even Slocombe's use of colour is immune from some criticism. In Sue Harper and Vincent Porter's *British Cinema of the 1950s: The Decline of Deference*, the application is 'uninventive, the high colour values are so uninflected that the little village and the toytown train lack emotional substance'.[57]

As for Charles Barr, he spends no fewer than six pages, in his 'Late Comedies' chapter, laying into – hammer to crack a nut? – a film that, he writes,

> marks a decadent stage, corresponding to the common identikit view of the genre, formed in retrospect, as something nice and whole and harmless, quaint and static and timeless ... Like *The Man in the White Suit*, it shows a society which has committed itself to the backward-looking soft option path which *Passport [to Pimlico]* settled for, and is thus a warning of some of the consequences. But it in every way lacks the critical perspective of Mackendrick's film.[58]

George Perry records a location report by Hugh Sansom in an edition of *Picturegoer*, a colourful British fan magazine that ran for nearly fifty years before closing down in 1960: 'Odd point about this railway location: not a single railway enthusiast to be found in the whole crew. T.E.B. Clarke, writer of the script, loathes trains. Producer Michael Truman can't get out of them quick enough. And director Crichton – well, you won't find him taking engine numbers at Paddington Station.'[59] In later years, Clarke, along with many others, would quote Alexander Mackendrick's own sharp analysis:

> At the time of *Passport to Pimlico* everybody wanted to share its characters' freedom from rationing and petty restrictions. And just about everybody would secretly like to rid themselves of tiresome relative as in *Kind Hearts and Coronets*, or get hold of unlimited free whisky, or remove a fortune in gold bars from the Bank of England. But not so many people have any great desire to run a railway.[60]

The Love Lottery (1954)

By 1972, a year after the publication of his best-selling memoir, *The Moon's a Balloon*, a compendium of funny if occasionally fanciful tales of his years in Hollywood, David Niven's working life mainly relied on the chat show circuit punctuated by lucrative commercials. For instance, he could be found, his official biographer Graham Lord explained, being chased along the Promenade des Anglais in Nice by a horde of Japanese girls shrieking 'David! David!' He turns round and says 'Girls, girls, how did you recognise me?' in dubbed Japanese, then sniffs his armpit and declares, 'Of course, now I understand. It's Who's Who!'[61] A few months later in London, Niven suddenly found himself being surrounded by a crowd of Japanese tourists. They raised their arms, dabbed at their armpits, and laughed hysterically. Who's Who was, of course, a popular Nipponese deodorant of the day.

Just under twenty years earlier, *The Love Lottery*, Niven's first and only film for Ealing, opens, presciently, with mass of female fans at the Hollywood premiere of his latest film, chanting his character Rex Allerton's first name, 'Rex!, Rex!' before breaking free of the cordon and then, excitedly, literally tearing him limb from limb, eventually lobbing his decapitated head though a box office window before he wakes up, eye-rollingly spooked from this grisly, Technicolor nightmare.

For a satirical comedy, which was derided then, and has been since, as, variously, 'deplorably weak' and 'stillborn', it is a genuinely disturbing introduction to Crichton's latest Ealing film about the use and abuse of, and by, celebrity that while mostly far too short on funny ha ha, still, rather unexpectedly, endures to this day as an often fascinating and also pleasingly subversive example of funny peculiar. Talk about biting the hand that feeds you. Quite what the newly crowned Queen Elizabeth II and Prince Philip must have made of this latest, and possibly strangest ever, offering from a studio best known for cosy comedies of contrary communities, one, sadly, will never likely know. They were attending a Royal Gala first night – a week ahead of its UK opening – not in London's West End but instead, almost twelve thousand miles away in Christchurch, New Zealand, on the first leg of their 1953–54 Australasian tour. Reporting the occasion, *The Times* could not resist noting, 'In some ways the theme [of the film] was not inappropriate to the occasion, for when the royal car had left for the Clarendon Hotel sections of the vast crowd waiting in Cathedral Square broke their ranks and surged after it in something of the manner that we had been watching on the screen.'[62]

The morning after the New Zealand premiere on 21 January 1954, the *Liverpool Daily Post* proclaimed a headline: 'Merseyside Master of the English Film'. Thankfully avoiding that old saw 'local boy made good' but emphasising 'Wallasey-born' was an article by Elizabeth Coxhead celebrating Crichton who 'has now in his early forties reached the top of the directorial tree'. After declaring a personal interest – 'My mother and his were fellow students at Liverpool University and to us country mice, the large and lively family of Crichton children represented the peak of town glamour on our regular Christmas visits to Merseyside' – Coxhead reflected on his career, 'I remember so well the toughness of his early struggles and his single-minded determination ... to become a film director, let it cost what it might.' Coxhead, a year older than Crichton and well known in her own right as a novelist, mountaineer and feminist, would also appear to have had the benefit of some input in her piece from the film-maker, whose public pronouncements tended to be few and far between.

THE FIFTIES: 1950–54

Most interestingly, especially in regard to *The Love Lottery*,

> He cites two actors of the first rank, Alec Guinness and David Niven, as examples of two types. Guinness broods on a part till he knows exactly how it should played, and woe betide the director who attempts to do more than follow in his footsteps. Niven is an infinitely pliable instrument prepared to execute whatever the director may wish, but the impetus has to come from outside. Adjusting his technique to such widely varying talents and getting the best out of each is a part of the director's job. He is no dictator; never more than a co-ordinator of a team. That's where the public school spirit comes in handy.

Finally, she writes, 'he does not believe that the answer to TV competition and dwindling audiences lies in 3D or any other form of gadgetry. It lies in better films – and gadgetry far from helping to achieve them is their active enemy' (Figure 5.6).

Figure 5.6 Crichton (centre) flanked by Herbert Lom and David Niven on the set of *The Love Lottery*

While he clearly claimed not to favour 'gadgetry' as such, *The Love Lottery* would prove to be easily the most cinematically tricks-filled film of all his twenty-one features, starting with that opening sequence in which the ravening mob turns out to consist of an endless multiplication of the face and form of one very pretty, petite blonde who we later discover to be Sally (Peggy Cummins), a simple English office girl who also happens to be Rex's most devoted fan. Despite his recurring dreams in which she always seems to appear and disrupt, he doesn't know it yet either.

After this nightmarish curtain-raiser, we learn that Rex, harried in reality by fans and beset by ever more desperate bouts of publicity and promotion to foster his popularity as a swashbuckling screen lover, is the disillusioned contract number two star of a top Hollywood studio, second only in popularity to 'Fang the Wonder Dog' (the film's best funny ha ha joke). Why not, Rex suggests, ironically, to the studio flaks, don't they just go the whole hog and organise a worldwide lottery with him as first prize? Unaware that Rex was merely being flippant, his suggestion is greedily seized on in all seriousness and handed over for implementation to the shadowy International Syndicate of Computation, whose lavish Italian waterside headquarters is in fictional Tremaggio (forever Lake Como).

With the 'story' credited to Charles Neilson-Gattey and Zelma Bramley-Moore, a rather mysterious pair of hyphenated British writers who collaborated on a number of projects in the fifties, the actual screenplay was by Harry Kurnitz, a seasoned Hollywood writer since arriving in Los Angeles in 1938. Appropriately for *The Love Lottery*, his scripts spanned Errol Flynn swashbucklers and Danny Kaye comedies. Just prior to this assignment, Kurnitz had written Carol Reed's Cold War Berlin thriller, *The Man Between* (1953), a rather bleaker portrait of a conflicted anti-hero.

After the opening credits have rolled over the image of a heart, initially with Niven's face on it, bisected by an arrow, the following legend is displayed: 'The scenes laid in the imaginary town of Tremaggio were shot in the Province of Como in Italy. But in Italy it is the gentlemen who serenade the ladies and not – as in our story – vice versa. We warmly thank the inhabitants and the authorities of the Province of Como for the generous help they gave us in establishing a fiction.' Thus, the whimsical tone is set from the very outset. One suspects that this declaration was likely the work of the producer Monja Danischewsky, with whom Crichton had been last associated during his brief but crucial intervention on 'Danny's' producing debut, *Whisky Galore*, four years earlier. 'Danny' received an 'additional dialogue' credit on *The Love Lottery*.

After being restricted to just Titfield's domestic rolling hills, green fields and a gaily painted locomotive, Crichton, reunited yet again with Slocombe, could now at least enjoy a much more ambitious palate of colour with which to play with, from the actuality of a beautiful Italian lakeside town to a series of fantasy dreams and nightmares allowing full rein for some vivid 'expressionist colour lighting techniques', wrote Josephine Botting in her 'Who'll Pay for Reality?' essay in *Ealing Revisited*.[63]

One of the earliest and most effective in the film arrives as Rex dozes in his dressing room following a short bout of romantic swashbuckling on the adjoining sound stage (here Crichton, Slocombe and camera operator Jeff Seaholme enjoy a brief clapperboard-only cameo). Reminiscent technically of the 'Haunted Mirror' segment in *Dead of Night*, we go through the looking glass and on to the stage of a large theatre where Rex is giving his Romeo to Sally's Juliet on the balcony above him. Soon the Bard is overtaken as, to Rex's horror, Sally segues into a lively song and dance routine. And there's more fantasy Terpsichore to come as, in another lavish staging, Rex and Sally swirl Astaire and Rogers-like until he's gradually transformed into a grey-bearded, hunched old man. The dance routines were devised by Australian-born choreographer, Freddie Carpenter, whose distinguished career would span more than thirty years in theatre, film and television.

The dream sequences obviously presage the inevitable, that Sally will win Rex and his promised hand in the lottery. But love, as the words of a rather queasy title song confirm, is a lottery, and Rex, just to complicate matters further, has fallen in love with Jane (French actress Anne Vernon), the mathematical genius of the computing syndicate in Tremaggio, where Rex has ended up fortuitously after trying to elude his fans in every other corner of the world. Once the fantasies – which also include an elaborate sword fight between Rex and studio head Stanton (former war correspondent Stanley Maxted) in the guise of Napoleon – the story plays out tritely, with romantic predictability and two moderate gags. The first is when Sally finally finds herself alone in a hotel room with her captive idol: 'Can I have your autograph, please?' she asks him, so politely. The very last shot of the film is set on the South Bank in London where syndicate head Amico (Herbert Lom) suddenly spots a faintly familiar figure peering out at the river: 'Sir, I am not a curiosity seeker nor an autograph hunter,' he says, handing his card to the man as he turns round. Humphrey Bogart takes the card and, wordlessly, offers instead just a withering look. Fade out. The film, you could say, has its cake and eats it, too.

Not even an uncredited appearance by Bogie, an old friend of Niven's – who was in England at the time filming *Beat the Devil*, John Huston's spoof follow-up to *The African Queen* – could help fully win over the critics. While acknowledging the film score's 'palpable, if gentle, hits', *The Times* carped, nevertheless, 'Mr Crichton ... seems to feel something, somewhere, has gone astray, and he is forced to fall back on some tiresome dream sequences – he is like a man condemned to drop catches off his own bowling.'[64]

C.A. Lejeune in the *Sketch* appeared to be more beguiled by the Italian locations, which 'seem a miracle of beauty to a shivering Londoner on a grey February day', than the film itself. The *Daily Herald*'s Paul Holt explained he would have 'enjoyed the film very much indeed had it not insisted on sinking me in seas of whimsy. There were so many dream sequences I felt in need of a psychiatrist.' The *Tatler* described it as 'a film ... which falters through running with the star and hunting with his hounds'.

'These days,' complained the *Kensington Post*, with some justification,

> film comedy itself seems to be a lottery. Where are the Capras of America and the Asquiths of Britain and the Clairs of France: The modern method even at Ealing is throw in Technicolor, a few wisecracks, situations dreamed up the night before that seemed awfully funny then, stars and girls galore, a pinch of satire and some fantasy ... and cross your fingers in the hope that what comes out of the tin can 'clicks'. *The Love Lottery* is the second Ealing comedy in a matter of weeks that generally misses. Maybe I'm losing my sense of humour, or maybe Sir Michael is losing his.

The first of those Ealing films, which the *Kensington Post* was referring to, was *Meet Mr Lucifer*, released in November 1953, another Danischewsky production also written by him, a feeble, wholly misfiring, satire – yes, that word again – about television, cinema's most dangerous competition, without an ounce of *The Love Lottery*'s undoubted ambition and resulting invention. One cannot help thinking that at least some of the negative reaction to *The Love Lottery* might have had to do with the inability of various critics and commentators to countenance the awful possibility that Ealing might suddenly seem to have strayed, as they saw it, way beyond its, by now, well-established, gently satirical, comedy remit. The term (and its implication) 'Ealing comedy' was, after all, firmly in the cinematic lexicon, and while it once may have been fine for eight members of the D'Ascoyne family to be cynically slaughtered for laughs, it was now quite another for a world-weary Hollywood screen idol to be dismembered in mordant jest.

In her 'Who'll Pay for Reality?' essay in *Ealing Revisited*, Ms Botting refreshingly embraced the film's fantasies whose 'Technicolor lavishness makes them effective parodies of Hollywood cinema', and praised Niven's performance as 'achieving just the right balance of conceit and self-mockery'. Botting then more directly addressed the problem:

> The film takes a dig at Hollywood as a dream factory and peddler of films as pure escapism. At one point Allerton demands of studio executive Stanton, 'Why does everything have to be an escape? ... What about reality?' to which Stanton replies, 'Who'll pay for reality? They've got reality. They hate it.' This ironic exchange is the nub of the film – was Ealing admitting that its adherence to realism was out of kilter with the public appetite? Or is Allerton the voice of Balcon, speaking out against the shallow commercialism of Hollywood?[65]

This potential dichotomy plainly contrived to help flummox audiences who gave the film short shrift in its day. If his views on Hollywood remained ambivalent, Balcon's assessment of *The Love Lottery* was, however, unequivocal. In a letter dated 14 December 1955 – almost two years after its UK release – to Sir Henry French, director-general of the British Film Producers' Association, he described the film as 'one of the worst pictures we made for years'. Of Crichton's own relationship with the film, there is, infuriatingly, very little available information. We learn, for instance, via the *Coventry Evening Telegraph*, just that he spent some time in Hollywood in early 1953 'getting some background material for the film'.

Christopher Barry, a lowly assistant director to Crichton on the film, who later rose to become one of the BBC's most prolific and successful directors, was, thankfully, a little more forthcoming, talking to Robert Sellers:

> My chief image of Charlie Crichton was of a smiley, pipe-smoking man, very approachable and easy-going, and, of course, an excellent director especially of comedy. I have to say I did enjoy working on this film immensely. Not only were the sets imaginatively designed with use of gauzes and clever lighting, but the dance dream sequences were all well-conceived, and being on the set with dozens of Peggy Cummins look-alikes was not unpleasant.[66]

Apart from the reference to David Niven in the Elizabeth Coxhead article, we can attribute just two pithy sentences from him on the subject: 'It wasn't successful, but I quite liked it. Perhaps it was too much a whimsy-whamsy thing.'⁶⁷ Although *The Love Lottery* proved to be, perhaps unsurprisingly, Crichton's last comedy for Ealing, within a year he had directed what Balcon would regard as one of the studio's best-ever pictures.

Notes

1 George Perry, *Forever Ealing* (Pavilion, 1981), p. 111.
2 Philip Kemp, *Lethal Innocence: The Cinema of Alexander Mackendrick* (Methuen, 1991), p. 42.
3 Brian McFarlane, *An Autobiography of British Cinema* (Methuen, 1997), p. 154.
4 Interview with the author, 4 December 2019.
5 McFarlane, *An Autobiography of British Cinema*, p. 591.
6 *Ibid.*, p. 420.
7 Kemp, *Lethal Innocence*, p. 42.
8 McFarlane, *An Autobiography of British Cinema*, p. 422.
9 Claire Langhammer, 'Review of *Going to the Palais: A Social and Cultural History of Dancing and Dance Halls in Britain*'. *Reviews in History*, no. 1976, https://reviews.history.ac.uk/review/1976 (accessed 7 January 2021).
10 *The Times*, 12 June 1950.
11 *BFI Screenonline*, 2003, www.screenonline.org.uk/film/id/587320/index.html#:~:text=BFI (accessed 16 January 2021).
12 *The Tatler*, 21 June 1950.
13 See www.derekwinnert.com.
14 *BFI Screenonline*, 2003, www.screenonline.org.uk/film/id/587320/index.html#:~:text=BFI (accessed 16 January 2021).
15 *BEHP*.
16 Lecture to Merseyside Film Institute Society, 1961 (henceforth MFIS lecture).
17 T.E.B. Clarke, *This Is Where I Came In* (Michael Joseph, 1974), p. 64.
18 *Ibid.*, p. 166.
19 *Ibid.*
20 MFIS lecture.
21 McFarlane, *An Autobiography of British Cinema*, p. 154.
22 *Ibid.*
23 Peter van Gelder, *That's Hollywood* (HarperCollins, 1990), p. 170.
24 McFarlane, *An Autobiography of British Cinema*, p. 154.
25 MFIS lecture.
26 Clarke, *This Is Where I Came In*, p. 164.
27 *Ibid.*
28 Alec Guinness, *My Name Escapes Me* (Hamish Hamilton, 1996), p. 172.
29 McFarlane, *An Autobiography of British Cinema*, p. 262.
30 *Ibid.*
31 Clarke, *This Is Where I Came In*, p. 168.
32 MFIS lecture.
33 *The Times*, 2 July 1951.
34 *New York Times*, 16 October 1951.
35 MFIS lecture.
36 Guinness, *My Name Escapes Me*, p. 171.
37 *BEHP*.
38 McFarlane, *An Autobiography of British Cinema*, p. 154.

39 Interview with the author, 14 November 2019.
40 *Ibid.*
41 *Ibid.*
42 McFarlane, *An Autobiography of British Cinema*, p. 154.
43 *Ibid.*, p. 69.
44 Interview with the author, 14 November 2019.
45 *Ibid.*
46 *Ibid.*
47 *Ibid.*
48 *New York Times*, 20 August 1952.
49 *Made in Ealing*, BBC Omnibus, 1986.
50 Clarke, *This Is Where I Came In*, p. 171.
51 *BEHP*.
52 McFarlane, *An Autobiography of British Cinema*, pp. 154–5.
53 *BEHP*.
54 *New York Times*, 6 October 1953.
55 Mark Duguid, *BFI Screenonline*, 2003, www.screenonline.org.uk/film/id/441558/index.html (accessed 16 January 2021).
56 Tim O'Sullivan, 'That Ealing Feeling' in Mark Duguid, Lee Freeman, Keith M. Johnston and Melanie Williams (eds) *Ealing Revisited* (BFI, 2012), p. 138.
57 Sue Harper and Vincent Porter, *British Cinema of the 1950s: The Decline of Deference* (Oxford University Press, 2003), p. 208.
58 Charles Barr, *Ealing Studios* (Studio Vista, 1977), p. 159.
59 Perry, *Forever Ealing*, p. 138.
60 Clarke, *This Is Where I Came In*, pp. 171–2.
61 Graham Lord, *Niv: The Authorised Biography of David Niven* (CB Creative Books, 2013).
62 *The Times*, 22 January 1954.
63 Josephine Botting, 'Who'll Pay for Reality? Ealing, Dreams and Fantasy', in Mark Duguid, Lee Freeman, Keith M. Johnston and Melanie Williams (eds) *Ealing Revisited* (BFI, 2012), p. 182.
64 *The Times*, 1 February 1954.
65 Botting, 'Who'll Pay for Reality?' p. 182.
66 Robert Sellers, *The Secret Life of Ealing Studios* (Aurum Press, 2015), p. 235.
67 *BEHP*.

The fifties: Exit Ealing, 1954-59 6

The Divided Heart (1954)

From the perceived lows of *The Love Lottery* to the widely acknowledged highs of *The Divided Heart*, how Crichton's critical fortunes, at least, would change within the course of less than twelve months. And following any possible misunderstanding about Ealing's preference for 'reality' over 'fantasy', Crichton's timely resurrection arrived triumphantly on the back of a subject that emphatically barked that well-worn journalistic screamer, 'torn from the headlines'. The subject in question received worldwide attention but probably nowhere more powerfully and with a wider global reach than *Life* magazine. 'The Story of Two Mothers', detailing the heart-breaking legal tug of love for a ten-year-old Slovenian boy in the chaos of post-war Europe, was unfolded coolly in the 13 October 1952 edition by its Bonn correspondent Roy Rowan.

The story itself actually began more than a decade before that with the birth of Ivan Pirecnik on New Year's Day 1941, in Sostanj, an industrial town in Slovenia. As war began to engulf the country, Ivan's father joined the local Resistance, was caught by the Gestapo and shot. The rest of the family went into hiding but was soon discovered, Ivan's older sister Marija was sent to Austria while his mother Pavla was deported to Auschwitz, which she miraculously managed to survive. Meanwhile Ivan disappeared into a kind of human black hole suffered by thousands of effectively orphaned children at the time.

After the war, Pavla managed to be reunited with her daughter but of Ivan there was no trace despite the best efforts of various refugee associations. Until, suddenly, she learned that her son was after all alive and living as Dieter Sirsch in Germany having been adopted during the war when the Sirsch couple were living in the Sudetenland and believed the child to be an ethic German war orphan. So began Pavla's long custody battle to have Ivan returned to her, a process that would drag out across no fewer than three trials before a trio of judges at the US Court of the Allied High Commission for Germany in Frankfurt. By an eventual ruling of 2–1 in her favour, little Ivan, despite claiming he wanted to remain with his adoptive parents, was handed back to his 'blood mother' and returned to Slovenia, in the northern part of Marshal Tito's Yugoslavia.

It is difficult to pinpoint exactly when the story might first have caught the attention of Balcon and his colleagues at Ealing in terms of its film potential. However, he wrote later in a memoir that 'part of its appeal for me was that it was about the mother–child relationship ... which, I recognise, was a recurring one in Ealing films'.[1] It seems likely though that once Balcon had been hooked by the facts, a screenplay was quickly sought from Richard Hughes, who, as explained in the previous chapter, had helped inspire *The Titfield Thunderbolt*. In fact, Hughes, a playwright and poet as well as a novelist, already had some more specific Ealing form having shared a writing credit with no fewer than four others on *A Run For Your Money* (1949). A modest, fish-out-of-water farce about gullible, rugby-mad Welshmen on the loose in London, it paled by comparison with the more celebrated trio of Ealing comedies from that same year.

How much of his work resided in the final draft of *The Divided Heart* one cannot tell but he was accorded the following at the front of the film: 'Grateful acknowledgement is due to Richard Hughes for his contribution to the film'. Full screenplay credit was instead given to Jack Whittingham, an incredibly versatile Ealing-contracted writer who already had *Cage of Gold*, *Pool of London*, *I Believe in You*, *Mandy* and *West of Zanzibar* under his belt, not to mention Crichton's extramural, *Hunted*. There was, as might be expected, some simplifying, streamlining and, to be sure, even some careful sanitising when Whittingham, with, doubtless, Crichton's connivance, came up with their film version of the original story. But even their careful tweaking did, despite Balcon's later assertions about the story's theme, still trouble him at the time, according to a 1955 interview he gave in *Films and Filming* to Kenneth Tynan, who wrote that 'it [the script] invaded territories of emotion where he felt uneasy'.

In reality, the German father was an SS officer and the boy was adopted under the Nazi-initiated 'Lebensborn' programme aimed at raising a new generation of 'racially pure' children. For the film, the father, Franz Hartl, is a simple Wehrmacht soldier and while there is a third-person reference to the Aryan purity project, there is no direct link between it and the childless Hartls' desperation to have a boy of their own. For the film, there is no suggestion that Pavla, now called

Sonja, has any other living child apart from the rediscovered Ivan, now known as Toni Hartl (not the 'Dieter Sirsch' of the original).

Along with the Hughes acknowledgement, 'The people of St Johann-in-Tirol and of Skofja Loka in Yugoslavia' were also 'thanked for their kind cooperation' at the front of the film. This followed location scouting in Germany, Austria and Yugoslavia in the winter of 1954 – ahead of a proposed spring shoot – by Crichton, together with associate producer Michael Truman, and, for their first and only collaboration, the great Czech cinematographer, Otto Heller, whose career in films had already spanned more than four decades. Instead of Germany and, in particular, the Hesse town of Kassel where the Sirschs actually lived, the film-makers opted instead for the Austrian ski resort of St Johann to double for an unnamed 'village in the Bavarian Alps', home of the Hartls, while Skofja Loka – for the film, 'Yugoslavia, a town in Slovenia' – would stand in for the original's Sostanj, Pavla/Sonja's home, about a hundred kilometres to the north-east.

As far as the casting was concerned, unusually for a Crichton film, there were none of the familiar faces that popped up so regularly in his Ealing canon – twelve titles at this stage and still counting. The director was, however, reunited with the ever-reliable Geoffrey Keen, dogged Detective Inspector Deakin from *Hunted*, who this time round, and in more sensitive vein, played the bilingual Marks, of the International Refugee Office, charged with investigating the Slovenian mother's claims. As the three presiding judges given the unenviable task of deciding the boy's fate – to be handed back to the 'blood mother' he no longer knew, or to the 'bread mother' who had looked after him often almost single-handed – were the Canadian Alexander Knox and two distinguished Irish actors, Eddie Byrne and Liam Redmond, who had both appeared in Basil Dearden's *The Gentle Gunman* (1952), Ealing's Irish Republican Army (IRA) thriller set during World War II.

But the real success, or otherwise, of the film would, necessarily, depend most on the casting of the four central roles – the Hartls, Sonja and, perhaps most crucially of all, little ten-year-old Toni aka Ivan. How much easier it might have been for the film-making team simply to select, for the adult roles anyway, from among the plethora of already well-established expatriate European actors who had been usefully employed adding authentic touches to more than a decade of British films dealing with aspects of the war.

Instead, for Inga and Franz Hartl, they ventured way beyond the usual suspects, signing up unknowns – certainly in UK audience terms – Cornell Borchers and Armin Dahlen.

Borchers, twenty-nine, of Lithuanian ancestry and with the looks of a younger Ingrid Bergman, had made only a handful of films in Germany before signing a seven-year deal with 20th Century Fox. But after just one film, *The Big Lift* (1950) she walked out of her contract and returned to Europe. Interestingly, her *Big Lift* co-star Montgomery Clift had just two years earlier made *The Search* (1948), playing an American soldier who manages to reunite a 'lost' Czech boy with his mother. As for Austrian-born Dahlen, thirty-five, he had, up until *The Divided Heart*, worked only in the German industry.

Between her first, uncredited, film performance in *Love on the Dole* (1941) and her next, a co-starring role eight years later opposite Edith Evans and Anton Walbrook in Thorold Dickinson's *The Queen of Spades* (1949), Yvonne Mitchell had become one of Britain's most accomplished young stage actors. Leading up to being cast as Sonja in *The Divided Heart*, Mitchell, also a budding playwright and novelist, could boast two more significant screen credits – on TV, as Cathy, in the BBC's *Wuthering Heights* (1953), and in the same year, as an ex-con in Jack Lee's film, *Turn the Key Softly*. As a Jewish woman, although her character was not, this latest role must have had extra resonance and poignancy for Mitchell, who was also required to learn Slovene and skiing for the film.

Michel Ray de Carvalho was exactly ten years old and with no previous acting experience when he was asked to play the boy. He was the son of a Brazilian diplomat and an English mother who married a wealthy leather merchant after his father died when Michel was very young. The couple used to have grand dinner parties at their London home and their guests included Balcon who told his hosts that he needed a young boy who could ski for his next film. Michel's mother was, however, against the idea of her son appearing on-screen, but as he told me: 'Sir Michael said it was only three months and who knows what will happen – this door has opened, why would you close it?'[2] It also helped that Michel was already a budding ski ace who, among many other things, would later go on to become twice a member of the British Winter Olympics team, at Grenoble in 1968 and Sapporo in 1972 (Figure 6.1).

Although the courtroom drama would inevitably provide the core of the film – Whittingham and Crichton cut down the original's three trials into a single hearing – the screenplay very expertly wove together the 'human factor' by means of contemporary action and some flashback.

The film opens on Toni's birthday 'seven years after the war', as he and his father ski expertly down slopes and back into town ahead of what we understand to be an impending youth competition. But no sooner are they home than they are confronted on their doorstep by

Figure 6.1 Yvonne Mitchell and Michel Ray in *The Divided Heart*

Marks and his colleague who have arrived with the shattering news that the boy's 'mother is alive' after all, wants him back and that his future will now likely have to be determined by an international court. The dreaded summons to attend court finally arrives, and the distraught Hartls must also prepare Toni to give testimony. They try to placate the boy with, 'It's not everyone who can say he's got two mothers', but not even that can comfort him especially when it leaks out to his more insensitive playmates that he might also be a 'foreigner'.

The court convenes and through Sonja's representative, we hear via flashback her tragic backstory following the Nazi occupation. In a street scene that closely resembles one in *Against the Wind* when, at a safe distance Simone Signoret agonisingly witnesses the capture of Gordon Jackson, so Sonja also looks on helplessly as her husband Josip (Theodore Bikel) is picked up by the Germans. At school, her daughters are fed the new propaganda: 'Adolf Hitler is a friend of all children', before being taken away by the authorities. Sonja and Ivan flee to the woods where they are looked after by the Resistance until she is captured and dispatched to 'a health resort', which we then understand to be Auschwitz. Ivan simply disappears. The flashback continues with the Hartls' 'past', from their visit to an orphanage in 1944 Leipzig where they are given a choice of two three-year-old boys, between the ebullient Hans and a very withdrawn Ivan, whom they call Toni. Opting for the latter, they return home and we see how the difficulties of readjusting as a family are exacerbated, first, by Toni's fear of uniforms, and, then, by the news that Franz, who had been posted back to the Russian front, is now 'missing believed killed'. When he finally returns to Germany after five years, having been a POW in Russia, the family is happily reunited and the future seems set fair – until the arrival of the International Refugee Organisation (IRO) representatives. So the scene is now set for the court judgment – requiring 'the wisdom of Solomon', barks a British journalist (Alec McCowen in just his third screen role) down the phone to London – and how it is actually implemented after the justices rule Toni/Ivan should go back to Slovenia.

Bringing this story to the screen clearly meant a great deal to Crichton, as he explained years later: 'I was deeply, emotionally, involved with *The Divided Heart*. After the war, when they were trying to reunite families, they discovered this boy and there were a series of trials to decide whether he should stay in Germany or go to the Slovenian woman who had survived Auschwitz. And the child was really put through the mill. It was very, very sad.' Crichton added,

> At the end of the third trial he was sent back to Slovenia which I think was a desperate mistake, and I think the whole thing was politically motivated. It wasn't the right thing for the child because he was very happy with his foster parents in Germany, and his mother was really a bit of a slut. He had to learn Slovene, and learn to love his mother, actually. I cannot judge whether it was right or wrong to bring the whole affair out into the open. Certainly it was a very tragic moment when the boy was removed from the care of those he had loved.[3]

The actors and technicians went first to Austria in March 1954, to make sure of filming the skiing sequences before the snow melted, then moved on to Yugoslavia in April. Although Michel Ray was already a medal-winning junior skier he was not allowed to go to Austria because of 'child actor' laws so a double had to be found for him from a school in Kitzbuhl. Although much taller than Michel, his outdoor action meant that with judicious use of back projection and skilful cutting his shots and Michel's skiing close-ups filmed later at Ealing were perfectly integrated. When the actors moved down from the slopes, including Mitchell, and into the village of St Johann, much of the snow had melted so lorries had to be sent out to collect snow from various districts to spread out in the village streets to give the proper appearance of winter.

An important scene involved Mitchell who, as Sonja, has arrived to meet Toni/Ivan properly for the first time. In her autobiography, the actress recalled:

> A number of the children were meant to be antipathetic to me and maliciously threw snowballs at me. The village children who played these parts were told by an interpreter what Charles Crichton wanted them to do. They treated me with such dislike that I felt as hurt as the real Sonja must have done. This experience, and not being able to communicate by language, and of being an outcast disliked by the children, was the first time I felt, instead of imagining, what the character I was playing was going through.[4]

In Skofja Loka, Mitchell also had vivid memories of another scene involving the 'locals'. She observed:

> There was one shot in the film of women and little girls being taken away in a lorry. Those that had been taken like this during the war had never returned. There was only one thing they resented doing – the men who were to play German soldiers at first resolutely refused to dress up in Nazi uniform. For a couple of days nothing would persuade any of them to play these parts in the film. However, apparently on the third day, one of them made a very rude remark when persuaded to try on [the] uniform; at which the others laughed heartily, and from that moment played at being Nazi soldiers with great verve.[5]

Once back at the studios, Crichton made the decision not to film one of the scenes in the script, of the concentration camp at Auschwitz. He thought it would be too painful, and also unnecessary to show it. That Sonja was at Auschwitz was mentioned in the court scene, and he thought that would quite suffice. Although the film may not have exactly mirrored the undiluted truth, it more than fulfilled the spirit of the original story in a remarkably strong but laudably unsentimental way across its taut eighty-nine minutes, complemented by Georges Auric's memorable score, his last for Ealing. So it is quite difficult to reconcile some of the latter-day criticisms about the film with the almost universal panoply of praise for *The Divided Heart* in the contemporary media.

Charles Barr dismissed it with, 'the verdict has to be: worthy but tame ... actressy ... afraid of getting into any deep emotional water'.[6] George Perry suggested, 'there is a characteristic reticence to become too deeply involved, almost as though, having uncovered an undoubtedly explosively charged affair of heart-breaking proportions, the filmmakers were reluctant to be drawn too closed and so risk being forced to make a commitment ... It is, in essence, far too British about everything.'[7]

Contrast that with the review in *The Times*:

> If there was one enormous wrong committed in the past, there are two present rights, the right of the mother to her own child, the right the foster parents have won by their love and self-sacrifice. Between the two, the script and the director, Mr Charles Crichton, pick a scrupulous way. They are determined to make a fair copy both of the proceedings of the court and of the events told in flashbacks, a copy free of the blots and smudges of false sentimentality and the underlinings of contrived heroics, and fair the copy is.[8]

Alan Dent, in the *Illustrated London News*, first invokes Virgil's famous quote in *The Aeneid*: 'Human deeds have their tears, and mortality touches the heart' before writing, 'too seldom in the cinema are we reminded of this deep, sad, truth. But a beautiful film like *The Divided Heart* reminds us of it poignantly ... this film is very remarkable for its lack of hysteria or exaggeration or of dwelling upon any scene to the point of mawkishness. The horror is suggested, not underlined.'

The *Belfast News-Letter* praises Crichton whose 'handling throughout is so objective, cool and yet sympathetic that the truth of the real life story on which the script is based never gets clouded.' The *Kensington Post* notes, 'the film is stark at times, warm at others, and holding throughout. And yet this very lack of heavy tear-jerking (a delicate accomplishment of the director Charles Crichton) tends to emphasise that the whole story is being carefully restrained for the sake of authenticity and research detail.' The *Western Mail* rightly makes special reference to the writer, too often a neglected creative in reviews:

> In the case of *The Divided Heart*, I would not go so far as to say that the (screen) play is the thing. That would be to discredit Mr Crichton's most accomplished direction and the actors' and cameraman's considerable achievement. But I must insist that not only is Jack Whittingham's screenplay as brilliant a piece of writing as we have had in any film this year but that it ranks with the best ever to come from Ealing Studios. I should like to see it published in book form and a copy distributed to every working and potential screenwriter. Perhaps then the spoken word would be able to make a stand against the current onslaught of the merely spectacular.

You would expect Crichton to draw the best even from a complete newcomer like Ray – although the director did remark much later, and rather uncharitably, he didn't think the boy was particularly good. After all he had coaxed extraordinary performances from the youthful cast in *Hue and Cry* as well as, like Ray, a similar novice in Jon Whiteley for *Hunted*. Whatever his apparent shortcomings, they certainly do not seem to the fore in the course of several complex scenes throughout the film as he runs, effortlessly, a gamut of emotions with each twist of the tale. When, towards the end, after Sonja has been granted custody and she arrives in Germany to try and sensitively begin the bonding process with her son on, for her, hostile foreign soil, his switch from sullen to supportive of her in the face of unfriendly locals is extraordinarily touching. It is as if he has finally come to embrace one of the judges' sage entreaties, that the court has now handed 'custody of the mother to the son'.

Mitchell, in particular, was full of praise for Crichton's direction:

> He had great taste leaving things unshown, as Georges Auric, who composed the music had an ear for silence in certain passages when music would've overladen the mood. At the moment in court when Sonja was told that she had won custody of the boy, Charles, instead of presenting a close-up of Sonja's feelings, left it to the audience to understand them, and instead filmed a long shot of the court, with Sonja silently sitting down, without expression. Another scene, which was cut, though we actually filmed it before he decided against it, was the final scene of the script, where the boy showed his mother conjuring tricks on the train journey. It was a good scene in itself, but not such a good ending to the film as the penultimate one, in which the boy assumed responsibility of his mother by quietly taking charge the train tickets.[9]

Crichton's sure touch with children is also palpable in a marvellous earlier scene where the Hartls visit a Leipzig orphanage to check out two little boys who have been offered for adoption. A younger version of Ivan was played by Martin Keller in what appears to be his only screen appearance. His fearful demeanour is in marked contrast to the other boy, the ebullient Hans, played by Martin Stephens (incorrectly credited 'Stevens') in his film debut. Stephens would go on to become one of Britain's most successful child actors in films like *Village of the Damned* (1960) and *The Innocents* (1961). Stephens, who gave up acting when he was seventeen to train as an architect, told me:

> I remember little about the audition process for *The Divided Heart* at the age of four, but I have one enduring memory of being on set [at Ealing Studios], waiting around until called to the scene. Maybe I got a little bored but I became fascinated with a rope ball that hung from the long mic boom. It was beautifully made but I had no idea why it was there (clearly it was to prevent people walking into the boom). So of course I wanted to swing on it – with interesting results![10]

So his skill with children and precision with editing – how, for instance, 'Tibby' Clarke's reputedly 112-minute script for *The Lavender Hill Mob* became an 81-minute movie, the perfect example – was by now a given. But the revelation, if one can dare call it that, here are the performances of Borchers and Mitchell, which are the glue for what I contend is Crichton's unarguably best 'serious' film.

Charles Barr called it 'actressy' pejoratively; more perceptively, Dilys Powell in the *Sunday Times* on 14 November 1954, wrote: 'The emphasis on maternal love ... has led some people to give the film the discouraging label of a woman's film. I should prefer to call it an actress's film.' Mitchell's portrayal, in particular, restricted as it is principally to just looks and gestures, was understandably picked out by most critics. This was how Jympson Harman, a doyen of reviewers, reacted in London's *Evening News*:

> Now at last Sir Michael Balcon gives the wider cinema public a complete demonstration of Miss Mitchell's dark, grave beauty and the exquisitely controlled emotion of her acting. Even if *The Divided Heart* were not such an admirably made picture of a compelling subject with profound international implications Miss Mitchell's performance would make it one of half a dozen outstanding films of the year.

Serendipitously, Harman's son, John, would, almost thirty-five years later, be the editor on Crichton's final film, *A Fish Called Wanda*.

Four months after *The Divided Heart* was released in the UK, the film became a firm contender in no fewer than five categories at the eighth annual British Academy Film Awards (now BAFTAs), held at the Odeon Leicester Square on 10 March 1955. In three of them – best film from any source (among twenty titles), best British film (among eight) and best screenplay – it was vying with another Ealing title, *The Maggie*, Alexander Mackendrick's much more traditional studio comedy, which Charles Barr would describe as 'an obvious twin of *The Titfield Thunderbolt*', about an old River Clyde 'puffer' boat threatened with the scrapyard. In the event, they cancelled each other out at the final prize-giving. However, considerable justice was seen to be done when Yvonne Mitchell and Cornell Borchers were named, respectively, best British actress and best foreign actress. One of Mitchell's fellow nominees, Audrey Hepburn, for *Sabrina Fair*, had clearly come a very long way fast since her almost wordless walk-on four years earlier in *The Lavender Hill Mob*, while Borchers's triumph must have felt particularly sweet coming in a category that included much better known names like Grace Kelly, Shirley Booth, Judy Holliday and Gina Lollobrigida.

That same evening, *The Divided Heart* also received the United Nations (UN) Award 'for the best film embodying one or more of the principles of the United Nations Charter in 1955'. The other contender was the Sanders brothers' twenty-minute American Civil War-set drama,

A Time Out of War, which got its reward three weeks later with an Oscar for Best Short. Crichton's work was further recognised as one of the top 'foreign films' of the year by America's National Board of Review, along with a Golden Laurel Award, presented annually 'to the film, other than American, making the greatest contribution to international understanding'.

The *New York Times* review underscored the positive tone with which the film was critically received Stateside: 'This is a bleak, heart-rending problem, as it is finely presented in this film with exceptionally sensitive understanding and scrupulous integrity ... director Charles Crichton has staged this in such swift, sharp, vivid documentary style that the nightmarish terror of those dark days is shudderingly revived.'[11]

Later that year, Mitchell was to be found at an event in Liverpool Philharmonic Hall, where, across two sessions organised by the Merseyside Film Institute Society, she addressed more than three thousand local grammar school students about the film and her award-winning role, which required learning some Slovene by 'listening to gramophone records'. Describing it as 'a part in a million', she had, the local paper reported, 'nothing but praise for the film's director'.

The film's acclaim earned Borchers another Hollywood contract, with a different studio, but by the end of the decade, she had retired from acting altogether opting instead for family life. Michel Ray's film and TV career continued for another ten years, culminating in a featured role as the teenage Farraj in David Lean's *Lawrence of Arabia* (1982). Later, under his full name, Michel Ray de Carvalho, he married the Heineken heiress and also became a billionaire businessman in his own right. As for Ivan, he received a hero's welcome on return to Slovenia and was given a new bicycle – a luxury then. In the years following the *Life* article and the film, his fame slowly faded but he remained the only boy in Sostanj, for a while at least, who owned a real leather soccer ball. Ivan never married and spent the rest of his life living with his sister Marija, while also continuing to correspond with his adoptive mother in Germany. He died of lung cancer in 1965, aged forty-four.

Despite the awards and fine reviews, the film performed only modestly in Britain and poorly in the States. In his memoirs, Balcon wrote: 'It seemed to me that the ordinary cinemagoer in those countries could not – even seven years after the war was over – become emotionally involved with a German woman and a Yugoslav child.'[12] The 'politics' of the time probably did not help the box office, either, according to Sue Harper and Vincent Porter, who reported: 'Davis [John Davis, the power behind the throne at Rank] refused wide German distribution of *The Divided Heart* because it dealt with some of the human consequences of Auschwitz and might upset audiences, noting that "*The Dam Busters* had very adverse comments in the German press".[13]

By the time Crichton returned to make his thirteenth and last film for Ealing eighteen months later, the studio had been sold to the BBC, and Balcon, the company and its leafy logo relocated from West London to MGM British Studios, Borehamwood, due north of the capital.

The Man in the Sky (1957)

The 'man' in question was Jack Hawkins, playing test pilot John Mitchell, in Ealing's first film at its new production base. Hawkins had also, coincidentally, been the star of *The Long Arm* (1956), an efficient police procedural, Ealing's very final film of more than ninety that had originated from West London following Balcon's takeover back in the thirties.

As various financial difficulties began to assail Balcon in the mid-fifties, the decision was taken to sell the studios to the BBC for £350,000 (over £9m in today's money). Balcon had, history relates, been led to believe that Rank would give Ealing space at Pinewood Studios including two new stages to be specially constructed for its exclusive use. According to George Perry: 'The two new stages were indeed built, but it was made clear that Ealing would have to take its chances with every other contender for the space.'[14] It seems that Rank, in the person of its autocratic managing director, John Davis, 'had no intention of allowing an autonomous group to operate on its special patch within the gates of Pinewood'.[15] For his part, Balcon believed that this would mean Ealing losing its independence and identity.

So Ealing's relationship with Rank, which had been initiated in 1944, was now severed altogether. Instead, Balcon signed up with MGM, with whom he had last worked for a little under two years from 1936 until he moved to Ealing. Despite some continuity for the company in collaboration with a 'major' of global significance, albeit in unfamiliar surroundings, Perry quotes Balcon admitting, 'It would be no use pretending that we did not have heavy hearts over leaving Ealing. To comfort myself, I used to say it was people that counted, not buildings. This was not strictly honest, as over the years there had developed at Ealing a spirit which had seeped into the very fabric of the place.'[16] 'Tibby' Clarke probably summed up the feelings of many of Balcon's once 'young gentlemen' when he said: 'I don't think any of us welcomed the change. There was little hope of the old team spirit being preserved now that we ceased to be a self-contained unit, and the intimate atmosphere of our previous home was sadly missing from these bleak new acres of characterless buildings.'[17]

Speaking some years after Clarke's observation, and well after Balcon's death in 1977, Crichton was rather more forthright, notably about when the company itself ceased to exist a little over three years and just seven films after moving to Borehamwood:

> I think to some extent that everyone at Ealing towards the late fifties was beginning to feel a bit incestuous, but this is not why the studio closed. Why the studio closed must be a secret that Mickey Balcon has taken with him. Whenever encouraged by good trade unionists like Sidney Cole, we asked for more money and he always said, 'What are you talking about, this is your studio, I'm getting old, I'm going to retire, and then the studio will be yours, so don't bloody well ask for any more money.' And then suddenly I wasn't there – I'd left already – and all those people who thought it was their studio were told, 'That's it, chums, fuck off.' People like Charlie Frend were absolutely shattered.[18]

Between *The Divided Heart* and *The Man in the Sky*, Crichton was attached, briefly, to the film version of *Lucky Jim*, an adaptation of Kingsley Amis's comic first novel, published in 1954, about life in a red-brick university. He had been loaned out by Balcon for just the second time – since *Hunted* in 1952 – because with Ealing's increasing money worries, it was believed that the studio could not afford to keep Crichton and Frend on the payroll at the same time. According to Andrew Pulver in the *Guardian*, Crichton had been shooting for two weeks with the star Ian Carmichael, in the title role, 'when he [and producer/co-writer Vivienne Knight] was forced out by John and Roy Boulting, the redoubtable producer-directors on the board of British Lion, the film's producing studio. John took over as director, his twin Roy as producer.'[19]

Crichton would remain tight-lipped about the course of events except to say, thirty years later, 'I don't like the Boulting Brothers. They cheated us. I think they made an awful picture. It wasn't the picture I would have made.'[20] He was more forthcoming about the reaction of Balcon when he heard Crichton was going to direct the film: 'The idea of an anti-hero or anything like that he couldn't understand [of *Lucky Jim*] "What do you mean, he burns holes in his bedclothes with his cigarettes! You can't make a picture about that kind of person." He had that puritan streak.'[21] As it turned out, the Boultings' version, which substituted slapstick for the novel's biting satire and made Carmichael's character more of a silly ass at odds, noted Pulver, 'with the original Dixon's simmering resentment,' received lukewarm reviews.

Instead, Crichton, with Seth Holt, who had been his editor on four films, as a first-time associate producer, and reunited with

THE FIFTIES: EXIT EALING, 1954-59   137

cinematographer Douglas Slocombe, swapped comedy for suspenseful drama, and a provincial university for life in and around a bustling Midlands aerodrome. *The Man in the Sky* was an original story by William Rose who also shared screenplay credit with John Eldridge. Rose, born in Missouri, made his home in England after the war during which he served with the Black Watch. Apparently he spent his demobilisation money on a screenwriting course, which clearly paid off as he earned Oscar nominations for two of his films, *Genevieve* and Ealing's *The Ladykillers* – a British Film Academy award winner – among five scripts, also including Mackendrick's *The Maggie*, he wrote for the studio between 1954 and 1957. Eldridge also had Ealing 'form' – *Pool of London*, of course, and *Out of the Clouds* (1955), a Heathrow-set drama, directed by Basil Dearden. He had also tangled with aircraft a year earlier, as director of *Conflict of Wings*, yet another one of Group 3's Ealing clones about a rural Norfolk community, crammed with eccentrics, protesting the use of a nearby bird sanctuary for RAF jet target practice.

Unlike the sleek jets and daredevil test pilots of David Lean's *The Sound Barrier* (1952), Jack Hawkins's Mitchell is a middle-aged family man required to demonstrate the new prototype of a pot-bellied freighter to secure the future of his cash-strapped, aero manufacturer employers. As misfortune would have it, and with the potential buyers on board, one of the plane's engines catches fire soon after take-off. Mitchell orders everyone to parachute out and, defying orders to crash the plane in the sea, is determined to try and land it intact: 'The moment I abandon this old cow, we're all out of business.'

Then in nail-biting real time, we watch as Mitchell has to keep flying, first diving to try and extinguish the fire, losing some aileron control in the process, then having to use up petrol ahead of any attempt at landing. The word soon goes round about the plane's plight and the crowds and press – naturally, an opportunistic freelance hack who is banking on disaster – begin to gather at the aerodrome, including, unknown to Mitchell, his distraught wife Mary (Elizabeth Sellars), to whom he has scrawled what may be a valedictory note. Happily, he lands safely before, in a kind of steely daze, walking from the plane to the buildings, taking off his overalls, tearing up the note, climbing into his car and driving home via the laundry where he'd promised Mary he'd pick up some dry-cleaning. Finally, home to his wife for a final confrontation, emotionally almost as fraught as anything he had experienced already that drama-packed day, beginning ominously: 'You're back early!'

In his autobiography, Jack Hawkins, explained what came next:

> My wife, beautifully played by Elizabeth Sellars, asks me how the day has gone, and I said, 'All right' in an offhand manner. Unknown to me

she had witnessed the near disaster and she rounds on me, accusing me of being prepared to sacrifice her and our children simply for the job. I then had a six-minute speech, which was really the justification of why a man does a job – any job – which was brilliantly written by Bill Rose, one of the finest screenwriters, who wrote perfectly for me. The speech attracted a lot of attention and for an actor, no feeling exceeds the satisfaction when people come up afterwards and say that the character you played was splendid, and you were just the right person to play it.[22]

In fact, the only 'drawback' about the film, Hawkins remarked, tersely, was having to spend twelve weeks away from home on location, much of it at Pendeford, a local municipal airport used at the time for private and training aircraft, about four miles north of Wolverhampton town centre (Figure 6.2).

If Alec Guinness was the 'face' of Ealing in its comedy pomp, then Hawkins surely provided the studio's most distinctive profile for its serious content; three of his films, *Mandy*, *The Cruel Sea* and *The Long Arm* all earned him British Film Academy award nominations; *The Man in the Sky*, his sixth and final film for Ealing, should have been added to that list. It was, though, Hawkins's first film for Crichton who, for

Figure 6.2 Jack Hawkins in *The Man in the Sky*

THE FIFTIES: EXIT EALING, 1954-59   **139**

the most part, was surrounded by actors with whom he had not worked before. The exceptions were Sellars – an actress Crichton compared to Bette Davis for 'intensity' – who had been Dirk Bogarde's adulterous wife in *Hunted*; Megs Jenkins, the flirty barmaid years earlier in *Painted Boats*; and Eddie Byrne, one of the judges in *The Divided Heart*, here playing Mitchell's American customer who, despite the flight failure, magnanimously places his order anyway presumably on the strength of Hawkins's stiff-upper-lip heroics.

The star may have had his reservations about Wolverhampton, but the town for its part came up trumps helping out the film. The *Birmingham Weekly Post* reported that,

> One hundred and fifty people have been invited to assist not only as bystanders during the dramatic action centred round the airport itself but in specific roles as, for example, ambulance men and firemen, a group of cyclists, clerks and car drivers. Despite the fact that in Wolverhampton there are more jobs than people to fill them, some of the biggest industrial firms have encouraged and given facilities for their shift workers during their off-duty time and others who might be on holiday to be employed from time to time on the film.

While the film was recreating airborne mayhem, Douglas Slocombe, during one particular chunk of his downtime, inadvertently devised his own. Stuck away for weeks in and around an aerodrome, he decided to learn how to fly. One long summer's evening, after shooting had finished for the day, the now-qualified Slocombe registered a flight plan and took off for a solo flight in a small Auster aircraft, aiming to return in good time for the evening's 'rushes'. Within half an hour, and after a series of prescribed turns, he began to get the distinct, increasingly sinking, feeling that he was lost.

As it started to get darker, he looked desperately for somewhere suitable to land; after one abortive attempt he flew on, eventually coming in on a somewhat bumpy surface only to be confronted by some RAF personnel who escorted him irately to a Nissen hut for a full explanation. Meanwhile, back at Pendeford, there was great concern for the missing cinematographer. When eventually, hours later, he returned shamefacedly to base, having missed the 'rushes' session, Crichton was, Slocombe would recall, 'very angry'. The reason for this pilot's error turned out to be strangely simple: his exposure meter, tucked away in a trouser pocket, had conflicted magnetically with the plane's compass situated between the seats, so, for example, a 180-degree turn registered instead as 360 degrees. His final destination proved to be some two hundred miles due north of Wolverhampton.[23]

After the almost universal praise for *The Divided Heart*, Crichton might reasonably have expected some sort of critical backlash this time round. But again the plaudits were plentiful, not just for the director, Hawkins and, in particular, that climactic domestic scene, but also, reassuringly, for Ealing itself. In the *Sketch*, C.A. Lejeune noted: 'It is splendid to find Ealing Films still hale and hearty after their sad exodus and the premature rumours of their death. From their new lodge at Elstree in care of MGM they have produced ... something well up to the best Ealing standards ... the last moments show both actor and director Charles Crichton at their full stature.' *The Times* praised the scene between Hawkins and Sellars as 'psychologically right' and 'perfectly acted' before declaring, 'it is good to see the Ealing insignia on this screen again'.[24] The *Tatler* concluded: 'I must say that the final scene – full of emotion and totally devoid of emotionalism – seems to me as true and poignant as any I have ever seen.'

That sentiment was underlined even more forcibly by Alan Dent in the *Illustrated London News*:

> When the wife – as wives will – lets out a whimper to the effect that she knows all and that he has not given his own wife and bairns a thought, husband Hawkins lets out a foaming gush of pent-up fury which will warm the cockles of the heart of every married man in the land. Furthermore it will make millions of wives stare at the screen in astonishment at so startling an intimation that many husbands may know and feel and think far more than many wives imagine.

Then there was the considered reaction of the *Birmingham Daily Post*'s twenty-five-year-old reviewer, Alex Walker, as he was bylined in those apprentice days before becoming at the end of the decade, and for the next forty-three years, the respected film critic of the *London Evening Standard*. He wrote:

> A situation then packed with incident but turning essentially on character. Crichton has developed it with enormous skill. I feel sure it is the finest thing he has done ... A disciplined, honest, performance Hawkins gives; and he has my thanks for it. Crichton partners him beautifully. He builds up in your mind not only the tension, but, far more important, the responsibility shouldered by the man who is at the centre of it ... Then suddenly comes the outburst of hysterical reproaches. How could he risk so much? He has not been brave – just foolhardy. The words, as Elizabeth Sellars delivers them with bitterness induced by strain, leaves Hawkins baffled and dumb. But it is the *reculer pour mieux sauter*; and as he gathers himself for a magnificent, surprising and psychologically satisfying comeback, the man and the film achieve their full height.

More than fifty years on, Professor Robert Murphy's take on the film for his 2012 essay, 'Dark Shadows Around Ealing', is equally positive as he describes *The Man in the Sky* as 'the sort of film that any national cinema ought to be proud of – sophisticated, economical, emotionally engaging, entirely convincing in character and action.' Although he might also have pointed out that, in these feminist times, Hawkins's furious outburst would now seem hopelessly dated, he makes no such cavil, suggesting instead that 'his motives were inspired by love as much as by duty'.²⁵ At today's equivalent of £3.5m, Crichton's budget was probably the steepest among all of his Ealing films but, he admitted later, despite the reviews, *The Man in the Sky* 'didn't do particularly well. I think the reason was that the climax was an emotional rather than a physical one.'²⁶

So, after sixteen years with Ealing as, variously, an editor, associate producer, and director, the studio tie was finally cut. He would reflect:

> Ealing was a snug nursery where one was surrounded by talented playmates and supervised by a tolerant headmaster – well, he was not *all* that tolerant. We were each expected to make one picture a year, or else! Outside, it was very much colder, more daunting, but once a script had been financed and a unit gathered together, things were not all that very much different from Ealing.²⁷

***

Almost exactly three weeks to the day after *The Man in the Sky* went on release in the UK, Ibsen's tragicomedy, *The Wild Duck*, Crichton's first work for television, aired on ITV. Since independent television was launched in 1955, there had been almost from the beginning, a weekly, live, *Play of the Week*, produced, variously, by the then mere handful of ITV companies, notably Associated-Rediffusion, which held the weekday franchise in London. Between 1955 and 1974, there would be nearly six hundred productions in all. Crichton's contribution was especially notable as it was the first recorded *Play of the Week*, shot as a 35 mm feature film on a sound stage at Shepperton Studios. The TV version, adapted by Alwyne Whatsley, was a recreation of a very successful stage production, 'presented' by John Clements, from a translation by Max Faber, at the Saville Theatre, which opened just before Christmas 1955.

The principal cast of Dorothy Tutin, as Hedwig, Emlyn Williams (Hjalmar Ekdal), Michael Gough (Gregers Werle), Laurence Hardy (Dr Relling), Angela Baddeley (Gina Ekdal), Robert Beaumont (Molvik) and George Relph (Old Ekdal) regrouped, along with the rest of the stage players, for Crichton and his director of photography, Walter – known as

'Jimmy' – Harvey, whose career in the camera department had begun in the silent days.

'Television came tantalisingly close to perfection in last night's ITV production', purred the *Liverpool Echo*. 'Of Dorothy Tutin, I can speak only in superlatives ... [she] has the kind of face that was made for the close-up of the television camera. The girl is brilliant. And this was her play.' The paper's critic did, however, have just one 'complaint ... at the quality of the sound reproduction, but the many other excellent features were more than enough to make me forget this'.

Professor John Wyver of the University of Westminster sought out a rediscovered print of the production, which was shown a few years back in a season at the BFI Southbank, and particularly noted the impact of being filmed:

> In part as a consequence of such an unconventional production process, this 'filmed play' has an entirely distinctive visual style and a rare dramatic effectiveness. Working with what I assume to be just a single film camera, Crichton and Harvey achieve far more than simply documentation of the production. Each shot is calculated, each choice of framing and camera lens motivated by the relationships between the characters. On occasions Crichton also scores striking visual coups, as when the shadow of Gregers Werle (Gough) looms up against the door of the Ekdal household, dominating and destroying the family that the character believes he is helping. The camera inhabits the rooms of this insistently interior Ibsen drama, constantly shifting its position and orientation, and just occasionally moving to adjacent spaces to look back into the central emotional area. Small lapses of continuity and breaks in performance development can also be recognised as the outcome of the shot-by-shot coverage and a film edit, but the gains in focus and visual intensity most definitely outweigh these negatives.[28]

It would be another five years before Crichton returned to the small screen, directing some episodes of the bland ITV series, *Man of the World*. Ibsen, it was not.

***

Law and Disorder (1958)

Considering Crichton's low opinion of the Boultings and what must have surely been some residual bitterness after his abortive tilt at *Lucky Jim*, it was perhaps a little surprising to find him so, comparatively, soon after at the helm of a new production from British Lion, the film company run by the Boultings in tandem with another pair of prolific British moviemakers, Frank Launder and Sidney Gilliat.

It may have had something to do with the possibility that, as noted in some but not all sources, he actually took the helm of *Law and Order* – as a favour? – when the original director, Henry Cornelius, had to quit because of what turned out to be a fatal illness. Cornelius, who, of course, worked with Crichton on *Painted Boats* and, more importantly, *Hue and Cry*, back in the forties, had just completed *Next to No Time*, a new romantic comedy for British Lion, before starting *Law and Disorder*. He died aged forty-four before either film was released. If there remains the slight mystery about a Cornelius/Crichton juggling act, then another must be that, curiously, in his enormously enjoyable memoir, 'Tibby' Clarke, who is credited as the main writer of *Law and Disorder*, makes not a single mention of the film in its two hundred or more pages despite covering, even briefly, all his other screen work in and around that same period. Maybe he also thought, like Crichton said later, the producer was 'a clot of the first order, and didn't know what he was doing',[29] and so, like Crichton had generally done, drawn a veil over the whole experience.

The producer was Paul Soskin, one of the legion of East European-born – in his case, Crimea – aspiring film people who had made their way to Britain before, during and after the war. Soskin's uncle Simon built Amalgamated Studios at Elstree in 1935 but a deal the nephew had hoped to secure with Columbia in the States failed to materialise, and that together with other increasing financial difficulties led to them losing the complex in 1939. Separate from any studio ambitions, Soskin produced a number of films between 1935 and 1958. For the Boultings, he produced *High Treason* (1951), a kind of sequel to the highly successful *Seven Days to Noon* (1950), and in the same year as *Law and Disorder*, was also behind the brothers' *Happy Is the Bride*, a breezy 'will-they-won't-they' wedding comedy.

Law and Disorder is often described, mostly dismissed, as 'a sub-Ealing comedy' probably because of Crichton's and Clarke's names on the credits. But in truth, it actually more resembles, certainly in its better moments, the kind of sharply satirical – even at times, quite mean-spirited – comedy that would come to characterise the best of the Boultings' work in films like *I'm All Right Jack* (1959) and *Heaven's Above* (1963), both far removed, in most cases, from the gently whimsical world conjured up at Ealing Green.

This point is underlined by Sue Harper and Vincent Porter: 'On the whole the output of British Lion in these years was very mixed with the best films being made by experienced Ealing refugees. There was one very competent comedy *Law and Disorder* which displayed the weary cynicism about the Establishment which was beginning to look like a British Lion requirement.'[30]

Clarke's autobiographical omission – airbrushing out? – seems stranger still when, in the final third of the film, some of the hijinks involving hapless policemen of all ranks are curiously reminiscent of the chaotic cavortings of the law in *The Lavender Hill Mob*. Clarke is, however, credited alongside two other writers, Patrick Campbell and Vivienne Martin, so perhaps his contribution had been considerably diminished by the final draft, which may, in its turn, explain his belated reticence about the whole assignment. Campbell, the immensely tall, stammering Irish peer and humorist, with screenwriting experience already across a decade, had remained on board *Lucky Jim* when the Boultings usurped Crichton and Knight. His teaming with Knight, who had spent a number of years as a publicity person with Powell and Pressburger, would presage a later union when the pair married in 1966, she becoming Campbell's third wife. By this time, Campbell and Knight had also become firm Crichton family friends, even holidaying together on occasion.

The project had originated with a comic novel, *Smugglers' Circuit*, published in 1954, the first of nine books by Denys Roberts, whose day job as, eventually, Sir Denys Tudor Emil Roberts, was as a much-travelled British colonial official and judge, becoming from 1979, the last non-Chinese to hold the post of chief justice of Hong Kong. At the time British Lion put *Law and Disorder* into production, Roberts was Crown counsel in Nyasaland (later Malawi).

The opening titles inform us that the two main stars, Michael Redgrave, as Percy Brand, and Robert Morley, are, respectively, on the 'wrong' and 'right' side of the law, ahead of the film's recurring joke that one is a charming but inept con man who, over almost twenty years, has the misfortune of always coming up in court against cantankerous judge Morley who unfailingly sentences Percy to steadily increasing terms of imprisonment. Percy takes these regular setbacks in surprisingly good heart despite the fact he has regularly to concoct stories of why he's an absent but devoted single father to growing son, Colin (Jeremy Burnham), who remains in the care of Percy's card-sharping sister, Florence (Joan Hickson). Percy's cunning guise is of a cleric, whose missionary work takes him 'abroad' for long periods, on and off from 1938 – when we first see him emerge from prison – right through World War II and well into the fifties, by which time he has been everything from an army chaplain to frocked bishop. But his best-laid plans threaten to go haywire when, on his latest return from 'abroad', he discovers that Colin is now a fully qualified barrister – and has, to Percy's horror, been assigned as a marshal to Morley, as the judge begins a round of circuit courts. Time to go straight, Percy reckons, so

THE FIFTIES: EXIT EALING, 1954-59   145

he and his sister move to a seaside cottage only then to become rather too easily embroiled in an ingenious local smuggling racket involving French sailors, brandy and a hollow shark.

When the smuggling scam escalates, Percy is inevitably seized by the authorities, so now the game changes to the question of how he, with the help of his ever loyal, if crooked, friends can avoid being hauled up before Morley who just happens to be presiding at the local court, without Colin, still entirely ignorant of his father's past, also being in attendance. So far, so mostly good, with Redgrave, in a variety of dog-collared disguises, and Hickson on very good form surrounded by about as classy a collection of British character actors – Ronald Squire, Lionel Jeffries, prissy Reginald Beckwith, John Le Mesurier, massively moustachioed Michael Trubshawe, George Coulouris ('Jacobean? It will be soon') and the ubiquitous Sam Kydd, to name but a few – as it must have been possible to muster in the day. Then there was Elizabeth Sellars, again in barely more than a cameo as a barrister, and even an amusing spit-and-cough role for Irene Handl. The straightest face had to belong to Burnham as guileless Colin; later he turned from acting to scriptwriting, including an episode of *The Avengers*, which Crichton directed in 1968.

Returning for his second film, this time uncredited, with Crichton was the by now seven-year-old Martin Stephens who told me he thought that his single scene in *The Divided Heart* must have made an impression on the director.

> After that I assumed my film career was over but three years later a call came from my agent. I think Charles remembered that cheekiness, because he wanted a cheeky boy for a small part in *Law and Disorder*. So I spent a wet and windy week in Fishguard, Wales with my dad waiting to shoot the couple of scenes in which I appeared on the beach. Robert Morley was fun and I was lucky to work with him again on a TV Dickens series in which he played Mr Micawber.[31]

The Pembrokeshire coast doubled for Kent, within spitting distance – notably from a smuggling point of view – of France, while the interiors were shot at ABPC Elstree, ironically, across the road from Soskin's once-dreamed of studio empire that was now the new base for Ealing.

The final third of the film, though endlessly madcap as Percy's pals resort to ever sillier ways of trying to keep him away from the judge – notably a rather tiresome legal subplot involving a slanderous parrot – contrive to make the absurdly brief running time of seventy-six minutes feel somehow much, much longer. The final line of the film, though, does at least neatly bring the story full circle as, with Colin now firmly believing his father has left for yet another priestly odyssey, Redgrave arrives back at the gates of the familiar nick to be greeted by an old friend (Michael Brennan):

> Scene 131. PRISON ENTRANCE, DAY. WARDER: Come along in, Percy. It's a pleasure to have you back. FADE OUT.

That scene is on page 97 of Crichton's own annotated script, which reveals bits of storyboarding, some rhetorical reminders like 'ADEQUATE?' and 'GOOD ENOUGH?', as well as the intriguing 'INSERT PARROT?' Crichton said later he had 'to fight him [Soskin] all the time, and in the end, and of course he had the privilege, he cut out a sequence without which the end of the picture is pretty incomprehensible. No matter how much I fought him on that, he got his way, which was a pity.'[32] That seventy-six-minute running time was, according to comments in *Variety*, the result of some fifteen minutes of cuts. Yet, despite the director's apparent concern, the end result still appears to be a near fit.

The Times, which did not refer back to 'Ealing', was dismissive: 'The plot has some good ideas, but they do not work out, and one is left with the suspicion that they probably seemed far funnier on paper then they do on the screen.'[33] The word 'Ealing' is not invoked either in the *Coventry Evening Telegraph*, which is a little more enthusiastic, noting Crichton's touch as 'sure and the film, while not the outstanding comedy of the era, has clever touches and a generally good standard.' The *Western Mail* does, however, make the connection: '[the film] is a frolic in the Ealing tradition which evokes more admiration than uproar'.

The response in the States, where the film opened a couple of months after the UK, was far more positive. *Variety* wrote, '*Law and Disorder* is a highly amusing offbeat comedy which notches guffaws and giggles with disarming ease. It has more than a little of the Ealing stamp.' A.H. Weiler in the *New York Times* developed the theme by reminding readers of the Clarke/Crichton team who 'mined loads of mirth from *The Lavender Hill Mob* some years ago, have uncovered another deposit of guffaws and chuckles in *Law and Disorder*'. Weiler reserves particular praise for Morley, 'who contributes an outstanding performance as the stern judge who finds himself as much outside the law as within it. Although he never cracks a smile, chances are he will force a few on the customers. As a matter of fact, they should find most of the cheerful disorders in *Law and Disorder* irreverently funny and diverting.'[34] After his clapperboard 'cameo' in *The Love Lottery*, the director seems to have enjoyed another 'nod' here as it is surely far too coincidental that Morley's character just happens to be called 'Judge Crichton'. On page 8 of the screenplay, he is described thus: 'He is a big man of strong personality. He is approaching his late forties.' Crichton, who passed forty-seven while filming in West Wales, would seem perfectly to have fitted the profile.

Floods of Fear (1958)

Just when you thought Crichton had proved that his versatility knew almost no bounds after more than more than a dozen features across the past decade, ranging from quirky and romantic comedies to wartime docudrama and chase thrillers, along came this astonishingly effective £300,000 disaster/jeopardy film. Although Crichton's cameras had ventured, albeit rarely, beyond his own native borders in the past – briefly, Belgium, Italy, Austria and Yugoslavia, for example – this was the first time he had taken on a wholly American subject, firmly set in the States, but filmed entirely, apart from some newsreel inserts, in England, principally in and around Pinewood Studios.

The review by the *Belfast Telegraph*'s Martin Wallace characterised many at the time when he wrote:

> *Floods of Fear* ... gives an amazingly accurate picture of an American community battling a river's rage. In fact, Charles Crichton is the first British director, working in Britain, to create a credible American landscape. *Floods of Fear* is remarkable in another sense. It is tough, unsqueamish, taut as a whiplash – one of a few recent movies which give hope that British film-making is shedding the middlebrow gentility which has strangled it for years.

The £300,000 *Floods of Fear* began life as a seven-part newspaper serial, 'A Girl, a Man, and a River' – 'He was fleeing prison – she was running from reality' – written by brothers John and Ward Hawkins for the *Saturday Evening Post* in the States. First published between January and March 1956, it reappeared the following year as a hardback retitled *The Floods of Fear*. The subject appealed to Sydney Box, then head of production at Rank, as part of the company's strategy, wrote Professor Andrew Spicer in his biography of Box, to try and 'conquer the American market'.[35] Box's career to that point had been about as interesting and varied as Crichton's. Three years his senior, Box had produced more than a hundred shorts for the government during the war before moving into features, most spectacularly with *The Seventh Veil* (1945), directed by Crichton's former editing assistant, Compton Bennett. The film also won Box and his second wife Muriel the Oscar for Best Original Screenplay. This led to his being appointed head of

Gainsborough Pictures, one of Ealing's great rivals for British cinema audiences at the back end of the forties where he stayed for a couple of prolific years before moving entirely in-house at Rank through the fifties. *Floods of Fear* would prove to be one of his final productions before switching to television.

Floods of Fear accorded Crichton a rare writing credit, with Vivienne Knight also acknowledged for her 'additional dialogue'. According to Crichton:

> It wasn't a subject I would have chosen myself. I had to make it [the film] because I wanted money. It had a writer who was so awful that the producer [Box] said, 'You take half the book and I'll take the other half; you write that half, I'll write this half.' We only had a little time to do it. So I wrote my half and asked him where was his half, and he said, 'I haven't started yet, you better go on, actually.'[36]

'You need never starve if you can write', Box had once told director Ken Annakin, who directed four of the Huggett family films for the producer. However for Box, 'genial, overweight ... with a malformed hip',[37] who had apparently written over a thousand one-act plays even before taking on films, *Floods of Fear* was a screenplay too far with all his other production responsibilities at Rank.

For the project, Crichton was rejoined by editor Peter Bezencenet with whom he had worked on *The Divided Heart*, and, for the first time, by art director Cedric Dawe and cinematographer Christopher Challis, as well as his old housemate, Muir Mathieson, who was musical director and conductor of composer Alan Rawsthorne's suitably epic score. Sadly, Challis, already a veteran of more than twenty-five features including *Genevieve* (1953) and *The Battle of the River Plate* (1956) reveals in his own autobiography, *They Aren't All Awful*, that he was a very reluctant recruit to the project and fails to enlarge on his very considerable contribution to, visually at least, a monochrome treat.

After we hear in voiceover, 'The Year of the Big Freeze', the snow melts rapidly causing increasing flood chaos in and around Nevada's Humboldt River. Convicts from the nearby 'Pen' are imported to help repair dykes, but as water levels inexorably rise, it is every man for himself. Two prisoners, Donavan, who we later learn may be innocent of an old flame's murder, and the psychopathic Peebles escape together picking up an injured guard Sharkey on their watery way to, fortuitously, some first-floor respite in the otherwise flooded home of a local doctor. 'Doc' is otherwise occupied helping victims in town. Alone and defenceless in the remote dwelling, however, is his beautiful daughter Elizabeth, who is about to get unexpected guests with very different agendas.

The original title, 'A Girl, A Man, and a River', posited an intriguing triple threat casting-wise, bearing in mind that the river had also to be a major 'character' in this combination of action and more traditional 'film noir', a genre with which Crichton had tangled before in a very English way with *Hunted*. For the 'man', Donovan, Rank first looked no further, it seems, than their own 'company of youth' – the so-called 'charm school' of contracted actors – of which the hell-raising Peter Finch was a reluctant player. London-born but Sydney-bred, he had already appeared in a slew of Rank films including three Australian-themed tales, most notably *A Town Like Alice* (1956). That the role went to Howard Keel instead may have had to do with the fact that Finch had been offered the male lead opposite Audrey Hepburn in Fred Zinnemann's *The Nun's Story*, a major Hollywood movie that promised international stardom rather than just an idol of the Gaumonts and Odeons.

The fact that Keel was best known at the time for being the singing star of, to date, at least five of cinema's greatest Hollywood musicals, including *Seven Brides for Seven Brothers* and *Kiss Me Kate*, made his non-singing selection seem even bolder. At thirty-eight, three years younger than Finch and seven inches taller, Keel was to prove, however, a perfect, authentic-looking and sounding fit for Donavan. Might the producers have also checked Keel's back catalogue, as it were, and discovered, that ten years earlier, when still known as 'Harold Keel', he had made his screen-acting debut in England (while playing in *Oklahoma* on stage) in *The Small Voice*, a British Film Academy award–nominated thriller, portraying a court-martialled American who has escaped from Dartmoor?

For the 'girl', the producers were rather less ambitious and selected Birmingham-born Anne Heywood, a former Miss Great Britain, from the 'charm school', who had for Rank added much sex appeal but no great acting talent to instantly forgettable Odeon fodder such as *Checkpoint* (1956) and *Dangerous Exile* (1957) (Figure 6.3). Her intermittent American accent in *Floods of Fear* is marginally – just – more coherent than Cyril Cusack's as the demonstrably unbalanced Peebles who affects, at times, an almost unintelligible high-pitched Southern drawl whether threatening rape or flashing a blade while on the lam. Cusack, an otherwise fine Irish actor, looks, with his buzz cut, a little like Steve McQueen's evil twin in the film, but despite some respectful reviews, this is not his finest hour. Fortunately, Keel was also surrounded by a host of expatriate American and Canadian actors to add credibility, among them John Crawford, Guy Kingsley Pointer, James Dyrenforth, Jerry Stovin, Gordon Tanner, and Graydon Gould. Home-grown Harry

150 CHARLES CRICHTON

Figure 6.3 Anne Heywood and Howard Keel in *Floods of Fear*

H. Corbett, as Sharkey, and Eddie Byrne, by now an old Crichton hand, as the Sheriff, also sounded entirely authentic.

What of the film's third 'main' character, arguably its 'lead', the 'river'? Earlier that same year, Rank had recreated the 1912 *Titanic* disaster in *A Night to Remember* (1968), in the tank at Pinewood and at the Ruislip Lido, a large reservoir less than seven miles to the north-west of the studios. While it took a million gallons of water to sink the 'unsinkable' *Titanic* in Pinewood's tank, *Floods of Fear* utilised 2.3 million gallons to recreate the rampaging Humboldt River and its stricken banks. Into the mix was added, along with some filming at the Lido, stock footage of the Zambesi River and authentic newsreel footage of flooded towns and countryside.

While, in much later recall, he may be forgiven, for misnaming his 'Humboldt' as the 'Mississippi', and although, surprisingly, not especially enamoured of the film itself, Crichton was clearly, and rightly, proud of what he and his team had accomplished technically: 'I think it was quite an achievement,' he said, giving much credit to Challis's black-and-white cinematography: 'Chris used very little light. It was suggested rather than the way, say, Lionel [Banes] would have lit it, [where] everything would have been floodlit.'[38]

Exposed – often literally as he spends much of the film stripped to the waist in *and* out of the 'river' – as an actor without the benefit of music and lyrics, Keel's 'straight' performance is as impressive as his six-foot-four frame. In his autobiography, he wrote: 'The water had to be both dirty and cold, and it was. They couldn't heat it for fear it might get rancid. That was [a] tough picture. Anne Heywood never once protested about the water. [Charles] Crichton ... had a great sense of humour.'[39] For the most part, Crichton's script is as lean as the film's slim running time – as usual, well under ninety minutes – with just enough noir-ish 'thick ear' and 'hard-boiled' dialogue to complement non-watery action like a skimpily clad Heywood menaced by lustful Cusack or a bloody climactic fist fight between Keel and his nemesis, played by Crawford.

Typically: 'Kill him, kill him – you're in for murder anyway!' screeches Cusack at Keel who instead saves Sharkey from the river rather than taking his life. Or, as Keel, with a sly grin, tells Heywood, 'Killers can't always be killing. Sometimes they need a rest.' Compared with the Hawkins's fairly rambling narrative, which resolves in a surprisingly conventional and rather sentimental way, the screenplay instead strips the story down to its barest essentials, almost (but not quite) fully in the case of both Elizabeth and Donavan, whose bodily charms are described with almost lip-smacking relish in the original but dealt with more matter-of-factly in the film. A few plot points are changed or compressed while Crichton's pay-off is much more agreeably noir than the book's softer outcome.

When the British Board of Film Censors, as today's BBFC ('Censors' became 'Classification' in 1984) was called then, the film was accorded an 'A' – 'passed as more suitable for adult audiences – which 'required cuts', noted the board, although those 'cuts' are not specified in the BBFC's archive. Subsequent DVD versions carry a '12' classification, warning, 'moderate violence; sexual threat'.

As suggested earlier, the 'authentic American-looking' theme was pretty much common to all the reviews – 'British film in an American Disguise',[40] headlined *The Times* – as well as a preoccupation in some with Heywood's beauty and Keel's manly torso. 'Strange that British studios who have yet to turn out a Western or musical film comparable with the varied winners from Hollywood should successfully turn out a taut melodrama about America and Americans. *Floods of Fear* has been so expertly directed by Charles Crichton that one ventures to doubt if it did, in fact emerge from our own Pinewood Studios,' opined the *Middlesex County Times*. Dick Richards in the *Daily Mirror*, wrote: 'The American setting (designed to woo the United States market) is excellently captured and the flood scenes are remarkably well handled … *Floods of Fear* is by no means a new idea but the unusual flood setting gives it a fresh look and director Charles Crichton and his special effects team have done wonders.'

Rather less impressed was the *Birmingham Daily Post*'s critic – probably Alex Walker again – with what he perceived as the film's principal mission: 'I imagine the makers of *Floods of Fear* went about their work with just one end in mind, and that to thrill. Not a very high aim, maybe, but an old one, an honourable one. The pity is they appear to have bungled the job and when one of them is the gifted director Charles Crichton, this is a cause for wonder as well as regret.' Yet, he adds, more positively, 'technically the film is good … newsreel shots of floods are dovetailed ingeniously into the narrative and despite the story's improbabilities, there is a seldom a dull moment – and never a dry one'. No such equivocation from the *People*'s Ernest Betts: 'One of the most exciting and savage British films for years.'

Perhaps the most enduring compliment of all came from the novelist Elspeth (*The Flame Trees of Thika*) Huxley, writing in the *Tatler* as Elspeth Grant: 'The flood scenes have been most effectively handled and the desolation of it all chills one to the bone … this should prove the intensity of my "audience participation" for I have never yet been a flood victim though it seemed to me for a short while that I had.' Nowadays, talk is often about film's 'immersive' qualities; Crichton's intimate epic was a groundbreaker of its kind.

Notes

1 Michael Balcon, *A Lifetime of Films* (Hutchinson, 1969), p. 181.
2 Interview with the author, 11 April 2020.
3 *BEHP*; Brian McFarlane, *An Autobiography of British Cinema* (Methuen, 1997), p. 155.

THE FIFTIES: EXIT EALING, 1954–59   153

4   Yvonne Mitchell, *Actress* (Routledge & Kegan Paul, 1957), p. 102.
5   *Ibid.*, p. 104.
6   Charles Barr, *Ealing Studios* (Studio Vista, 1977), p. 205.
7   George Perry, *Forever Ealing* (Pavilion, 1981), p. 164.
8   *The Times*, 15 November 1954.
9   Mitchell, *Actress*, p. 105.
10 Email to the author, 6 March 2020.
11 *New York Times*, 4 August 1955.
12 Balcon, *A Lifetime of Films*, p. 181.
13 Sue Harper and Vincent Porter, *British Cinema of the 1950s: The Decline of Deference* (Oxford University Press, 2003), p. 64.
14 Perry, *Forever Ealing*, p. 167.
15 *Ibid.*
16 *Ibid.*
17 T.E.B. Clarke, *This Is Where I Came In* (Michael Joseph, 1974), p. 181.
18 BEHP.
19 *The Guardian*, 17 April 2004.
20 Crichton interviewed by Brian McFarlane, October 1992.
21 *Made in Ealing*, BBC Omnibus, 1986.
22 Jack Hawkins, *Anything for a Quiet Life* (Coronet, 1973), pp. 167–8.
23 BEHP.
24 *The Times*, 28 January 1957.
25 Robert Murphy, 'Dark Shadows Around Ealing', in Mark Duguid, Lee Freeman, Keith M. Johnston and Melanie Williams (eds) *Ealing Revisited* (BFI, 2012), p. 89.
26 BEHP.
27 McFarlane, *An Autobiography of British Cinema*, p. 153.
28 John Wyver, *Theatre Plays on British Television*, 19 July 2011.
29 BEHP.
30 Harper and Porter, *British Cinema of the 1950s*, p. 111.
31 Email to the author, 6 March 2020.
32 BEHP.
33 *The Times*, 30 June 1958.
34 *New York Times*, 6 August 1958.
35 Andrew Spicer, *Sydney Box* (Manchester University Press, 2006), p. 159.
36 BEHP.
37 Ken Annakin, *So You Wanna Be a Film Director* (Tomahawk Press, 2001), p. 17.
38 BEHP.
39 Howard Keel with Joyce Spizer, *Only Make Believe: My Life in Showbusiness* (Barricade Books, 2005), p. 192.
40 *The Times*, 17 November 1958.

The sixties: 1960–64

One of the stranger Ealing 'sequels', which had its first manifestation when the studio was still in its final throes, was in the form of a rather unlikely and, indeed, ultimately turbulent relationship between some of Balcon's finest and a powerful Hollywood production company called Hecht-Hill-Lancaster (HHL). Harold Hecht, a producer-manager, and Burt Lancaster first teamed up in 1948 to form Norma Productions (after Lancaster's second wife, Norma Anderson) by which time the actor had already attained leading man status and was desperately craving some kind of film-making autonomy. Norma became Hecht-Lancaster in 1952 and following hits like *Apache, Vera Cruz* and the Oscar-winning *Marty*, finally evolved into a triumvirate, HHL, when joined by another producer, James Hill, in 1956.

Hecht and Lancaster first had plans to adapt James Thurber's 1942 short story, *The Catbird Seat*, before the turn of the fifties – by which time the author's even more famous short story, *The Secret Life of Walter Mitty* (1947), had already been turned into a successful film – to be written and directed by Frank Tashlin with Jose Ferrer as star. The project then went permanently on the back burner because of the unconnected combination of the Hollywood 'blacklist', the Korean War and Lancaster's ever-busier acting career. Soon after Hill joined the pair, and as 1957 dawned, HHL announced an incredibly ambitious list of future film projects including a resuscitated *The Catbird Seat*, to be scripted this time round by George Axelrod. But as far as 'Tibby' Clarke was concerned, when the call came from America to come over and take on his first Hollywood assignment, 'I proudly thought in my innocence that I had been specially picked for this prestigious undertaking; it was some time before I discovered I was something like the seventh writer to have a go at it.'[1]

Before Clarke came to New York to begin his research for *The Catbird Seat*, HHL had already employed another Ealing alumnus, Alexander

Mackendrick, to direct *The Sweet Smell of Success*, the sharp-edged tale, alternately funny and cruel, of a ruthless gossip columnist, his hangers-on and his victims. The dark comedy of Mackendrick's *The Ladykillers*, though endlessly stylish, was hardly in the same league. Mackendrick was a replacement for Ernest Lehman, who had written a screenplay based on his own novel before retiring from the project through illness. Suffice it to say that Mackendrick had a very tough time on the film, a combination of star Lancaster's antagonism (he could not get over Lehman's withdrawal from the project) and the exigencies of Lehman's writing replacement, Clifford Odets.

The Sweet Smell of Success was a flop in its day but has rightly since become regarded as a 'film noir' classic. Its failure at the time may have further impacted on Mackendrick after he had been announced as director of HHL's *The Devil's Disciple*, an adaptation of Shaw's satire set during the American War of Independence. Just a week into filming on location in the UK, 'the too meticulous'[2] Mackendrick was fired, to be quickly replaced by another British director, Guy Hamilton. Meanwhile, as Clarke, by now in Hollywood, was continuing his research for *The Catbird Seat*, his old colleague and collaborator, Crichton, had been invited by Harold Hecht to fly stateside to discuss helming the project, He recalled: 'So I got my ticket, and flew over. I had no dollars with me, got to the other end, nobody to meet me, usually bit of red carpet, borrowed 25 cents from a fellow passenger to ring up the studio. Someone gasped at the other end. Eventually a car comes for me, I go to see Harold and he said, "Didn't anyone tell you, Charlie, we've given it to somebody else".'[3]

As for Clarke, 'I thought I had made a rather good job of adapting *The Catbird Seat*. This view was not shared by those who were calling the tune. I was paid off and replaced by another writer who in due course had the same experience.'[4] Recalled Crichton: 'Anyway, they were going to combine it with another [Thurber] story. I said, "You'll never make it," and they never did because the combination was impossible.'[5] The 'somebody else' was reputed to be Billy Wilder. At the same time HHL originally announced Crichton would direct *The Catbird Seat*, the company also reported that he would be making a film version of Turgenev's *First Love*, which turned out to be another empty promise.

Crichton's unfortunate association with HHL did not end there. Once bitten though clearly not, quite yet, twice shy, he was back in California towards the end of 1960 shooting *The Birdman of Alcatraz*, the remarkable if harrowing story of real-life convicted killer Robert Stroud who became an expert ornithologist during his long incarceration at Leavenworth and then, latterly, on 'The Rock' between 1942 and 1959. Crichton explained:

> Very interesting, of course, and I wanted to make it. But we'd have a script conference and all sorts of things would be decided, and then Burt [who was also playing Stroud] would go off for about three weeks to play golf and come back again, and it was as if nothing had happened. We just started all over again; there was a sort of vacuum, and we only had half the script the week before we were due to go on the floor. And Burt said, 'We're in marvellous shape, aren't we? We've never been in such good shape as this before.' Of course, remembering the Korda days, I should not have been unhappy about that. I think, by the way, he decided he didn't want me even before that.[6]

When Crichton was deciding whether to go to America, he had said to Hecht, '"Are you the producer, or is Burt the producer? If Burt is the producer, I don't want to go, but if you're the producer, fine." Oh yes, he was the producer [according to Hecht] and then I got to America, and Burt had all the power. Yes, I know he wanted me off even before we started to shoot, actually.'[7]

According to Kate Buford's biography of Lancaster, *An American Life*, Jules Dassin was first slated to direct the film, an idea that initially appealed to the star. But, in his heart of hearts, he really wanted to continue his association with John Frankenheimer, twenty years younger than Crichton, with whom he had just made *The Young Savages*. So Crichton was effectively doomed from day one. Writes Buford: 'Crichton ... lasted less than a month, a casualty of the actor's impatience and the director's own unsuitability for the subject.'[8] Probably to nobody's great surprise, Frankenheimer suddenly became available and took over the film with, it must be said, great success.

Quite why Crichton had been chosen in the first place for *Birdman* still remains an unanswered question. It may have had to do with the fact that by now he had been responsible for directing a revived, renamed and relocated, *Catbird Seat*, no longer HHL's project, which had also enjoyed a very fine review in the *New York Times*. Or maybe there had been some residual guilt on Hecht's part over Crichton's abortive trip to California a couple of years earlier. 'Less than a month' on *Birdman*? Crichton remembered it being 'a week, which was just marking time for them while they got another director. Then I went to New York to make another picture and walked out of that one because it was terrible, really terrible.'[9] He claimed he could not remember the film he'd quit so peremptorily. According to a report in the *Stage*, it could have been *The Major and The Private*, due to have co-starred Sammy Davis Jr and Peter Lawford, two of Frank Sinatra's so-called

'Ratpack', which also never came to fruition. Had, Crichton was asked, he learned anything from the experience? 'Yes,' he replied. 'I learned to be jolly careful about going to America.'

The Battle of the Sexes (1960)

Following the best attempts of ex-Ealing people to get *The Catbird Seat* on its feet in Thurber's original New York setting, how ironic that it should be two other former studio grandees who finally, together with Crichton, helped to effect its successful transfer from the word to the big screen. Monja Danischewsky had been the umpteenth writer to try and make a go of it in Hollywood but like all the others, without success. So, instead, he acquired the rights, brought the project back to Britain and rewrote it this time round with a Scottish setting – Edinburgh to be precise – perhaps inspired by the triumph he had enjoyed a decade earlier as producer of *Whisky Galore*. To complete the circle, the re-energised project, now also retitled *The Battle of the Sexes*, was to be the first film from Bryanston, a brand new production company, headed up by Sir Michael Balcon with fellow producer Maxwell Setton, and created, you might almost say, out of the ashes of Ealing.

As Charles Barr writes in *Balcon After Ealing*, a sort of sequel to his book, *Ealing Studios*, Bryanston Films was neither a studio nor a distributor rather a consortium of partners whose financial 'commitment and ... collective film-making authority earned them a guarantee of distribution of their films through British Lion, and, on the strength of this, of bank financing'.[10] Over five years until it was sold in 1964 to Associated-Rediffusion, Bryanston would be behind some of the key films of the British 'new wave', including *Saturday Night and Sunday Morning* (1960), *A Taste of Honey* (1961) and *The Loneliness of the Long Distance Runner* (1962).

However, at Bryanston's outset you might have been forgiven for thinking that it was simply a case of Ealing redux, with two of its initial slate directed by Crichton – *The Boy Who Stole a Million* following speedily after *The Battle of the Sexes* – and a third, *Cone of Silence* in the same year, helmed by Charles Frend, who had been only marginally less prolific at Ealing than his old friend, Crichton. Certainly, as far as *The Battle of the Sexes* is concerned, it is difficult to dispute Barr's contention that 'the whole film is intensely evocative of Ealing, in terms equally of personnel and of themes'.[11]

Thurber's comic story, which first appeared in the *New Yorker*, concerns the increasingly desperate attempts of Mr Martin, the otherwise exemplary employee of the firm of F & S, to thwart Mrs Ulgine Barrows, special adviser to the company's president, who wants to reorganise his precious filing department. First he plans to murder her but when that goes awry realises it might be better simply to make her appear insane. The title, incidentally, originated with a baseball term meaning 'sitting pretty' that became popularised via Thurber's tale.

Danischewsky's screenplay switched the action across the pond to the House of MacPherson, an old-fashioned Scottish tweed weaving company where Mr Martin is chief accountant. When the aged owner dies suddenly, his middle-aged, more English than English son Robert heads north of the border to take over and immediately hires Mrs Angela Barrows, an American efficiency expert, to draw up plans to modernise the business. These will include replacing not only all the old, island-based, weavers with, instead, workers in a large single factory but also, horror of horrors, substituting synthetic fibres for the company's trademark wool. The normally mild-mannered Mr Martin is now set on an inevitable collision course with Mrs Barrows.

Peter Sellers was, by the time he took on the role of Mr Martin, in his early thirties, and following radio stardom with the Goons, had become Britain's most gifted film comedy character actor after roles in Ealing's *The Ladykillers*, quickly followed by *The Smallest Show on Earth* (1957), *The Naked Truth* (1957), *The Mouse That Roared* (1959) – in which he played three roles, presaging his later versatility in *Dr Strangelove* (1964) – *Two-Way Stretch* (1960) and his award-winning breakthrough, *I'm All Right, Jack* (1960), as the implacable shop steward Fred Kite, which was released to huge acclaim *after* he'd completed his role in *The Battle of the Sexes*. According to Danischewsky's autobiography:

> Peter Sellers, whom I had barely met, had heard about it and phoned me out of the blue, saying he would like to play the part of the little middle-aged Edinburgh clerk. It was a brilliant piece of casting which frankly had not occurred to me. It was a fight, at that time, to get the finance people to agree he was a big enough 'name' for the budget. He also proved a tower of strength – a pleasure to work with, and a practical help to me as producer, for he found me two 'angels' for the end money.[12]

As Barr notes, the main cast, along with Sellers, were all Ealing alumni in varying degrees: Constance Cummings (Mrs Barrows) Robert Morley (Robert MacPherson), Donald Pleasence (Irwin Hoffman), Jameson Clark (Andrew Darling), Crichton's old friend Moultrie Kelsall (Graham), and eighty-year-old Ernest Thesiger (Old MacPherson), who had played a similar role in *The Man in the White Suit*.

The reunions behind the camera included Seth Holt, who had made *Nowhere to Go* (1958), his directing debut and Ealing's final film a year earlier, and rejoined Crichton as editor for the fifth and last time, along with art director Edward Carrick and Norman 'Spike' Priggen, who moved up from being an assistant director on four of Crichton's films to production supervisor. Last but not least, there was Danischewsky himself of less-than-blessed *Love Lottery* memory. As for the film's 'theme', its kinship with Ealing's oft recurring motifs of revolt, gentle anarchy and, let it be said, mild misogyny, is also self-evident.

In fact, the last of the three is considerably, and by today's standards, rather uncomfortably, more in evidence in Danischewsky's ninety-one-page screenplay than in any of the old Ealing canon or, for that matter, Thurber's typically droll and eight-page story. The battle lines of this so-called sex war are drawn from the very outset despite a rather off-putting opening image somewhat belying the notion of any enmity in extreme monochrome close-up of man and woman in an apparently tender lip-on-lip embrace. Over this, followed by aerial image of New York, a narrator (Sam Wanamaker) declares in stentorian tones:

> In this timeless struggle between man and woman, man had held his own until that fateful day in 1492 when Christopher Columbus discovered America. Out of this new world emerged the new woman destined to turn man the hunter into man the hunted. America's great Mr James Thurber, chronicler of man's losing battle has warned us all we are living at a time when in a moth-proof closet dwells a moth.

It has become very quickly very clear that any of Thurber's subtlety has been replaced in the screenplay's 'opening out' instead by broad strokes and, as very soon becomes apparent in the film's preliminaries – but not anywhere in Thurber's original – cross-cultural clash. For in a generic, high-powered high-rise in the Big Apple, Mrs Angela – no longer Ulgine – Barrows is clearly already considered the bane of an otherwise all-male boardroom. She must be sent away, it is unanimously agreed, somewhere 'really wild, really remote'. Our narrator returns, this time to justify the story's transatlantic leap: 'So destiny sent Mrs Barrows to carry the sex wars into one of the last bastions of man's supremacy ... Scotland. A man's world in which the shortest skirts are worn by men.' Quite why a Russian émigré like Danischewsky, who had with his family left the old country for Britain when he was eight, appeared to be so enamoured of Scotland – this was his third venture north of the border following *Whisky Galore*'s 'sequel', *Rockets Galore*, in 1957 – seems unclear, but for Crichton, as has been previously explained, no second bidding was necessary. 'Now every war produces its hero, the man with that little extra something that other men haven't got, the superman.

Mr Martin may not be cast in the heroic mould but he is a hero just the same.' And with that, out of the shadows of an Edinburgh alleyway, in what proved to be a sort of flash forward, emerges Peter Sellers, indeterminately middle-aged, grey-haired, spectacled, moustachioed, rain-coated, walking-sticked and flat-capped, on his way to secure what he hopes will be two of his most effective 'weapons' – cigarettes and whisky, both of which he is, we soon understand, a lifelong abstainer (a major plot point) – in the final resolution of this particular sex war.

Meanwhile, before the chief protagonists first meet, we are firmly situated within the dusty, musty confines of the House of MacPherson, where Mr Martin, as chief accountant, clearly rules the roost from his inner sanctum, the filing department. In the first of the film's two most memorable sequences, his two underlings, even older and more decrepit than him, are scratching away at their respective ledgers.

'Could you try and find a quieter nib?' chides Mr Martin, uttering, arguably, the film's most memorable line, before being summoned to the presence of the boss, Old MacPherson, on his deathbed, to be explained the imminent succession at the company after he joins 'the great weaver himself' – almost immediately as it happens following the downing of a large dram of whisky. This, Martin is informed, will be the old man's 'soft' son, Robert, 'Pity we sent him to school in England – careering around Windsor in frock coats' – whom we then meet almost straightaway in the form of the hippo-like Morley, in full silly-ass mode, absurdly clad in a kilt and tam-o'-shanter, setting off from London for Scotland on, coincidentally, the very same train as Mrs Barrows.

Once Mrs Barrows has inevitably insinuated herself into the firm – and also, possibly, MacPherson's affections – you know it is just a matter of time before Martin, whose old-fashioned, ordered world is terminally threatened with everything from time clocks, intercoms, adding machines, metal filing cabinets and to synthetics instead of sheep, begins planning murder – actually from about half an hour into Crichton's predictably spare eighty-four-minute running time. But it also has to be said that the comedy, brief thought it is, and despite being populated by a host of enjoyable character actors – not, Morley, though, whose shrill performance simply grates – does sag noticeably in the middle before igniting once again towards the end as Martin, having finally elicited a suitable murder plot thanks to watching a B-movie, *The Case of the Unknown Killer*, subtitled 'A Story of the Perfect Crime', at his local fleapit, now feels properly prepped for the role of avenging angel.

In the film's other memorable sequence – a small masterpiece of timing and farce – which, according to Ed Sikov's biography of Peter Sellers, was 'mainly improvised while shooting',[13] Martin, having wormed his way into Mrs Barrows' flat, tries to kill her with any sharp object that might come to usefully to hand. Of course, he doesn't succeed, not because he has completely lost his nerve but because, as in Thurber's story, an even more devious and far less messy plan B suddenly presents itself: to make it seem that Mrs B has lost her mind. While Thurber's resolution confers Martin's unequivocal triumph, the film, in its very final frame, settles for a slightly softer option; a battle won, but probably not the war, as he hands the tearful, ex-employee Mrs Barrows a consolation nosegay, an affectionate homage, one critic suggested, to a famous scene in Chaplin's *City Lights* (1931).

After being given the 'green light' in May 1959, *Battle* was filmed throughout that summer on a budget of £133,060 (a little over £3m today). According to Professor Duncan Petrie's informative paper, 'Bryanston Films: An Experiment in Cooperative Independent Production and Distribution', based on extensive research in the files of Film Finances, completion guarantors since 1950, and the Balcon papers at the BFI, company budgets were kept low in part by regular recourse to deferrals and direct contributions by the producers. In the case of *The Battle of the Sexes*, deferred payments were agreed with Sellers (£6,000), Danischewsky (£3,000), Morley (£1,250), Crichton (£875 – 2020 equivalent, £20,000) and Rank Labs (£2,000).[14]

Edinburgh was used extensively including 45 George Street, home of, variously, the publishers Blackwoods and, later, the wine merchants, Justerini & Brooks, as 'the House of MacPherson'. In addition, Waverley Station, the Royal Mile, Balmoral Hotel and Prince's Street also featured. More ingeniously, the tweed weavers' outpost in the Hebrides was recreated about a mile from the city centre in Holyrood Park as well as in and around its highest point, Arthur's Seat, a perfect double for a wild Highlands landscape. Interiors were completed at Beaconsfield Studios.

Graham Greene once said how, in terms of literary adaptation, he believed the short story, 'which can be enlarged', was an inherently more satisfactory source than the novel in which the inevitable 'process of cutting down must detract from aspects of all-important characterization'.[15] Would Thurber feel the same way when he saw how his creation had been 'enlarged'? In a letter to Danischewsky, dated 25 April 1960, he wrote, enthusiastically, 'We caught the movie at a special showing and everybody with us seemed to like it as much as we did.' He also showered praise on Sellers 'as an artist and a gentleman and a good companion [they had met for the first time at a small party after the screening]'.[16]

Crichton, who thought his producer's screenplay 'very good', considered Sellers's performance 'about the best thing he ever did. [It] was a part with every opportunity for overplaying, but Peter didn't take the bait.'[17] Danischewsky wrote that Sellers gave 'a wonderful performance ... [that] helped put [him] at the top of his profession'.[18] After nearly ten years of comedy characterisations and funny voices on radio, records and then in films, Sellers was already beginning to attain the status of national treasure while still on the cusp of an international stardom that would start to reveal increasingly large cracks in his already fragile psyche, likely to infuriate and, on many occasions, even alienate future film-making collaborators. The great Billy Wilder, who, in a different life, might have directed Thurber's story, famously provided a bitter two-liner after Sellers had to withdraw from *Kiss Me, Stupid* (1964) following a heart attack: 'Heart attack?' he said. 'You need a heart to have a heart attack!'

Wilder's barb is especially interesting, and also worth bearing in mind, when assessing some of the mostly very fine reviews – 'quite the funniest British comedy since *Genevieve*' – of *Battle of the Sexes* at the time of its release, which, in the main, rather than evoking any echoes of Ealing tended to be all about Sellers's performance. 'Much as I admire Mr Sellers' astonishing ability to get into the skin of any role he plays he has always (except as the shop steward in *I'm All Right, Jack*) seemed to lack human warmth. He is like a man who has looked upon a gorgon and been turned to stone within,' noted Elspeth Grant in the *Tatler*. Jympson Harman wrote in the *Liverpool Echo*: 'He once more plays a straight character so beautifully and realistically that it hardly seems to belong to a comedy. If he continues to play dead straight while all around are trying to be funny Peter Sellers is likely to stick out like a sore thumb in comedy.' Keith Bruce, who had just taken over from Alex Walker on the *Birmingham Daily Post*, opined: 'The film sets a standard for gentle, sharp-edged comedy which it is difficult to imagine equalled for a long time certainly not in this key and with this range of material. Sellers is impeccable, rounded, deeply human, deeply funny, though perhaps he sometimes underplays in his concern for dignity.'

The Times, however, was much less impressed:

> As a middle-aged clock in an old-fashioned firm of tweed manufacturers, he [Sellers] moves with slow and deliberate gait, pores lovingly over his jumbled files, and scratches laboriously in his ledgers with his pen. It

is a careful portrait, fondly observed, but it is all painfully slow ... The plot was an allegiance to a short story by James Thurber, but it remains a stubbornly distant one.[19]

In Thurber's own backyard, where one might have expected some demur from his own countrymen baulking at the story's huge cultural switch, A.H. Weiler from the *New York Times* enthused:

> It is to the credit of the production team headed by Monja Danischewsky, who also adapted the fragile work to the screen, that a minimum of slapstick and a maximum of wit and characterization have been chosen to accomplish Mr. Thurber's ends. As a result, *The Battle of the Sexes* is gentle, tongue-in-cheek ribbing that cleaves to the spirit, if not entirely to the letter of Thurber's lampoon ... They and a supporting cast expertly guided by director Charles Crichton make the transition from word to film a pleasant comedy spiked with farce. Fun, in this case, is being poked at both American efficiency and ancient British custom. Although this is not a new gambit, it comes off with charm and a few belly laughs.[20]

Not unexpectedly, Weiler brackets Crichton, probably for reader identification, with *The Lavender Hill Mob* despite the seven films he had directed since. That and *The Battle of the Sexes* were the only films on which he worked with, respectively, Guinness and Sellers. Though separated in age by more than ten years, the two actors were near contemporary masters of comic characterisation and versatility, both also possessed of very complicated private lives. In a *New Yorker* article to commemorate what would have been Guinness's birth centenary, Anthony Lane, in a single but penetrating observation, compared and contrasted the two talents in a way that somehow makes Wilder's acerbic outburst seem slightly less outrageous, as well as lending some credence to Elspeth Grant's more measured assessment. 'Shifting shape', Lane wrote, 'he [Guinness] remained unmistakable; who knew that chameleons possessed so robust a soul? Where Peter Sellers – who worshipped Guinness, and scrutinized him avidly when they worked on *The Ladykillers*, would spend himself in a fury of impersonation, Guinness gave no hint of a hollow core. He found a still point in the turning world.'[21]

Perhaps then, it was just a matter of warmth, something that Crichton managed to extract from Guinness in *The Lavender Hill Mob*, while Sellers's Mr Martin remains resolutely a brilliant but impersonal piece of artifice; like so many of the actor's performances before and right up to his premature death in 1980 at fifty-five, a comic 'turn'. Aside from an obvious delight in his actual performance, Crichton said of Sellers: 'He was very keen at one time that Danischewsky, he, and I should continue together and make more films. I don't know what happened. He lost belief in all of us, and *Battle of the Sexes*, before it came out. Then, years afterwards, Princess Margaret said it was the best thing he'd ever done ... and then perhaps he regained his belief?' Crichton also added: 'The picture was damaged by Robert Morley who *overflows* ... Morley plays it like a great baby. He's not right. But at the time he was much more famous than Peter Sellers.'[22]

Another appraisal of Sellers in the filming of *The Battle of the Sexes* arrived fascinatingly in the memoirs of cinematographer Freddie Francis, working with Crichton and the star for the first and only time. A brilliant black-and-white cameraman who in the same year as *Battle* won an Oscar for *Sons and Lovers*, Francis was positively withering about the actor:

> The surprise on the picture to me was how unfunny Peter Sellers actually was. I will go so far as to say I found him dull. This was Peter Sellers before Peter Sellers invented himself, although to have one of the Goons who, in life, is not funny, is a bit frightening. During the filming, Sellers was reluctant to have any conversation or to share anything with anybody on the picture. Normally with a leading actor or actress you're talking with them all the time and you become quite friendly, but Sellers hardly ever spoke to anybody. He was determined to be his character, a form of Sellers method acting, which didn't work well at all.[23]

Francis was almost equally ungenerous about his collaboration with the director:

> I pictured both of us getting on very well, which we did up to a point. The problem was Charlie Crichton loved Charlie Crichton and wouldn't ever consider suggestions and comments from the technical staff, including the cinematographer. I remember on one occasion I made a comment to Charlie about how a shot might be done, and he said, 'I know you think I'm an old-fashioned buffer, but I am doing it my way,' and that was it. No discussion and certainly no 'interference', as Charlie saw it, from the underlings. There is no doubt Charlie was a good director of light comedies but once he had made his mind up, nothing would move him.[24]

To add insult to injury, Francis, who, apart from joking around the set with Morley and Cummings, seems to have been disappointed generally with the entire collaboration, finally condemned the film 'as very much a sub-Ealing picture'.[25]

Battle's obvious antecedents and their latest 'incarnation', which had, as I suggested, been almost wholly ignored by reviewers, are more thoughtfully discussed by Charles Barr in *Balcon After Ealing*:

THE SIXTIES: 1960-64 **165**

Thematically, *The Battle of the Sexes* is reminiscent of Ealing in being centred on a conflict between traditional and modern, small-scale and large-scale ... 'Just an old family firm' is how MacPherson junior describes his tweed business.

Like the Greenleaf Brewery [in *Cheer, Boys, Cheer* (1939), one of the earliest of Balcon's Ealing output], it is given a foundation date of 1789, as if to establish good democratic credentials for it; its small-scale traditional character is threatened in the course of the film, then triumphantly restored. The first Bryanston film, then, is like a nostalgic celebration: an assurance that things can go on as they used to both on and off screen, within a new family firm run by the same lovable headmaster-boss who can be affectionately joked about ... But of course Bryanston was not Ealing, and Balcon was not filling quite the same role as he had done there ... *The Battle of the Sexes* then represents less a renewal of the old ways than a nostalgic farewell to them.[26]

Despite, presumably, the best of intentions, there was an immediate problem when Bryanston actually launched its trailblazing production following a West End premiere in February 1960, because British Lion also released another high-profile British film, *The Angry Silence*, in the same week. While from British Lion's perspective, notes Professor Petrie,

> this may have demonstrated the current vitality of low-budget independent production, the decision greatly upset Balcon and prompted Setton to write to David Kingsley [of British Lion], urging that 'this kind of duplication and rivalry "within the family" should be avoided whenever possible in the future'. Bryanston were also concerned that British Lion were failing to give them sufficient acknowledgement in the promotion of individual films and in their general publicity and annual accounts.[27]

On the plus side, *The Battle of the Sexes* went on to become a small commercial hit, earning Bryanston a profit of £10,894, or little under £250,000 in today's money.

The Boy Who Stole a Million (1960)

The spectre of Ealing also continued to haunt Crichton after he had completed *The Boy Who Stole a Million*, his second film in just over a year for Bryanston. In a remarkably good way, as it happens, if you can believe the surprisingly respectable reviews for this slightest of Anglo-Spanish adventure comedies recorded in some of the more influential corners of the American press. Following its US opening towards the end of the year just a few months after its patchy release in the UK, *Variety* trilled: 'It's difficult to go wrong with the combo of an appealing kid, the inevitable pooch and a chase in which the youngster's up against the world. This one is marred by some slightly uneasy dubbing, and an occasional lapse into slapstick when only light comedy was needed, but overall it's a warm little piece.' But that was merely the overture to a much longer and more glowing appraisal by Howard Thompson in the *New York Times*. Thompson, following fast on the Ealing-echoing plaudits initially laid down by his colleague, A.H. Weiler, for *The Battle of the Sexes* earlier that same year, contributed a veritable Christmas card as he purred about a film that 'sheds a pleasant Yuletide glow, and all the way from Spain'. Reminding his readers of the 'eagle-eyed' director's CV, he rules that 'kids will like it, and parents should relish some typical, subtle embroidery by Charles Crichton'. Ah, yes, that chase.

> The chase is the thing – leave it to Mr. Crichton. As the young fugitive, expressively played by Maurice Reyna, and his cute dog, leg it all over Valencia, Douglas Slocombe, photographer, superbly catches the city's picturesque facade, brisk tempo and bustling working-quarter atmosphere. The only real crime is that the picture wasn't shot in color.[28]

There is no doubt these American critics at least greeted the film, which cost £115,802, considerably more warmly than the British public, which, as they say, deserted the film in droves. 'A perfunctory attempt at a British *Bicycle Thieves*, packed with clichés both in script and in Charles Crichton's direction', was the *Monthly Bulletin*'s ruthless and, sad to report, rather more accurate assessment of this equal low (alongside *Another Shore*) in Crichton's filmography. So how come there seems to be such a disconnect between the reactions on either side of the Atlantic?

Before the emerging 'kitchen sink' strand of new British dramas would come to epitomise the best of Bryanston, it seemed that safety first was the order of the day, and a cosy, Ealing-ish product must have felt the best bet certainly to Balcon, if not to the other members of the consortium as the company started out. While *The Battle of the Sexes* effectively speaks for itself, *The Boy Who Stole a Million* appeared also to have had, going in, all the right sort of ingredients. The producer, George H. Brown, had just come off an enormous domestic hit, *Tommy the Toreador*, starring pop idol Tommy Steele on some colourful Andalusian locations in Spain. Already an industry veteran, who had even done some time at Ealing (on *The Proud Valley* (1940), starring Paul Robeson), Brown, British born but raised in Barcelona, was an old Spanish hand, so this Valencia-based tale with, like *Tommy*, a Fiesta

THE SIXTIES: 1960–64   **167**

backdrop, might have appeared right up his street. The story involving children, chases, colourful villains and inept police was, surely, right out of the Crichton playbook.

From an 'original screenplay' and 'story' by a Danish writer, Niels West-Larsen, the 'scenario' – shooting script, by any other name – was by Crichton and John Eldridge, who had last collaborated on *The Man in the Sky* three years earlier. The opening credits also trumpet, 'Introducing Maurice Reyna as ... The Boy Who Stole a Million' (Figure 7.1). The black-and-white cinematography – courtesy of Douglas Slocombe, reunited with the director after a three-film break – immerses us instantly into the bustle of busy Valencia where the women are hanging out washing on their apartment balconies. The camera pans across to settle finally on father and son (Virgilio Teixeira, Reyna) cheerfully following suit before preparing to head out to work; Miguel (Teixeira), a local taxi driver; little Paco (Reyna), a bank page, in formal outfit and peaked cap, a little like his father: 'Remember, bank managers wash behind their ears,' says Miguel.

Figure 7.1 Maurice Reyna as *The Boy Who Stole a Million*

Within minutes, the first major plot point is set up as Miguel's rather beautiful but ancient cab breaks down in the street en route for the station, leaving his infuriated passenger (producer Brown in a Hitchcock-style cameo) to walk. When his garage-owning pal, Luis (Harold Kasket), tells him the repair job will cost ten thousand pesetas, Miguel is horrified, explaining there is no way he way he can afford such a bill and that his entire livelihood is threatened. What he does not realise is that Paco, who has overheard the conversation after heading out for his lunch break, now heads back to the bank with a plan. By great good fortune, the vault door has been left open carelessly by the chief cashier, so Paco sneaks in, grabs what he can, wrapping it up in some handy cloth, and makes his getaway before the cashier returns and, horrified, discovers the cash shortfall, yelling, 'The bank's been robbed, a million pesetas gone!' The news spreads round town like wildfire. First the police are alerted, then some local gangsters, thanks to a tip off from a boozy crook Pedro (Warren Mitchell) who had overheard about the theft while being briefly detained in the local cop shop. So everyone is now after Paco, whose best attempts to try and return the loot when he discovers the extent of his haul, keep getting thwarted. When he tries to reconnect with Miguel, he again overhears his distraught father who, not realising Paco was merely trying to help him out with his cash flow, declares his son surely cannot be a thief; if he is, 'I would disown him!' Paco goes back on the run.

This increasingly 'mad, mad, mad, mad world' set-up – which would, ironically, get the eponymous film treatment on a vaster Hollywood scale three years on by a former Ealing scribe, William Rose – is joined by Miguel, Luis and pretty Maria (Marianne Benet), desperate to retrieve Paco before he gets into even worse straits, including being beaten with a stick by a blind beggar. Being a family-friendly film, all is finally resolved blandly, and any misunderstandings cleared up. Paco is even reinstated at the bank, although must now pay back the accumulated interest on the returned million (about £200,000 today) out of his wages, at two pesetas a week.

Of the four main actors, Teixeira and Kasket had both appeared in *Tommy the Toreador* while Benet, Spanish-born like Teixeira, had already been in two Hollywood films about the IRA, co-starring opposite, respectively, James Cagney and Robert Mitchum. How little twelve-year-old Maurice Reyna got the title role was a fascinating story in itself, as he explained to me. He and his two siblings had arrived in England with their parents in 1957 after fleeing their native Venezuela and the repressive right-wing regime of President Marcos Pérez Jiménez.

THE SIXTIES: 1960–64 **169**

When he was deposed early the following year, Maurice's father became cultural attaché at the Venezuelan Embassy in London.

> So I happened to be on a London Underground train, arguing with my sister Tatiana, when a talent scout spotted me and asked me if I would like to make an audition for a film. I was a bit startled, but not too surprised as my family had been surrounded by actors, poets, painters, writers and intellectuals all my life. The discussion in Spanish between Tatiana and me had been rather lively. Anyway, he wanted my phone number – Tatiana didn't agree with that – but when we arrived at Notting Hill Gate station near where we lived, I wrote the phone number on the dirty glass door of the carriage, back to front, so the scout, who had introduced himself as 'Mr Dangerfield', could read it. It was all quite amusing.
> Anyway, when we got home I was very excited about the whole experience and told the family. They thought it all a bit farfetched, and took it with a pinch of salt. The days went by and no phone call. Tatiana and Federico (my elder brother) made fun of me. 'Hahaha! An actor? Maybe just a pervert, that Mr Dangerfield.' After two agonising weeks, the phone finally rang and my mother took the call, from Mr Dangerfield, or it could have been George Brown. After they'd had a long talk, an appointment was made, and I went to Pinewood Studios for the audition along with about four hundred other kids. I later learned that Curt Christian was the runner-up for the leading part, but I looked more like my father in the film. And that is how I became 'The Boy Who Stole a Million!'

What memories, if any, did Reyna who, after a brief career as a child actor became a successful musician and diplomat, have of the director?

> I remember Mr Crichton as a very fine gentleman, kind but firm in his directing, and very thorough explaining the sequence to be shot and the mood that had to be conveyed. He also was very special during the studio recordings of the dialogue that had to be redone due to the city noise or 'bad takes' on location, much of which was done running around Valencia. Outside of the filming, especially on location in Spain, he was a cheerful person, sharing paella and the other catering food brought to the set, with the rest of the actors and crew. In general, I remember him as a thoughtful and dedicated director, who took great care to explain his filmic wishes to the actors, and to me, in particular.[29]

On the fiftieth anniversary of the film in 2010, he told *Valencia International*, the city's English-language newspaper, that although his memory had mostly dimmed about the filming, he did remember shooting 'in the gypsy quarter when I am with Currito [Curt Christian] trying to get away from the blind man and we had to shoot it several times because of the night setting in. Another time we had difficulty with the dog [which follows the boy in his flight]; he didn't want to have anything to do with the *Fallas* [the city's annual fiesta] and the fireworks.'

A glance at Crichton's annotated scripts suggests shooting went well. Up front is scrawled, 'As a matter of INTEREST have covered 14 pp in 12 days shooting.' The film closed with an aerial shot, high above Valencia's rooftops, of Miguel's repaired taxi driving away from the city. The final scene, as originally set out on page 83 of the script, was rather different. It is Warren Mitchell's character, Pedro, who had effectively set the film's long chase sequence in motion, reprising, 'I know where there's a million', before taking to his heels, as one of the street villains 'turns threateningly on him. FADE OUT'. So despite on paper, at least, some encouraging elements, the stark reality is revealed by Professor Petrie in his authoritative paper:

> The omens ... had never been promising, with the initial assessment by Film Finances' consultant John Croydon indicating a number of serious concerns with script, schedule and budget. The report concludes with an unequivocal condemnation: 'My own personal opinion is that it is one of the craziest propositions it has ever been my misfortune to examine and report upon.' Despite Croydon's reservations, Film Finances provided a completion guarantee on a budget of £100,000 the costs covered by £49,500 from Lloyds Bank/Bryanston, £49,500 from [US distributors] Paramount (a mixture of sterling and pesetas) and a £1,000 deferment from Charles Crichton. Problems with bad weather on location and delays in the studio shoot led to the film going over budget by £11,000 which Film Finances were obliged to cover by the terms of their guarantee. This resulted in rather strained relations between Brown and Michael Balcon who considered the disastrous performance of *The Boy Who Stole a Million* to be in part due to Brown's failure to control the production. Balcon also noted that Kenneth Shipman [a studio-owning member of the consortium] was concerned about the number of projects associated with Brown – the implication being that 'he is spreading himself too thin and the commercial potential of individual projects is suffering as a result'.[30]

The box office results spoke for themselves. After pitiful takings of just £7,525 at the UK box office, the film overall incurred a loss to Bryanston of over £52,000 in today's money, and with an unfortunate echo of the film's title, just over £1m. It was a depressing outcome for what the ever-optimistic *Tatler* critic, Elspeth Grant, found 'all tremendous fun'. While George Brown would soon bounce back with a couple of successful Miss Marple film mysteries, starring the ineffable, if initially reluctant, Margaret Rutherford, Crichton headed back to America and his abortive (second, and even more painful) fling with Hollywood. It was more than three years before he returned to a feature-film set, during which time he, like so many of his contemporaries, began to flirt more and more, mostly out of financial necessity, with the small screen instead.

***

Seven years after commercial television was launched in the UK, ITC Productions, a subsidiary of ATV, had become – thanks in no small part to the entrepreneurial flair of the colourful Lew Grade – the most prolific provider of filmed TV entertainment, following the spectacular success of its inaugural show, *The Adventures of Robin Hood* (1956–60). Grade's holy grail was the American market, so many of his shows, though UK based, were carefully packaged with that transatlantic objective.

Following his first foray into television with a single play five years earlier, Crichton, now divorced from Pearl and remarried, in 1962, to Nadine (Haze), who had been in the French Resistance during the war, plunged back into the medium with a vengeance directing four, hour-long episodes of a typically banal ITC series called *Man of the World*. The set-up was simple enough: Mike Strait was a globe-trotting, American freelance photo-journalist who somehow always managed to end up in some of the hotter spots. As a former Office of Strategic Services (OSS) agent during the war he also knew how to handle himself. Strait was played by Craig Stevens, a solid, second-string Hollywood leading man who had moved into television with some success, most notably as the eponymous star of NBC's *Peter Gunn*, created and produced by Blake Edwards, about a cool, private detective. It ran for four years and 114 episodes. *Man of the World* survived 20 episodes in 1962 and 1963 across just one and a half seasons.

Crichton's four episodes – two in the first season ('The Runaways', 'Portrait of a Girl'), two in the second ('The Bandit', 'The Prince') – were typical of the series, which always opened with a jaunty Henry Mancini theme and a rather inventive title sequence as if shot through a camera lens; then a Strait voiceover for some exotic overseas footage before settling into sets that were forever in and around Shepperton Studios. The plots were often faintly exotic, recreating faraway places, and the dialogue strictly functional relying on gnomic utterances like, 'It is said the camera does not lie, but it can distort the truth'; or as one Red Chinese villain (played by a British actor with sloe-eyed make-up) says of Strait, 'a man of independence and integrity ... despite his Western education'.

The Third Secret (1964)

'I hope,' the American writer-producer Robert L. Joseph told Eddy Gilmore of the *Arizona Daily Star*,

> no one gets angry with me for not picking a bus conductress or a waitress to star, or a man who's never seen the inside of a studio to direct the film. Movies are the only field in the world where inexperienced, unknown people are pitchforked into an arena and often praised for their amateurism. The only thing I really believe in is professionalism – as long as there's real talent behind it, and in *The Third Secret* I've got plenty of both.

Headlined 'Producer Tackles Movies', the interview, dated 8 December 1963, unsurprisingly offers no clue as to the problems that beset the film after it had finished shooting in the UK throughout that late spring and summer.

Following three years away from the big screen and having just established a toehold in the burgeoning medium of filmed TV, *The Third Secret* would seem, at first glance, a rather unlikely 'vehicle' for Crichton's big screen return. Yet, a much closer examination of what turned out to be an ambitious, star-laden, if flawed thriller – about remote as can possibly be imagined from his signature work at Ealing – reveals it is veritably stuffed with recurring motifs from some of his past films. This in turn gives considerably more substance to the suggestion by Professor Neil Sinyard, in his typically perceptive analysis of the film found among the 'special features' on the 2019 Blu-ray DVD release of *The Third Secret*, that the idea for the film originally stemmed from Crichton himself. According to Sinyard, after Crichton had been fired from *The Birdman of Alcatraz*, he returned to the UK with 'an idea about making a psychological thriller similar in manner to *Psycho* but not a gothic horror. The interesting thing for him was that the suspense and solution came from the psychology of the main character ... that it was a new twist to a murderous impulse from a psychological imbalance of which [the] perpetrator may not be aware.'[31]

While It is not unreasonable to imagine Crichton would have seen and possibly admired Hitchcock's sensational, tongue-in-cheek shocker when it opened in the States while he was prepping *Birdman*, there seems to be no concrete evidence to support Professor Sinyard's notion, least of all from Crichton himself whose own motive for making the film was, he claimed later, 'because I needed a job'.[32] Might Crichton have met Joseph during his American misadventure? The latter had produced a number of classic revivals on Broadway including some Shakespeare and a couple of Shaws before his own play, *Face of a Hero*, starring

Jack Lemmon and Sandy Dennis, opened in New York four months on from *Psycho* (and closed after just thirty-six performances). Joseph had also some years earlier co-written, with the director Ida Lupino, *The Hitch-Hiker* (1953), a much-admired B-movie about a psychopathic serial killer. Following his screenplay for a minor western in 1958 and some episodic TV, including a *Playhouse 90* version of *Face of a Hero*, which predated its Broadway flop, *The Third Secret* was, as writer and producer, by far and away Joseph's most ambitious screen venture. He even persuaded the distributor, 20th Century Fox, to allow him two weeks of rehearsal before production.

In its bare bones: Dr Leo Whitset, a well-connected London psychoanalyst, is found by his cleaner one morning dying with a bloody head wound, everything seems to point to suicide, especially as his last words to her are, 'Tell them I messed up. Nobody to blame but me.' His fourteen-year-old daughter Catherine, who lives unhappily with adoptive parents (her kindly aunt and gruff uncle) has, however, other ideas; she's absolutely convinced he has been murdered by one of his patients and seeks the help of Alex Stedman, a UK-based American reporter/pundit with his own popular British TV show, who had also been in therapy with Dr Whitset since the tragic death of his own wife and daughter. The fact that suicide contradicts everything the good doctor stood for finally persuades Stedman to come on board.

Still troubled himself and, as we witness, subject to occasionally violent mood swings, Stedman begins his halting investigation that appears to centre on three people: Alfred Price-Gorham, an art gallery owner; Anne Tanner, an attractive but mousy secretary; and Sir Frederick Belline, a distinguished judge. As the labyrinthine tale further unfolds, it seems two more names can be added to the possible suspect list: Catherine, who was also being treated by her father, and, of course, Alex, hence the film's pleasingly cryptic teaser line, 'The Story of a Man Searching for a Killer Who Might Be Himself!'

Joseph and Crichton gathered, on paper at least, a superb cast for the film. Stephen Boyd, in the final throes of a long contract with 20th Century Fox, during which time, from 1958, had mostly consisted of loan-outs to other major Hollywood companies like MGM for whom he enjoyed his signature role, as villainous Messala in the multi-Oscar-winning *Ben-Hur* (1959). Thereafter sword-and-sandal parts pursued him, first as Mark Anthony in the aborted version of *Cleopatra* (1963), and then as heroic Livius in producer Samuel Bronston's glorious failure, *The Fall of the Roman Empire* (1964), opposite Sophia Loren, Alec Guinness and Christopher Plummer. Stedman was a rare, and gratefully accepted, contemporary role for the actor born and raised in Northern Ireland.

The film's other major role, Catherine, went to thirteen-year-old Pamela Franklin, who had been plucked from ballet school to co-star in *The Innocents* (1961), Jack Clayton's masterly version of Henry James's chilling ghost story, *The Turn of the Screw*. By the time she joined the cast of *The Third Secret*, the precociously talented Franklin had already completed a couple more features as well as a two-part TV film for Disney. Filling out featured roles as other prime suspects were Richard Attenborough (Price-Gorham), Diane Cilento (Anne Tanner) and Jack Hawkins (Judge Belline).

Making her rather belated film debut at twenty-nine playing Price-Gorham's pliant assistant, Miss Humphries, was Judi Dench, already long a leading light in the British theatre for her work with the Royal Shakespeare Company both at home and on Broadway. 'I was extremely frightened,' she told Brian McFarlane. 'I said to the runner [sic] who came to get me and show me to my room, "Is he frightening? Will I like him?" and he said, "Oh, no, he is not at all intimidating and you'll probably like him very much." It wasn't until four or five days later I found out I'd been talking to his son.'[33] Like Dench, David Crichton was also making his first tentative steps in the film industry as, in fact, third assistant director before abandoning it soon after for the relatively securer shores of television (Figure 7.2).

Along with the film's own built-in mystery, as a 'who-if-any-dunit?', was also the case of the missing film star who had filmed her role and then disappeared altogether from the final print. This was Patricia Neal, who just two weeks after *The Third Secret* opened in New York – six months before the UK release and without Neal – won the Academy Award for Best Actress in *Hud*. Because the film was so compartmentalised, almost a portmanteau affair, with, apart from Stedman, none of the main characters interacting despite their common link with the psychiatrist, Dench would say later that she never realised that Neal had even filmed a role. Married to British writer Roald Dahl, and no stranger to filming in the UK, Neal was playing another of Dr Whitset's patients, the suicidal Claudia Sorilla Boucher, described in the script as '35, noticeably underweight. We see the remnants of a once great beauty. She is exquisitely dressed.' Like all the principal characters in the film, her psychopathy is evident but never fully explained. She does, though, add to the enigma when in a clearly heartfelt outburst to Stedman, she cries: 'This man was a healer – a man who helped – a man who journeyed with people all the way to the centre of hell and stood with us deep in darkness and challenged the demons to come out and fight. Alex, why should such a man die that way? Why?'

THE SIXTIES: 1960–64 **175**

Figure 7.2 Crichton (rear) with camera crew, including director of photography Douglas Slocombe (second left), camera operator Chic Waterson (front centre) and focus puller Robin Vidgeon (front right), track Pamela Franklin on *The Third Secret*

So Neal ended up on the cutting-room floor along with much of Dench's already fairly brief role as, what the script but not the final film, overtly suggests, the victim of an abusive relationship with her employer – 'I'm sorry, Alfred ... please don't hurt me – Alfred, I'm sorry, please.' Why? According to Crichton: 'The top man at Fox changed. [Darryl F.] Zanuck got in and decided he wanted to make pictures for the family, and this was a strange mad picture, so he cut out most of the mad bits which didn't help; another reason for not going to America.'[34]

Professor Robert Murphy, who contributed a very informative essay, 'A Startling Journey into "A World of Nightmare"' for the Blu-ray release, thinks Crichton's explanation a little too simplistic:

> When Zanuck returned to the helm of the company after a long spell as an independent producer, he was not pleased with the resulting film. The screenplay shows her [Neal's] role in the film to be superfluous and poorly written (Crichton made more extensive changes to her scenes than anything else in the final script). Her suicide and her claim that she murdered Dr Whitset look neither necessary nor convincing.

Instead, careful editing displaced 'Claudia's most useful function into Cilento's more interesting character'.[35]

As for the savage paring of Dench's role, Crichton offered no 'on the record' explanation. Instead, Murphy writes: '[It] looks more like a directorial decision than a producer's cut.'[36] Indicating some of the notes in Crichton's annotated script – Price-Gorham 'was quite a nice little boy – but he is a horrid middle-aged man … he is a frustrated painter. And the talent for a delicate appreciation but lack of creative talent has spread to his sex life … He is a cripple' – Murphy suggests that 'endowing him with a sadomasochistic relationship with Miss Humphries and a bitter hatred of his psychoanalyst might have worked if he really was the murderer, but the film works better without such lurid red herrings'.[37] As we will see, Crichton made up for what effectively was reduced to nothing much more than a spit-and-cough by giving Dench a substantial co-starring role in his next film.

For *The Third Secret*, Crichton (Figure 7.3) was reunited with a couple of key crew: for the twelfth and final time, Douglas Slocombe, and production designer Tom Morahan, another Ealing alumnus, who had worked with the director on *The Love Lottery*. Since their last collaboration on *The Boy Who Stole a Million*, Slocombe, together with his regular camera operator, Chic Waterson, had shot three particularly stylish black-and-white films, Seth Holt's *Taste of Fear* (1961), Bryan Forbes's *The L-Shaped Room* (1962) and Joseph Losey's *The Servant* (1963), which deservedly earned Slocombe a BAFTA and the British Society of Cinematographers' annual award. Now, filming in Cinemascope, one of the last black and white films to do so, added a shimmering width to some of the locations, in particular, the muddy riverbank on the Thames below Strand-on-the-Green at Chiswick where Stedman and Catherine walk, talk and play strange, chalked, word games on the river wall below her late father's house.

Sinyard's analysis of the film refers to an 'unusual script, very literary'.[38] This observation is suitably underlined by the rather surprising appearance Thameside, during a Stedman–Catherine walk-and-talk, of Georg J. Lober's celebrated bronze sculpture, a copy naturally, of Hans Christian Andersen – 'the master fantasist', notes Sinyard – the original of which helps decorate Central Park in New York.[39]

Christian 'Kits' Browning, Daphne du Maurier's son, who was second assistant director, recalls some of the crew being rather 'contemptuous of the dialogue' with certain phrases bandied about the set about accompanied by sly laughter. Favourite 'funny lines' were 'There's no money, none' (uttered by Catherine's uncle, played by Alan Webb); 'I think that's an unconscionable thing to have done' (delivered by Jack Hawkins

Figure 7.3 Crichton relaxes on *The Third Secret*

who, Browning also said, had to be plied with a half a bottle of vodka before he could manage to produce some required tears for a scene); and the rather more self-explanatory, 'Anything wrong, go and see Dr Whitset'.[40] This may well explain David Crichton's still vivid memory of experienced first assistant director Peter Bolton's regular rallying cry, 'Be loyal, guys, be loyal!'[41] Browning claimed it was 'not a particularly happy film',[42] that Crichton was 'rather bullied'[43] by Joseph. From a showbusiness family, Andrew Birkin, the seventeen-year-old runner on *The Third Secret*, who would later become a successful writer-director in his own right, suggested instead that the director had more problems with the associate producer, Shirley Bernstein, the feisty younger sister of musical maestro Leonard Bernstein, who ran her own theatrical literary agency.

Birkin's fondest memory of Crichton – who, said Browning, was 'always courteous and kind to his assistants' – occurred during a night shoot:

> We were filming a scene down by the river. The crew broke for dinner and I was left in charge of camera gear, which had been prepared for a tracking shot. Looking up from the book I was reading, I suddenly noticed the river was rising and the water was beginning to lap round wheels of the camera dolly. I flung my book aside and pulled the camera back from the water so it was well out of the way, and put the brake back on. I then ran off quickly to where [the] crew was having dinner, and told them I'd just 'saved the camera because the tide's coming in'. Instead of being declared a hero, I was lambasted by the shop steward who told me I had 'no business touching the camera' as I was not in the union. 'What about the film,' I asked? 'It's all insured,' he said. Charlie Crichton came to my rescue and said, 'Well done – that's what's wrong with the business' [referring to the knee-jerk union 'intervention'].[44]

The film's solution, revealed in a very striking climactic scene between Stedman and Catherine replete with a knife-wielding, *Psycho*-style moment, is not altogether a surprise: that she, suffering from severe mental illness – paranoid schizophrenia, no less – and with her father agonising over whether to commit her, actually turns out to be the killer. As the film's line has it: 'The first secret is what we don't tell people, the second secret is what we don't tell ourselves, and the third secret is the truth.'

Pamela Franklin would be the last in a line of child actors from whom Crichton had, since *Hue and Cry*, then on through *Hunted*, *The Divided Heart* and *The Boy Who Stole a Million*, helped coax a scene-stealing performance, which suggested, according to one critic, 'a suspiciously seasoned thespian within her youthful exterior'. If a facility with youthful performers was one of what I referred to earlier as 'recurring motifs' then also the director's ability to refine that to their close if often confused interaction with stressed adults is surely another, especially reminiscent of the relationship between Jon Whiteley and Dirk Bogarde in *Hunted*.

Neil Sinyard says the film strongly reminded him of Serge Bourguignon's Oscar-winning *Sundays and Cybele* (1962) about the unlikely friendship between a disturbed adult and a lonely girl, who has been deserted by her parents. He also bracketed *The Third Secret* with what he describes as other rather 'moody, slightly arty black and white thrillers'[45] slightly to one side of the mainstream in the early sixties, like Bryan Forbes's *Séance on a Wet Afternoon* (1964), John Guillermin's *Rapture* (1965), Polanski's *Repulsion* (1965) and, he might also have added, Preminger's *Bunny Lake Is Missing* (1965), most of them reflecting different aspects of mental illness.

These are films, which Robert Murphy, like Sinyard, believed contrasted strangely even starkly with what seemed to be the prevailing mood at the time in a Britain where Beatlemania was rampant, Bond had been unleashed and the sixties were in full swing.

The two commentators also appear to have much more time for Joseph's screenplay, which attracted the main brunt of criticism when the film opened, first, in the States and then in the UK towards the end of 1964. The *New York Times* wrote that 'the film uncoils and meanders so deviously and pretentiously, and the dialogue slips into such metaphorical mishmash that the result is more often exasperating than entertaining – or convincing'. The *Belfast Telegraph* considered that 'the plot has possibilities but the writing breaks down in midstream and Boyd's man-to-girl talk consists largely of woolly homespun philosophy and screen clichés'. *Monthly Film Bulletin* commented that 'this is an unappealing and irritatingly muddled scribble of a film, thoroughly lacking in suspense, veracity and justification'. The *Sun* criticised it for getting 'bogged down in a series of artificial conversations' and the *Liverpool Echo* described it as a 'banal and hiccupping story with stilted dialogue'.

The Times was conflicted: 'The director, Mr Charles Crichton, manages to conjure up very well the odd, haunted atmosphere in which these people lead their lives ... The film is marred only by a certain indulgence of the producer Mr Robert L. Joseph towards the more pretentiously would-be philosophical lines of his own otherwise intelligent and ingenious original screenplay.'[46] Alexander Walker in the *Evening Standard* opined that 'the film is dark and moody, sombre and gloomy but, apart from star spotting, there is much to applaud, specifically the necessarily uneasy tone established by the accomplished director, Crichton'.

Murphy clearly sides with the Walker school of thought when he declares, in an essay included in the booklet for the 2019 DVD release of the film, 'What critics pooh-poohed as pretentious and obscure now looks bold and innovative'. His championing of the film – 'a *film noir* nightmare' – even goes so far as to compare it favourably with two classic movies of the genre from the forties, Orson Welles's *Lady From Shanghai* (1947) and Rudolph Maté's *DOA* (1949). Murphy and, to a lesser extent, Sinyard are, frankly, overgenerous with their assessments of the film, which feels now for the most part as heavy-handed as it seemed to most critics at the time. As well as the possible influence of *Psycho* – and what film-maker at the time would not be – Sinyard also posits two more 'Hitch' references: of the ostensible hero who might be a murderer as in *Suspicion* (1941) or *Spellbound* (1945); and *Marnie* (1964), about a heroine who needs help. The more Catherine investigates the suspicious suicide of her father, the more, Sinyard neatly argues, she begins to penetrate her own psychology and her own repressions.[47]

Hitch-influenced or not, the Catherine strand is far and away the most compelling element in the film, thanks in no small measure to Franklin's remarkably mature performance. She switches from being a clearly bright, almost scarily articulate young schoolgirl on a mission to tragically damaged adolescent, without ever resorting to the kind of more obviously rehearsed neuroses enacted, variously, by the film's 'guest stars', as they are billed in the opening credits. That said, Hawkins's brief turn as a judge with an unexplained dark past is quite touching in one of his final roles before throat cancer robbed him of a wonderfully distinctive speaking voice. Cilento and Attenborough are simply wasted. Boyd's studiedly world-weary – 'Cheer up, Alex, you're off camera now,' smiles his producer – and increasingly tortured performance eventually becomes quite irritating, while his relationship with Catherine moves beyond ambivalence into downright creepy, and not in a good way.

'What I did not realise before,' Robert Joseph added, in that *Arizona Daily Star* interview of 8 December 1963 mentioned earlier, 'is that in the movies – once the film is delivered to the distributors – it is more or less irrevocable,' which may, finally, have been a hint that all had not been quite as first hoped for with Fox following post-production. The film's box office arithmetic confirmed the worst. According to the distributor's records, *The Third Secret* needed to earn $1.3m ($10.8m today) in rentals just to break even; in the event it recorded less than half that total. The company that actually made the film was called Hubris Productions; as they say, pride comes before a fall. Despite any problems he might have had on or after the filming, Crichton thought it 'quite an interesting picture', and that students at the London International Film School, where he taught in the seventies and early eighties, always seemed to like it and, particularly, Richard Arnell's superbly evocative score, whenever it was screened there.

***

Almost exactly a month before *The Third Secret* opened in the UK, a new, more extravagantly devised, version of a once-popular ITV series returned to British television. *Danger Man*, starring Patrick McGoohan as globe-trotting lone wolf security agent, John Drake, working covertly for NATO, had run for thirty-nine half-hour episodes between 1960 and 1962. Following a two-year hiatus, during which time James Bond 007 had been introduced into popular screen culture, Drake was reborn on 13 October 1964, as an agent working for MI9, part of Britain's secret intelligence service, with episodes now doubled in running time. In fact, the 007 connection had originated when *Danger Man* was just a twinkle in the eye of creator Ralph Smart, and Ian Fleming was involved at the initial development stage. Was it just coincidence that in the first series, two years before *Dr No*, a McGoohan opening voiceover would intone, 'My name is Drake ... John Drake'?

With Smart as executive producer, the two line producers assigned to the revived show were Aida Young and Sidney Cole, Crichton's old friend and colleague from Ealing days, so perhaps it was no great surprise when the director was invited to helm the opener, which was filmed at MGM Borehamwood between 10 and 23 July 1964. Written by Donald Jonson, the episode had been called 'The Network' during shooting, before being changed in post-production to 'Yesterday's Enemies', from a line in the script. Still in black and white, Drake's eagerly awaited reintroduction begins with a close-up of McGoohan's eyes staring out at us before we are then transported to a filmed insert of (possibly) Beirut. The action opens on businessman Brett (Peter Copley, Dr Whitset in *The Third Secret*), who we soon discover is part of an independent spy ring run by sacked MI9 operative Archer (Howard Marion-Crawford, an opportunist reporter in *The Man In The Sky*), who has gone rogue in the Middle East. After doing one of those traditional secret-document handovers in a bar, the hapless recipient is shortly machine-gunned down by an unknown assailant.

Cue credits unreeled over a pounding Edwin Astley score – apparently upped in tempo from the first series – called 'High Wire'. Back in London, Drake pulls up in his Mini just beyond St Paul's Cathedral, and disappears into a building addressed '70 World Travel' to be briefed on his next mission by grim-faced MI9 chief Admiral Hobbs (Peter Madden). Within five minutes we're off and running on a rather stately international adventure mostly set in Beirut – actually, in and around Borehamwood – enlivened by a few fist fights, the threat of torture, no sex, almost non-stop smoking and some cynical Cold War-esque dialogue – 'Nothing to choose between East and West; they're both making a hash of the world' – ahead of an uncompromisingly bleak denouement. Following the release a month earlier of the spectacular, technicoloured, *Goldfinger*, this was very 007-lite by comparison, with cool McGoohan, ever neatly suited, barely moving out of second gear.

Directorially, it was all fairly anonymous, like most episodic filmed television back in the day – apart, that is, from one sequence, which portrayed beautifully Crichton's precisely timed comic antecedents. Drake is being held captive by Archer and a couple of locally recruited thugs when just as our hero is about to have a lighted cigarette applied to one of his eyes, suddenly in breezes Joan Hickson, as a plum-voiced pillar of the expat community. This, unwittingly, saves him from a fate worse than death as she witters on about a cancelled am-dram performance thereby distracting the captors enough so he can make his getaway. This was twenty years before Hickson's own reincarnation as TV's most fondly remembered Miss Marple, and also a reminder of her unique comedy chops, which were one of the few highlights of *Law and Disorder*.

It proved a successful launch, and four episodes on – the second, incidentally, having been directed by another old Ealing close colleague and friend, Michael Truman – Crichton was back in the driving seat for 'A Fair Exchange', co-written by Wilfred Greatorex (series script editor) and Marc Brandel. This one takes Drake to East Germany where a former MI9 colleague (American actress, Lelia Goldoni) has been captured while on a personal revenge mission to kill the country's security chief responsible for her torture after an earlier assignment. Ordered by his boss, the series' other 'M' figure, Gorton (Raymond Adamson, a less bulky Jack Hawkins look and soundalike), to stop her, Drake devises a crafty kidnap plan to leverage her release. Like the first episode, and all his *Man of the World* contributions, this show was photographed by Brendan J. Stafford.

Despite McGoohan's reputation for being prickly, he and Crichton seemed to get on very well; so well, in fact, said Crichton, 'that later on, when the actor had his own [created] series, *The Prisoner*, he kept on saying, "You must come and do one, Charlie," but never *actually* asked me'. Quizzed by Sidney Cole if he felt the actor never quite fulfilled his potential, that his was all 'personality acting', Crichton agreed, adding that there was 'too much of himself' in what he did and that he 'didn't spread himself into other characters very much'.[48]

Another old industry relationship was rekindled when Crichton was invited by *Hunted* producer Julian Wintle – a lifelong haemophiliac who rarely complained about his disability – to direct a fifty-minute episode in the second season of an ITV psycho-drama, *The Human Jungle*, revolving around the case file of Harley Street psychiatrist Dr Roger Corder. It was a rare sympathetic starring role for the ubiquitous Czech-born Herbert Lom, whose usual exotic villainy spanned comic gangsters (*The Ladykillers*) to vengeful Moor (*El Cid*). Roy Ward Baker, who directed eight of the thirteen episodes in season two, was awed by Lom's ability to 'to spout reams of dialogue as he analysed the mental problems of each patient. He said once that when he went out to dinner and the waiter handed him the menu he started to learn it by heart.'[49]

The first series in 1963 had been shot at Wintle's and partner Leslie Parkyn's own studio at Beaconsfield. By the time their show revved up second time round, the studios had been sold and the production moved to ABPC Elstree. Crichton's episode, lit by Gerry Turpin, later a double BAFTA winner for his work on *The Whisperers* (1967) and *Oh, What a Lovely War* (1969), was called 'Ring of Hate', whose two 'guest stars', Dudley Sutton and Bernard Lee, play long-estranged father and son, Jim and Leigh Garner. Scripted by the series' story editor, John Kruse, from a story by Leo Lieberman, Leigh is a promising boxer considered a contender but when his folk-singing father suddenly comes back into his life, the young man's innate volatility is suddenly unleashed as unhappy childhood memories – especially of a cruel aunt who used to lock him in a cupboard – come flooding back; a suitable case for Corder treatment, using LSD, no less – 'It'll relax you, make your mind more pliable'.

Apart from a toe-curling sequence in which a clearly dubbed (by Val Doonican) Lee is required to trill a song at his lad's gym, the rest of the action with the requisite amount of suitable psychobabble, is decent enough and includes a very well-choreographed, eight-minute climactic boxing bout for 'the light-heavyweight championship of Great Britain', with celebrated stuntman and fight arranger, Peter Diamond, officiating uncredited as the referee.

After shooting more than, to date, eight hours of television, Crichton felt that, aside from the obvious strictures of budget and schedule, there was for him no great difference technically between shooting for the big or small screen. 'Usually there's one right place for a camera; anyway we were working on film and weren't using multiple cameras. When shooting with one camera, the technique's exactly the same as far as I'm concerned.'[50]

Notes

1 T.E.B. Clarke, *This Is Where I Came In* (Michael Joseph, 1974), p. 186.
2 Kate Buford, *Burt Lancaster: An American Life* (Aurum, 2008), p. 191.
3 BEHP.

4 Clarke, *This Is Where I Came In*, p. 194.
5 BEHP.
6 *Ibid.*
7 *Ibid.*
8 Buford, *Burt Lancaster*, p. 209.
9 BEHP.
10 Charles Barr, *Balcon After Ealing* (Berlin: Volker Press, 1981), p. 4.
11 *Ibid.*
12 Monja Danischewsky, *White Russian – Red Face* (Gollancz, 1966), p. 190.
13 Ed Sikov, *Mr Strangelove: A Biography of Peter Sellers* (Hyperion, 2003), p. 134.
14 Duncan Petrie, 'Bryanston Films: An Experiment in Cooperative Independent Production and Distribution'. *Historical Journal of Film, Radio and Television* 38, no. 1 (2018), pp. 95–115.
15 Quentin Falk, *Travels in Greeneland: The Cinema of Graham Greene* (UPNG, 2014), p. xvii.
16 Danischewsky, *White Russian – Red Face*, p. 191.
17 BEHP.
18 Danischewsky, *White Russian – Red Face*, p. 191.
19 *The Times*, 29 February 1960.
20 *New York Times*, 19 April 1960.
21 Anthony Lane, *Smart Alec* (New Yorker, 2014).
22 Roger Lewis, *The Life and Death of Peter Sellers* (Century, 1995), pp. 269–71 (original emphasis).
23 Freddie Francis with Tony Dalton, *The Straight Story from Moby Dick to Glory* (Scarecrow Press, 2013), p. 92.
24 *Ibid.*, p. 91.
25 *Ibid.*
26 Barr, *Balcon After Ealing*, p. 2.
27 Petrie, 'Bryanston Films', p. 5.
28 *New York Times*, 31 December 1960.
29 Emails to the author, 8 and 20 May 2020.
30 Petrie, 'Bryanston Films', p. 8.
31 Neil Sinyard, *Lost Souls* [documentary] (Indicator, 2019).
32 BEHP.
33 Brian McFarlane, *An Autobiography of British Cinema* (Methuen, 1997), p. 162.
34 BEHP.
35 Robert Murphy, *A World of Nightmare* (Indicator, 2019), p. 11.
36 *Ibid.*, p. 13.
37 *Ibid.*
38 Sinyard, *Lost Souls*.
39 *Ibid.*
40 Email to the author, 11 January 2020.
41 Interview with the author, 9 May 2020.
42 Email to the author, 11 January 2020.
43 *Ibid.*
44 Interview with the author, 9 January 2020.
45 Sinyard, *Lost Souls*.
46 *The Times*, 19 November 1964.
47 Sinyard, *Lost Souls*.
48 BEHP (original emphasis).
49 Roy Ward Baker, *A Director's Cut* (Reynolds & Hearn, 2000), p. 121.
50 BEHP.

The sixties: 1965–69   8

He Who Rides a Tiger (1965)

On the way, Roger awarded himself his first black mark in Peter's eyes. He drove too fast, throwing the Triumph into corners with the zest of youth. Peter noted the fault, but made no comment. They engaged in mainly monosyllabic conversation until, settled comfortably on one of the half-moon couches, they had ordered their food.

'I saw *He Who Rides the Tiger* at Blundestone [HM Prison Blundeston],' Roger confided in his quiet voice. 'I rate it. I remember every detail.'

It had been over fifteen years since a film had been made of Peter's exploits as a cat burglar, but it was still occasionally screened on TV. He had been played by the actor Tom Bell.

'You're very like him, you know,' Roger remarked with a sly smile. 'Only you're more bloody arrogant.'

'What were you in Blundestone for?'

'I was doing a nevis [seven years] for a couple of screwers [burglaries].'

'How long have you been home?'

'Just over a year.'

'And are you up for a bit of work?'¹¹

'Peter' is Peter Scott, author of *Gentleman Thief*, from which the above extract is taken. It was published in 1995 when Scott, real name Peter Gulston, had allegedly retired from his dubious, lifelong profession, revealed in his autobiography's prominent strapline, 'Recollections of a Cat Burglar'.

A curious blend of self-aggrandisement and self-laceration ('this is a degenerate tale'), the memoir, written rather oddly in the third person, plays particular attention to Scott/Gulston's glory years, principally between 1953 and 1985 when he burgled, he claims, over £30m worth of high-end items, including furs, jewellery and artworks, often from the rich and famous, including film stars like Sophia Loren, Lauren Bacall, Zsa Zsa Gabor, Natalie Wood and Vivien Leigh.

Back in the late fifties and early sixties before his acting career properly took off, Trevor Peacock became fascinated with Scott/Gulston's much-publicised life of crime and made contact with him. In between prison sentences, which punctuated the burglaries, the Ulster-born crook even invited him to observe him on a job (Peacock politely declined).

Long before acclaimed roles in the theatre, the screen and on TV, latterly as the confused old rustic, Jim Trott, in the much-loved *The Vicar of Dibley*, Peacock was a prolific writer, providing scripts for everything from *Look at Life* cinema featurettes to early pop music shows such as *Oh Boy!* and *Six-Five Special*. But apart from a 'based on an idea' screen credit for *What a Whopper* (1961), an Adam Faith–Sidney James comedy, *He Who Rides a Tiger* was Peacock's only produced feature film script as acting eventually took over completely from writing, which had also included lyrics for pop songs ('Mrs Brown, You've Got a Lovely Daughter') and musicals ('The Passion Flower Hotel').

Ditching the name-dropping celebrity element, regular bouts of cell time, tennis-playing sideline and four marriages (and divorces) that constantly decorate the real-life story, Peacock, though inspired by Scott/Gulston's exploits, concentrated mainly on his own character's psychopathy: his often dangerously edgy criminal compulsion and shamelessly amoral lifestyle. Filmed suitably in shadow-packed black and white, he has etched many powerful elements of classic film noir. The result is a B-movie thriller in the best tradition and, probably Crichton's most unjustly neglected film. It was also, as will be shown, a production haunted by money problems and undisclosed legal difficulties.

For *He Who Rides Tiger*, Peter Gulston became 'Peter Rayston', still, apparently, as irresistible to women and hooked on crime and fast cars as his inspiration, while his real-life criminal mentor, George 'Taters' Chatham, the doyen of cat burglars and nearly twenty years Gulston's senior, took on the screen guise of 'Peepers' Woodley. They, together with a young thief known as 'The Panda', embark on a spectacular via-rooftop robbery, which climaxes the film and ends in tragedy. Prior to the big heist, we have been following Rayston from the moment he picks up his life after the latest 'stretch' inside. Contemptuous of the prison authorities – he has a reputation as a 'spitter' (spitting at 'screws') – he collects his 'valuables' and, no sooner as he has signed for them, then he is – nice touch – signing in, smartly suited, at a fashionable London nightclub after which he ends up spending the night with a beautiful blonde who had eyed him up earlier.

Rayston is portrayed as brusque and unsympathetic from the very start and there is no let up as he pushes his one-night stand around, barks at a waiter and when questioned by a rather wary detective after his next job – 'You do have a reputation for violence', he tells the suspect – is bought off with a hefty bribe. Apart from a brief moment when Rayston picks up a teddy bear dropped by a child in the park and hands it back to the nanny, Peacock is vividly painting the time-honoured anti-hero.

When the character goes on to mingle his life of crime while romancing a single mother, Joanne, he picked up at the roadside one night – she was hitch-hiking home after missing the last bus – while preparing to case the joint of a possible victim in stockbroker country, all kinds of potentially sentimental subplots (he loves children and animals) threaten to derail the narrative. But the tale finally has the courage of its own convictions and as we reach the nocturnal denouement, the very final pay-off is suitably bleak, almost as pitch black as the night. The title, referring to Rayston's criminal addiction, is said to be an Indian proverb, 'He who rides a tiger can never dismount'.

From the same British working-class generation as Michael Caine, Richard Harris, Albert Finney, Tom Courtenay, Anthony Hopkins, Alan Bates and Peter O'Toole, Liverpool-born Tom Bell somehow never achieved the same kind of international fame enjoyed by his contemporaries. But then again it is difficult to imagine any of those fellow actors being quite as perfect as Bell for the role of Rayston. After a breakthrough role in *The L-Shaped Room* (1962), which should have set him on the same sort of big-screen trajectory as his contemporaries, it was not until he had reached his mid-forties that, in series television, he would begin to produce his best work since *He Who Rides a Tiger*. From *Out* (1978), in which he played an armed robber, to *Prime Suspect* (1991–2006), as a sardonic detective sergeant in three of the police procedural's seven series (right up to the actor's death at seventy-three in 2006), he was never less than charismatic while also being utterly uncompromising as an actor. Those roles on either side of the law also earned him his two BAFTA nominations.

At the time he was cast in *Tiger*, his career was in something of a slump as so-called 'hell-raising' antics, which included drunkenly heckling Prince Philip at an awards dinner, were said to have condemned him to an unofficial casting 'blacklist'. However, not only was Bell absolutely right for Rayston he also, as a sort of added bonus, must have been considerably cheaper than any of his contemporaries because of his 'rep'.

The most mysterious figure in the *Tiger* set-up was the producer, David Newman, about whom there is precious little information apart from a long list of credits between 1960 and 1978 on a BFI website, which, on closer inspection, do not, apart from *Tiger*, appear to have ever made it into production. 'He was a terrible bullshitter, a very pushy guy',[2] recalled Peacock's second wife, Tilly, indeed pushy enough to have insisted his name was above the title, 'A David Newman film', as if he was somehow a latter-day Selznick or Goldwyn. Edina Ronay, who had one quite violent scene with Bell, remembered Newman, 'as a bit of a wide boy. I didn't like him very much.'[3] Some years later, long after *Tiger*, a paperback titled *Three Men Went to War* was published in the UK. The author was Newman, but if you flip a couple of pages, there, in much smaller print, is 'Based on an original screenplay by Trevor Peacock'. Set in and around the ill-fated Siege of Kut in Mesopotamia between December 1915 and April 1916 during World War I, this intended follow-up to *Tiger* between the writer and Crichton finally proved abortive. Newman was also, briefly, in the news a couple of years after *Tiger* when he unsuccessfully sued actor Richard Harris for libel.

How Peacock and Crichton ever became embroiled with Newman, who died on 27 June 2003 in his mid-eighties, nobody quite seems to know. Crichton would, sadly in view of the film's quality, remain more tight-lipped about the film than about almost any of his others and, years after, still blanch at the memory of Newman and all his works.

He recalled, painfully:

> That was a bad experience which I prefer not to talk about. All I can say is the producer was a shit, a cheat and a bastard. This is the sort of thing that happened. I had been paid according to my contract a cheque one day quite early in the week. Friday night we had a crowd at Marylebone Studios and nobody had been paid, and nobody was being paid. The crowd refused to leave until they were paid. The producer arrived about nine o'clock with a bagful of money. He said, 'I want to talk to you afterwards, and have a drink with you.' So he paid the crowd and we went to have a drink. I said, 'What's so important?' He said, 'You know that cheque that I paid you last week? Well, I managed to stop it; that's how I paid them all.'[4]

At the outset all seemed perfectly shipshape as Crichton gathered together a very fine cast including a number of actors from his own earlier body of work like Ralph Michael who had co-starred in *For Those in Peril*, two decades before. The cadaverous-looking Peter Madden, playing 'Peepers' Woodley, had been in one of Crichton's *Danger Man* episodes. Then there was Kay Walsh who, like Frederick Piper, was in *Hunted*. Back from *The Third Secret* was Paul Rogers, this time round in the much meatier role of Rayston's nemesis, Superintendent Taylor, and, of course, Judi Dench (Figure 8.1).

THE SIXTIES: 1965–69 **189**

Figure 8.1 Tom Bell and Judi Dench in *He Who Rides a Tiger*

Having had her role decimated in *The Third Secret*, Dench, now turned thirty, enjoyed much more serious screen time as quiet, refined, Joanne, quite unlike the kind of 'dolly birds' (Annette Andre, Ronay) – this was, after all, the time of swinging London – who normally and often only briefly populated Rayston's promiscuous downtime. It seems that Peacock had to 'push' for Dench as Crichton initially seemed less keen, thinking, he apparently told the writer, that she had not 'got very good legs'. Dench, who by this time already had a bulging and already much-lauded stage CV promised, believed Peacock, 'a reality and a tenderness'. Whether he and the director's discussions began before Crichton used her in *The Third Secret* is unclear, but the problem of 'the legs' seemed to have been resolved by the time *Tiger* started shooting. Good legs or not, Dame Judi Dench says she still remembers Crichton

> with such fondness. It was after several years at the Vic and at Stratford that Charlie asked me to be in *The Third Secret* and then subsequently *He Who Rides A Tiger*. I had been told, while I was at the Vic, that I had the wrong face for films so I was eternally indebted to Charlie, who not only employed me but also gave me a love for filming which I never believed I would ever have. I have never seen either film, but I have never forgotten Charlie.[5]

Apart from recalling Crichton as 'a quiet guy who got on with the job and didn't give you a hard time', Ronay's most vivid memories of the film were Bell – 'he was moody but incredibly charismatic, had a great presence. I think he was a wasted talent' – and Dench. 'I must have watched her do a couple of scenes at the studio while I was waiting to do mine; at the time I was going out with Michael Caine, and after filming finished that day I later told him I thought that Judi was a great actress.'[6]

Crichton's cinematographer was John von Kotze, who, despite his name and fluency in German, was British, with Freddie Cooper, like von Kotze in his mid-thirties, as camera operator. After beginning his apprenticeship in the camera department on major films like *The Small Back Room* (1949), *The Third Man* (1949) and *The African Queen* (1951), von Kotze finally graduated to director of photography on Jack Cardiff's *Scent of Mystery* (1960), notable, perhaps infamous, as cinema's first and only film in smell-o-vision.

Giving full rein for the moodiest black-and-white imagery, predominantly night scenes, on the ground, on roofs, in darkened rooms with characters often picked out by street lamps or headlights, *Tiger* was filmed on various locations around London and at Marylebone Studios, Goldhawk Studios and, according to Steven Webb, lead singer of the Rapiers, the pop group featured at the film's climax, Twickenham Studios. The Rapiers, an Essex group comprising Webb and three of his school friends, are performing the title track (by Peacock) for a 'Beat Night' concert at the Playhouse, Northumberland Avenue, which is dramatically cross-cut with the Rayston and Woodley's diamond heist next door. However, the band and its screaming fans were actually recreating the gig at Twickenham. Webb said that the group were recruited about six weeks before shooting began and introduced to the song – 'quite a sweet little song,' he recalled, 'not really the sort that would inspire fans to scream like that'.[7]

First indications of money problems appeared in June 1965 when the *Hammersmith and Shepherd's Bush Gazette* reported that 'a new film is being finished at Goldhawk Studios', conveniently on the paper's home patch. 'Filming had to stop suddenly last November when the film company ran into financial difficulties. For a while nothing happened. But because a great deal of money was already invested, several film financiers decided to put up the money to get production going again.' The paper's source would appear to have been Newman who was anxious to point out that the film was 'not a crime thriller. It would be more accurately described as a love tragedy'. There would not be, the paper relayed, 'a conventional, standing-at-the-altar happy ending'.

The reviews were, to say the least, mixed. Felix Barker writing in the London *Evening News*, syndicated in the *Liverpool Echo*, was enthusiastic, 'an unambitious but smoothly made crime film'. He was particularly taken with the two leads:

> As the outwardly smooth, inwardly twisted jewel thief, [Bell] is very compelling. The amused, hawk-like features and easy manner are perfectly suited to this modern-day Raffles. The same film produces a delicately shaded study from Judi Dench in the sort of screen part – unmarried mother, working in an orphanage to keep her child who falls for the crook – that could have been awful but which she makes completely believable.

The *Daily Mirror*'s Dick Richards added, 'a crisp, competent, cops-and-robbers picture with an edgy ending'.

Lynn Fenton in the *Newcastle Journal* was more half-hearted – 'I found a great deal of this story hard to accept,' while admitting the film had 'suspense and excitement while Rayston was cracking his cribs'. She picked out Bell and von Kotze's camerawork for special mention. *The Times* derided 'a cliché-ridden script,' but then admitted, 'the film, like all directed by Charles Crichton, has a certain grace and freshness in its treatment which are appealing'.

It took two years for the film to reach American cinemas, but perhaps it should have not bothered if you believed Vincent Canby's excoriating review in the *New York Times* on 10 September 1968:

> Its London locations look gritty and real; its actors have conviction, and its photography is in black and white, which, at a time when almost every movie is shot in color for an eventual TV sale, is sometimes equated with honesty. *He Who Rides a Tiger*, however, is both small and pretentious, which means it's even more boring than a movie that's big and pretentious (and that may possess a sort of vulgar charm). The film was directed by Charles Crichton ... Here he displays a really numbing appreciation for the visual and narrative cliché – lyricism is moonlight shimmering on water, sentiment is a bunch of sweet-faced orphans having fun at a party, and profundity is an unhappy ending.

Inevitably, Canby also mentions, just in passing, two of the director's earlier comedies and there is perhaps the suspicion that some of his remarks could be predicated on the fact that the film does not remotely deliver what the critic might have first expected when confronted with a Crichton work.

Although Peacock's screenplay flirts with potentially saccharine moments, they are nearly always undercut by doses of sharp reality. For instance, during Rayston's first encounter with Dench's Joanne, they come across a fox caught in a trap. Taking it to a country vet late at night, animal-loving Bell suddenly explodes with rage when the vet, who says he has no other alternative, puts down the damaged creature. Joanne supports herself and little son Dan by teaching painting in an orphanage – an authentic Dr Barnado's home – and selling encyclopedias. When Rayston offers to buy several sets, she refuses his 'charity'; his response is to storm off and rough up Ronay's character, Anna, instead, chucking cash at her as he walks out of their smart love nest.

It is clear that Rayston is falling seriously for Joanne but when she discovers via his press cuttings what he does for a living, beats a hasty retreat leaving behind an expensive necklace he'd given her. Rayston's response is savagely to deface an expensive artwork.

There is another excellent scene near the end when Superintendent Taylor tracks Joanne down to the orphanage and confronts her with the truth of Rayston: 'He's a dangerous, ruthless, useless man, and a notorious criminal,' he tells her. 'Is that all he is?' she replies, quietly. Then when Dan shows Taylor something Rayston painted earlier with the kids, the policeman turns it over to find a map of the impending robbery; we see that Joanne's son has inadvertently betrayed Rayston. All this is very far removed from the cosily comical capers in Crichton's Ealing pomp.

He Who Rides a Tiger would be, rather remarkably, some might even suggest inexplicably, Crichton's last feature film for more than twenty-three years. But by the time Canby's review appeared, he had already directed in the interim another nine hours of prime-time television, the medium that would dominate his working days over the next two decades.

***

The Avengers was more than three years and eighty episodes old when Crichton first encountered the popular ITV series shortly after it had embarked on its fourth season towards the end of 1964, during, as it turned out, the shutdown of production on *He Who Rides a Tiger*. Two significant changes had also taken place with the format when Crichton was invited to direct 'Death at Bargain Prices', the fourth episode of the new batch. Video with multi-cameras was replaced by single-camera shooting on 35 mm film, and Diana Rigg, as Emma Peel, had taken the place of Honor Blackman's Cathy Gale as John Steed's (Patrick Macnee) sidekick.

Newly in charge of the series was Julian Wintle, who having completed two seasons of *The Human Jungle*, gathered his team at Elstree Studios, including Albert Fennell, whose credit was 'in charge of production', and an already experienced *Avengers* writer, Brian Clemens, as associate producer and unofficial script editor. A number of regular crew from the old *Jungle* team were also signed up. Crichton's availability and past history with Wintle suggests that it was no great surprise to see him begin an irregular involvement with the series over the next three years.

According to Michael Richardson's *Bowler Hats and Kinky Boots*, his very informative 'unofficial and unauthorised guide' to the *Avengers* phenomenon:

> The differences between making the series on film as opposed to videotape were enormous. Whereas the taped episodes were recorded in one evening, generally in a single take, and had no post-synch or dubbing carried out, the standard shooting time for a filmed episode was ten days, and there was significant post-production work done.
>
> However, the taped episodes were preceded by several days of rehearsals, whereas the filmed episodes generally allowed for only a couple of runthroughs before each shot – although retakes could always be done if necessary. Directors working on a filmed series were expected to get at least five minutes of finished footage in the can every day, but it was not an all-or-nothing situation as with videotape. If the required footage was not captured in the allocated time, then the crew either continued filming until it was, or a smaller second unit would take over and finish things off.[8]

Richardson quotes the per-episode budget as £29,000 – an increase of £4,000 over the original allocation due to scheduling overruns. This would rise, it was reported elsewhere, to £56,000 (£1.1m in 2020).

As its title might suggest, Crichton's debut involved shenanigans in the London department store, more specifically, a dastardly plan to detonate an atomic bomb in the basement of Pinters, where Mrs Peel and Steed has gone undercover to try and infiltrate the would-be bombers. Written by Brian Clemens, the episode was almost a compendium of what would become the series' signatures: more tongue-in-cheek, increased use of Steed's lethal umbrella and bowler hat and Rigg's outfits including the famous leather catsuit. There was also room for another of the director's very rare 'cameos', in this case, most fleetingly, as the name of a brand of ceramics – Royal Crichton – on show in the store. In a neat twist on one of his most famous roles as Superintendent Folland foiling an atomic threat to London in the classic Boultings' thriller, *Seven Days to Noon* (1950), Andre Morell played the villain, wheelchair-bound Horatio Kane. Neither he nor any of the other main actors had worked before with Crichton but there were, for the director, reunions with, as well as the producer, cinematographer Gerry Turpin and editor Peter Tanner. According to Michael Richardson, the episode was one of Patrick Macnee's favourites.

Launched at the beginning of October 1965, the fourth season had been on air for a month when Crichton returned to the set to begin rehearsals for 'The Danger Makers' – twentieth of the twenty-six episodes in the season – written by Roger Marshall, a veteran of the series since 1962, who would eventually rack up fifteen produced screenplays for *The Avengers* across five years. A variation on a very regular theme of the series, the episode featured a secret clique of eccentrics, some borderline psychopaths, in this case ex-military men who are unable to come to terms with civilian life, live dangerously and often illegally on the edge – from playing chicken with motorbikes and scaling St Paul's to planning a heist of the Crown Jewels from the Tower of London. One of the two main baddies (the other was Douglas Wilmer) was played by Nigel Davenport, who had been Stephen Boyd's TV producer in *The Third Secret*. Paired for the first time with cinematographer Alan Hume (who would light *A Fish Called Wanda*), Crichton directed a typically bizarre tale replete with outrageous stunts, fights, a couple of cliffhangers and Mrs Peel's fetching catsuit.

There were also, Michael Richardson points out, a couple of 'bloopers':

> In a stock footage mix-up, [a] Supermarine Swift jet fighter ... becomes a propeller-driven de Havilland Chipmunk just before it disappears behind some trees, followed by the sound of an explosion and then huge plumes of thick black smoke. Steed and some RAF personnel watch proceedings from beside Stage 5 on the studio lot, with the traffic lights used to facilitate the movement of large pieces of scenery in and out of the soundstage clearly visible.[9]

After more than a year away from the series, and after *Adam Adamant Lives!*, the BBC's pale imitation had been seen off, Crichton was recalled for *Avengers* duty in January 1967 for episode nine of the fifth season, by which time the show was being in shot in colour to appease the ABC network in the States to whom the series had been successfully sold. Written by Brian Clemens, 'The Correct Way to Kill' was, in fact, a reworking of 'The Charmers', one of his own episodes from season three in which Steed and Cathy Gale liaised with their Russian counterparts to track down as assassins killing Soviet agents. The show gave Crichton the most scope yet to demonstrate his familiar ease and precision with comedy. After all, how serious could a storyline be when the main villain is called Nutski (Michael Gough) and his organisation SNOB (Sociability, Nobility, Omnipotence, Breeding Inc)? To aid the laughs, Crichton cast five-foot-ten Anna Quayle as Russian agent Olga after seeing her some years earlier playing, among a number of roles, an outrageously exaggerated Bolshevik in the Newley-Bricusse stage musical, *Stop the World – I Want to Get Off*.

By the time Crichton rejoined the *Avengers* team sixteen months later for 'False Witness', episode fourteen in season six, there had been two major changes in the series: Diana Rigg had been replaced by Canadian Linda Thorson, at twenty-one, youngest of Steed's sidekicks, as Tara King, and 'Mother', a kind of 'M' figure but rather more louche and rotund introduced in the form of actor Patrick Newell. There were also two significant reunions for Crichton on the show. It was written by Jeremy Burnham with whom the director had last worked ten years before when Burnham played Michael Redgrave's strait-laced son in *Law and Disorder*; and Alan Hume's veteran camera operator was Jeff Seaholme, who had also operated on six of Crichton's Ealing films between 1947 and 1954.

Regularly cited as one of the best ever episodes of the series, 'False Witness' also displayed a strong streak of comedy, both in Burnham's dialogue and with some excellent visual gags, typically when Steed parks his Rolls-Royce by a housing estate, erects a portable bus stop sign just as a double-decker arrives, housing, on the upper deck, Mother's mobile office complete with drinks decanters, telephones and statuesque 'helpmate' Rhonda, who never, ever, utters a word. The typically convoluted plot had something to do with trying to discover why witnesses keep failing to provide evidence against a proven blackmailer, Lord Edgefield (William Job).

Crichton's final *Avengers* stint, in September and October 1968, was 'The Interrogators', co-written by Richard Harris and Clemens, which, according to Michael Richardson, is one of Thorson's own half a dozen favourite episodes. It also saw the return of Christopher Lee to the show at a time when he was also a major star of Hammer films. Last time out, in 'Never, Never Say Die', he had played a mad professor attempting to create a race of invincible duplicates. This time round he was the rather saner but still villainous Colonel Mannering who has devised an ingenious way of extracting information from secret agents, including his latest kidnap victim, Tara King.

Filmed on location in central London and on Hampstead Heath, the episode also involved some helicopter hijinks, which due to fog caused shooting delays that, in turn, necessitated the axing of several scenes. The 'chopper' finally arrived at Brocket Hall in Hertfordshire, a stately home that has since become a regular country house location for films and TV. Michael Richardson notes that Thorson considered herself 'privileged' to have worked with both Crichton and Lee. More than fifty years later, Thorson, recalled by Crichton long after as 'that pretty girl', confirmed how thrilled she had been to have worked with the director

> who had come to us on *The Avengers* out of the stratosphere. When I arrived in England from Canada as a sixteen-year-old, the first Ealing comedy I saw was *The Lavender Hill Mob* and I loved it.
> When I heard that this famous director was coming to work with us, I could hardly believe it. He had white hair by that time, was incredibly lean and handsome, and always wore a sort of safari jacket. I loved the smell of his pipe, which reminded me of my father who also smoked a pipe. He was very lovely to me, and I always felt completely looked after. When I went to see *A Fish Called Wanda* all those years later, his name came up on the screen and I remember thinking, 'That can't be the same guy who directed ...' Like a lot of other people I hadn't heard a thing about him since I had worked with him ... what was it, twenty years earlier?[10]

You might suspect that Crichton would have been invited to direct many more than just the five episodes he helmed over a period of four years, but mingled in with his *Avengers* work were six and five instalments, respectively, of two more high-profile ITV series, *Man in a Suitcase* and *The Strange Report*, like *Man of the World* and *Danger Man*, off Lew Grade's seemingly relentless ITC conveyor belt. Said to be a replacement for *Danger Man* after Patrick McGoohan quit to pursue his own dream project, *The Prisoner*, *Man in a Suitcase* was dreamed up by experienced television writers Dennis Spooner and Richard Harris who, curiously, never actually contributed any scripts to the series they created. The premise was that loner McGill – he only ever had a surname – had been fired by the CIA as a scapegoat following a scientist's defection to Russia, and relocated to England from his native America to work as a private investigator – the proverbial righter of wrongs – while also trying to prove his innocence.

Texan Richard Bradford, a prematurely grey-haired method actor in the Brando tradition – he had actually beaten up Brando in Arthur Penn's *The Chase* (1966) – was signed up to play McGill, or 'Mac', as he was generally known, in thirty episodes aired between September 1967 and April 1968. Based at Pinewood, the series – first titled *McGill* before being changed during filming to *Man in a Suitcase* – was produced by Crichton's old friend Sidney Cole, and his cameraman on two of the episodes – 'Brainwash', which launched the title, and 'Day of Execution' – was Lionel Banes, who had worked on both *Against the Wind* and *Train of Events*.

'Brainwash' was never intended to be the trailblazer, but, in the event, it was chosen to supersede the actual pilot episode, which explained McGill's backstory. So we first meet him on a railway platform somewhere in the English countryside – actually, Denham Golf Club, a stone's throw from Crichton's old home in Denham village – where within the first couple of minutes he has been coshed and bundled into the back of a car. Howard Marion Crawford, who had played the treasonous Archer in one of Crichton's *Danger Man* episodes, was even more viciously villainous this time round as the former president of an African country who, together with his sidekick (Colin Blakely), first kidnaps then tries to brainwash McGill into confessing that the American government had been behind the coup that toppled him.

Although, according to Michael Richardson in his exhaustive survey of the whole series in an autumn 2001 edition of *Action TV* magazine, Bradford cited the episode as his personal favourite, filming was not plain-sailing:

> What should have taken two weeks to complete overran into four and it's likely that Bradford's reluctance to rehearse was causing problems on set, More than once it was reported that when a director called for action, [Bradford] would simply stand there getting himself into character and this approach caused further friction as [he] refused to rehearse intricate fight scenes.[11]

In this particular episode, stunt man George Leech had firmly to persuade the actor to prepare properly or else it was likely he'd be injured.

Peter Duffell, who directed six episodes, explained some of the potential difficulties of working with Bradford that would likely have impinged on Crichton:

> Following the Brando philosophy, Richard's tendency to do things that had not been planned in rehearsal and to change his dialogue at the last minute so that the other actors were uncertain of their own cues often gave us terrible problems. Sometimes during a take Richard would do something completely [different] from what we had rehearsed, which was particularly difficult for the camera operator who could never be quite sure where Richard was going to move. He also has a distressing habit of lighting up a cigarette during a shot, which he had not done in rehearsal and which could totally alter the ensuing action. He would even stand them on end on a desk in front of another character he might be interviewing so that one's eyes were inevitably drawn towards the precariously balanced cigarette that might fall over at any moment.[12]

Crichton's remaining episodes took McGill twice to Africa – 'The Whisper' with Colin Blakely back this time as a former mercenary turned Jesuit priest, and 'No Friend of Mine', where he was caught up in a revolution – and France for 'Three Blinks of the Eye', where McGill was investigating mock executions in a Paris nightclub called La Guillotine. Like 'Brainwash' and 'Day of Execution', in which McGill was dodging death threats, shooting was always confined to Pinewood with occasional locations nearby and in London. Crichton was once asked if he felt he was somehow 'slumming' with this kind of frantic, non-stop episodic television work after all his earlier years on features: 'It's a difficult question; after all, I had been slumming on features,' was his splendidly sanguine riposte, adding, 'Even if the story wasn't ok it was always interesting trying to do the best one possibly could with the material."[3]

Of all his leading men in television, Anthony Quayle was easily Crichton's most experienced, not to say distinguished, with more than thirty years of theatre and film already behind him when he played the eponymous ex-Scotland Yard commissioner called in to consult on quirky cases in *Strange Report*, a Pinewood-based co-production between Grade and the American network, NBC. The original plan was to shoot two seasons with the second moving from a very obviously swinging London to an American base. However, Quayle and one of his co-stars, Anneke Wills, a former *Doctor Who* companion, had no desire to relocate to Los Angeles so the series was scrapped after just one sixteen-episode season. Wills played Evelyn, Strange's modishly dressed young neighbour from across the hall, who regularly found herself caught up in his cases. Third member of the investigative team was, as doubtless the US deal demanded, a square-jawed, motorbike riding, wise-cracking, twenty-something American, Hamlyn 'Ham' Gynt, played by Lithuanian-born Kaz Garas.

Crichton directed five episodes including the opener, 'Report 5055: Cult – Murder Shrieks Out', which first aired in the UK on 21 September 1969. Produced during the era of flower power, love and peace, its plot, about a murder and shady financial dealings behind the scenes of a happy-clappy, global-giving, cultish charity, probably fitted in with the overall attempt of the series to produce some storylines 'torn from the headlines' such as student unrest, racism and human trafficking.

But the script – by writer-actor Moris Farhi, who had written one of Crichton's *Man in a Suitcase* episodes – is perfunctory at best, required as it is to fill in bits of back story about the main characters in between some excruciating slices of dialogue. Evelyn on her middle-aged, pipe-smoking bearded neighbour who drives an old taxi: 'You're really a cold-blooded monster – and I dote on you!' or, Strange, furious that 'Ham' has tried to rescue a kidnap victim on his own – 'the mutton-headed Minnesota fool'.

The episode begins with a helicopter returning three of the charity's key personnel to its modernist headquarters, including musical duo, guitarist Jay, shortly to be electrocuted in mid performance; singer Maggie (Pamela Franklin), soon to be kidnapped; and leader Lars. The episode ends with the same helicopter carrying Lars off to Paris unaware there is a bomb on board. Unselfishly – especially as we thought he was the main villain – he sacrifices himself by crashing the chopper well away from any housing. It is perhaps in keeping with the sheer tackiness of the episode that the fatal crash itself is out of sight and merely signalled by noise and a plume of black smoke.

Considering the Anglo-American talent involved, the episode suggests that, on this occasion anyway, Crichton's 'best' simply was not good enough to lift such dire material. Executive producer Norman Felton and script editor Edward DeBlasio, two of the three principal Americans on the series, had hours of prime-time US television behind them; producer Robert 'Buzz' Berger was, admittedly, very inexperienced at the time. Director of photography (for the entire colour series), Gerald Gibbs, was a highly experienced British cinematographer who in his eclectic list of credits since 1935, included *Whisky Galore*. Another intriguing credit was the series 'forensic advisor', Dr Francis Camps, the Home Office pathologist, best known for his work in the case of serial killer John Christie in the early fifties.

In terms of the better-known cast, along with the dependable Quayle, who almost but not quite rises above the material, was a pair of Crichton returnees: Pamela Franklin, now five years on from *The Third Secret*, as Maggie; and as an unlikely Lars, a charismatic Norwegian, the Irish actor Ray McAnally – last directed by Crichton as a kindly orphanage superintendent in *He Who Rides A Tiger* – dressed until his selfless passing in a sort of absurd-looking beige smock top with a blue logo. Franklin's ghastly, shrill, intermittently tearful, performance as Maggie even threatened to dim memories of her brilliance as the complex Cathy in *The Third Secret*. Quite why they decided to lead off with such a dire script remains a mystery; apart from filling in bits of the investigative trio's previous history, perhaps they felt it chimed best at the time with the series' faintly forensic brief, in this case, probing corrupted love and peace, which was also in reality beginning to stale a little at the time.

In fact, the series picked up considerably after this misstep. Crichton's four other episodes – 'Hostage – If You Won't Learn, Die!', 'Grenade – What Price Change?', 'Revenge – When a Man Hates', and 'X-Ray – Who

Weeps for the Doctor?' – all enjoyed much grittier settings and storylines such as kidnapping with international implications, controversial defence research protests, and euthanasia.

Years later, as a plethora of online fan sites would attest, the series would as a result of DVD afterlife enjoy plenty of positive attention. Typical is Mark Trevor-Owen's 2019 assessment on the *We Are Cult* website. Praising *Strange Report*'s regular engagement with 'issues' while also noting the unevenness of its plotline, he also observes:

> To a modern viewer, it's intoxicatingly swinging sixties London in its style. Compared to other ITC programmes of the time though, *Strange Report* has a grittier, earthier feel. Consciously stripped of the glamour and gadgets of its stablemates, it veers towards realism. The settings are recognisably real world. This is a London that goes beyond Carnaby Street to embrace dingy bedsits, brutalist tower blocks and glass-lined polytechnics.[14]

***

In 1969, some months before *Monty Python's Flying Circus* first aired on the BBC changing sketch humour forever, John Cleese and his regular writing partner, Graham Chapman, since Cambridge University student days, resumed working on a screenplay called *Rentasleuth*, an 'out-and-out comedy', as Cleese described it. Funny men like the two Ronnies, Barker and Corbett, as well as Marty Feldman and Tim Brooke-Taylor were being rounded up as the likely stars for this David Frost production but, as yet, no director had been signed.

First choice was the hugely experienced comedy writer Denis Norden who had never directed a film and had absolutely no desire to do so. Next they approached Jay Lewis, who had been directing shorts, documentaries and the occasional comedy feature, like *The Baby and the Battleship* (1956), since the early forties. But between sending him the script and catching up with him again a few days later for a reaction, Lewis suddenly died aged fifty-five. 'Now,' Cleese wrote in his autobiography,

> We were asked if we knew a Charles Crichton. We looked him up, and leapt about excitedly when we discovered that he had directed for the Ealing Studios ... Charlie had made my second favourite (after *The Ladykillers*), *The Lavender Hill Mob*, so we sent our script off to him – and then recalled that our ending was a complete and deliberate steal from that very film (or, let us say, it had influenced us greatly).
>
> Fortunately, we discovered that when we went to meet him that he had not noticed. Even better we realised after about five minutes that we had stumbled across a treasure, a man who knew so much more about film than anyone we'd ever met that it was almost embarrassing. We'd pack up for the day, having left some problem unresolved, and then the

next morning Charlie would push a sheet of paper towards us, rather shyly, while puffing on his pipe, and we would glance at it and realise that he had not only come up with the solution but somehow also clarified a plot point and added a good joke. Under his tutelage the script improved rapidly.[15]

Despite a report in the film trade press that the film was firmed up with Crichton at the helm, it never happened, for it turned out that Frost had sold the script to Ned Sherrin, who after years of producing satirical news shows for the BBC, had turned, principally, to films. It was very soon clear that in this later sixties age of youth culture, a director on the cusp of sixty was not an option. With Crichton rejected, Cleese and Chapman also walked away from the project.

The film was eventually made three years later, retitled unsubtly *Rentadick*, rewritten by John Wells and John Fortune, with a cast that included none of the original comedy names, and directed by Jim Clark, better known as an ace editor. Critically savaged, *Rentadick* was also a box office flop. Clark said that when they saw the film, Cleese and Chapman

> demanded all trace of their names be removed [they appear on the credits as, respectively, 'Kurt Loggerhead' and 'Jim Viles'] and we were lucky not to be sued. There was precious little left of their work anyway. If their script had formed the basis of the Cleese/Crichton partnership, *A Fish Called Wanda* might never have been made. So, in a roundabout way, we did them a service.[16]

Notes

1 Peter Scott, *Gentleman Thief* (HarperCollins, 1995), p. 26.
2 Interview with the author, 22 October 2019 and 27 May 2020.
3 Interview with the author, 27 May 2020.
4 BEHP.
5 Email to the author, 9 June 2020.
6 Interview with the author, 27 May 2020.
7 Interview with the author, 30 October 2019.
8 Michael Richardson, *Bowler Hats and Kinky Boots* (Telos, 2014), p. 131.
9 *Ibid.*, p. 166.
10 Interview with the author, June 2020.
11 Michael Richardson, 'You Crazy Idiot. My Name's McGill' (Action TV, 2001), p. 19.
12 Peter Duffell, *Playing Piano in a Brothel* (BearManor Media, 2011), p. 72.
13 BEHP.
14 Mark Trevor-Owen, 'Turn and Face the Strange: Strange Report'. *We Are Cult*, 2 February 2019, http://wearecult.rocks/strange-report (accessed 9 September 2020).
15 John Cleese, *So, Anyway* (Arrow Books, 2014), p. 380.
16 Jim Clark, *Dream Repairman* (Landmarc Press, 2010), p. 82.

The seventies: Downsizing 9

How tempting it would be to speculate, more likely plain fantasise, that Crichton's first two filmed television projects of the new decade, on paper seemingly as different as chalk and cheese, were assigned to him directly as a result of his distinguished Ealing comedy past. The unlikely first, an episode of the children's adventure sitcom *Here Come the Double Deckers*, about a gang of seven kids who hang out in a disused red London bus, had irresistible echoes of *Hue and Cry*. As for 'The Colonel', his single, half-hour, contribution to *Shirley's World*, starring Shirley MacLaine as the proverbial 'globe-trotting photojournalist', it might have been hewn from Balcon's back catalogue.

From 20th Century Fox Television and aimed squarely at an American audience, *Here Come the Double Deckers*, effectively spun off from a popular series of Children's Film Foundation (CFF) cinema shorts called *The Magnificent Six and ½* (1968), was also shown the following year in 1971 on the BBC, which makes it the only recorded piece of small-screen material that Crichton ever made, albeit indirectly, for the corporation. Two of the original CFF cast, Michael Audreson and Brinsley Forde, made it across to the TV series, renamed Brains and Spring, and the gang was filled out by, among others, seventeen-year-old Peter Firth before his eventual stage fame in *Equus*, as leader Scooper, and, to add some transatlantic credibility, an authentic American, twelve-year-old, Detroit-born Bruce Clark, as Sticks, named for his drumming skills.

Described by *The Encyclopedia of Daytime Television* as 'a sort of Limey update of [Hal Roach's] *Little Rascals* [aka *Our Gang*] film troupe [of slapstick shorts from the twenties]', it also quoted *Variety*'s assessment of the seventeen-part series as 'low farce, but very substantial fare against the one-dimensional characterisations of the cartoons. It also has a uniquely refreshing score – no rock.' Endearingly low-tech, with occasional singing and dancing, the series' resident adult was Albert, played by Melvyn Hayes, who also co-wrote some of the music.[1]

Crichton's thirty-minute offering was 'The Go-Karters', a reworking by writer Peter Miller of an old CFF title, *Go Kart Go* (1964), which had starred fourteen-year-old Dennis Waterman. Ahead of the big race, Spring is up before the magistrate for driving his go-kart recklessly through the town, so the gang must prove that it was tampered with by an unscrupulous fellow competitor. Filmed mostly on location in Hertfordshire, there's a spectacular extended motorcycle cop pursuit though the streets of Aldenham and nearby Elstree Studios as well as official go-kart action at the world famous Rye House track, within spitting distance of where Crichton's two sons went to boarding school.

There's also a distinctly Home Counties feel to his *Shirley's World* episode, which despite boasting its eponymous star's range of modern outfits and modish headwear is pure *Titfield Thunderbolt*, even down to two of the episode's stars, John Gregson and Michael Trubshawe. Also on show was another Ealing 'graduate', Bill Owen. The storyline, also by Peter Miller, concerned a disgruntled colonel, an old buffer (Trubshawe), attempting to sabotage the building of an oil refinery in his tranquil corner of the English countryside. Taking time out from the usual globe-trotting assignments for *World Illustrated* magazine, edited by perpetually harassed Dennis Croft (Gregson), Shirley Logan (MacLaine) is on the case.

If ever a series defined the expression 'star vehicle' it was *Shirley's World*. From its extended opening credits featuring an interminable montage of MacLaine head shots, to, in this episode, her driving a heavy digger helping the Colonel gleefully destroy the oil company's building site. Even its progenitor, Sir Lew (later Lord) Grade, the eternal optimist, was forced to admit that despite a sale to an American network, the series 'wasn't a success'. He claimed that the show's American producer, Sheldon Leonard, was 'too much in awe of Shirley and allowed the production to slip away from him ... What was really lacking was Shirley's effervescent personality. It just didn't come through.'[2]

To give Crichton credit, on this occasion, MacLaine really did look as though she was having fun smashing stuff up while also observing amusedly a series of British stereotypes going through their predictable paces against some eye-catching rural backdrops, photographed by Alan Hume. According to the website Nostalgia Central, 'Shirley MacLaine and her British crew developed a mutual loathing of each other during the making of this series. All were mutually happy when it was cancelled.'[3] Another of Crichton's old Ealing colleagues, 'Tibby' Clarke, also contributed a script to the series. It was one of his last screen credits, but, tellingly, he does not mention it anywhere in his memoirs.

After several futuristic series of trail-blazing television puppetry, such as *Fireball XL5* (1962), *Stingray* (1964), *Thunderbirds* (1965) and *Joe 90* (1968) followed by a first live-action creation, *UFO*, Gerry Anderson, in cahoots with Lew Grade, who provided the one-line concept, produced his first contemporary action show, *The Protectors*, in 1972. The set-up for the series, which ran for a total of fifty-two half-hour episodes across two seasons on ITV, was the varied caseload of a stylish trio of international, trouble-shooting, private detectives 'outside the law', as Grade conceived it: Harry Rule (Robert Vaughn), the Contessa di Contini (Nyree Dawn Porter) and Paul Buchet (Tony Anholt), based, respectively, out of London, Rome and Paris.

Unsurprisingly, Crichton, with several hours of ITC filmed production already behind him, took on five episodes in the second season by which time the format – cramming often globe-trotting crime tales into twenty-five minutes screen time – was probably beginning to flag. Following just a year on from Grade's altogether more lavishly produced, *The Persuaders!*, *The Protectors* rather tended to smack of a cheap knock-off, despite the starry presence of the one-time *Man From U.N.C.L.E.* Crichton did what he could with a quintet of hasty storylines, which spanned Cold War political dramas ('The Last Frontier', 'Dragon Chase', 'Border Line') to more purely home-grown plots involving everything from protecting a millionaire's teenage daughter ('Sugar and Spice') to preventing a disturbed mental patient from killing a judge ('Trial').

Following the tightly budgeted and slim scheduling of *The Protectors*, shot for more speed on 16 mm, Crichton's next Anderson assignment was something of a sea change as the producer returned to the kind of material he knew best when, in 1974, he and his wife Sylvia came up with the live-action *Space: 1999*, their most ambitious and visionary project yet. At $275,000 per fifty-two-minute episode – a total of $6.5m (£31m in 2020) – it was the most expensive television series to date. Between the autumns of 1974 and 1976, Crichton, by now in his early sixties, directed no fewer than fourteen of the forty-eight episodes of this ambitious intergalactic adventure, making him by far the most prolific director on the ITC series across its two twenty-four-episode seasons.

Set thirty years after the first lunar landing, the story centres on Moonbase Alpha, on the dark side of the moon, peopled by more than three hundred men and women from all over the world. The base is being used to store atomic waste disposal from Earth but when the debris begins generating its own magnetic energy a huge thermonuclear explosion is triggered, blasting the moon out of Earth's orbit. Careering through the cosmos, Alpha and its principal personnel dressed in dull beige unisex jumpsuits are set on, and off, course, for a series of weekly encounters with all manner of likely jeopardy from fantastic life forms and odd monsters to interplanetary humanoids while trying to hunt down a compatible planet.

Although firmly based at Pinewood and with a domestic special effects team led by Brian Johnson and Nick Allder who, between them, would later win Oscars and BAFTAs for films like *Alien* (1979), *The Empire Strikes Back* (1980), *Aliens* (1986), and *The Fifth Element* (1997), three of the four main cast members were American. Husband and wife Martin Landau and Barbara Bain had co-starred together for three years in TV's *Mission: Impossible*, and Barry Morse, British born, was best known as the relentless Lieutenant Gerard on the trail of *The Fugitive* for four years between 1963 and 1967. The fourth was a young Australian actor, Nick Tate.

Between October 1974 and the following February, Crichton directed 'War Games' and Death's Other Dominion', two of the first five *Space: 1999* episodes to air in the UK from September 1975. Written by Christopher Penfold, the show's story consultant for most of the first season, 'War Games' was one of the original storylines prepared before the series began and proves a handy guide for the kind of straight-faced, design-heavy, sci-fi shenanigans to follow. On the subject of 'straight-faced', Crichton did have some trouble with two of his actors, Isla Blair and Anthony Valentine, who were both burdened with some extraordinary prosthetic make-up for the episode, which pitches the Alphans against an unknown enemy. As they could not look at each other without laughing, they ended up having to do their scenes facing away from each other.

There was a different kind of concern affecting two of the actors on 'Death's Other Dominion' in which the Alphans come across a group of people who seem to have found the secret of immortality. Landau and Bain apparently refused to work on an ice cavern set until a specialist confirmed that fumes given off were non-toxic. In his preview of the series on 19 September 1975, John J. O'Connor from the *New York Times* remarked of the American leads, 'All three have developed cool robot styles entirely suited to the sci-fi genre. Miss Bain is particularly proficient at serious lifelessness.'

Thanks to *Moonbase Alpha Space: 1999 Wiki* (on fandom.com), one of a number of latter-day fan websites devoted to the memory of the series, there is a plethora of information and trivia about all the show's episodes, none more so than those helmed by Crichton: of 'Dragon's Domain', 'perhaps the most overtly mythological episode of *Space: 1999*', Christopher Penfold's script was 'revised probably by Crichton, Anderson and Landau'; on 'Guardian of Piri', a young actor, Gareth Hunt, who would later become a huge TV star for his role in *The New Avengers*, can be seen briefly as a spacecraft pilot; however, 'the role was intended to be larger but he left the production after a disagreement with Crichton'.[4]

Filming on 'Matter of Life and Death', the first episode actually to be completed, suddenly stopped during an important scene when everybody heard Crichton call 'Cut!' It turned out to be a parrot. On 'Space Brain', Crichton's final contribution to the first season, the fan site reports that 'as foam filled Main Mission, Crichton tried to cut the scene but could not be heard above the sound of the aircraft engines whipping up the foam. He ran forward waving his arms, slipped and disappeared into the foam. He emerged covered in it. The foam continued until it filled the set.'[5]

The second season started airing in September 1976 with 'The Metamorph', written by Johnny Byrne, one of Crichton's six contributions to the follow-up series. Byrne, who had been the most prolific scenarist on the first series, was invited to be the show's creative consultant on the second. However, with an eye still firmly on the American market, the producers decided instead to import Fred Freiberger, an old *Star Trek* hand, to do the job. As far as Landau – and possibly, Bain too – was concerned this was the beginning of the end. Landau, who claimed later that he had turned down the role of Mr Spock in *Star Trek*, became increasingly disenchanted with Freiberger's priorities for the show. On the script for 'A Matter of Balance', directed by Crichton, he wrote, testily,

> I'm not going out on a limb for this show because I'm not in accord with what you're doing as a result ... I don't think I even want to do the promos – I don't want to push the show as I have in the past. It's not my idea of what the show should be. It's embarrassing to me if I am not the star of it and in the way I feel it should be. This year should be more important to it not less important ... I might as well work less hard in all of them.[6]

Landau's concerns about this episode in particular, which revolved around an exploration by some crew members of the planet Sunin, were echoed by fans who took it to task for everything from 'setting back feminism by 40 years' to 'a ridiculous-looking alien'. Another chirped, 'Oh, Freddy [Freiberger], what did you do to this show?'[7] Interviewed in 1999 on the occasion of the show's twenty-fifth anniversary since its launch, Landau berated Freiberger for allowing 'the actors to serve the script rather than the characters' and that, 'he turned the show into a cartoon'. Landau's dissatisfaction seemed to echo Robert Vaughn's with *The Protectors*, the latter said, it was reported later, to have acted like a prima donna, unhappy with everything from the scripts to his fellow actors.

The proof of the pudding was that all three major US networks turned the show down. So instead, the producers managed to sell it directly to individual stations via syndication and managed to get it scheduled in all the major cities. But after, noted the *Complete Directory to Prime Time Network and Cable TV Shows*, 'heavy curiosity viewing, audiences realized that *Space: 1999* had the same problem as most space epics: all hardware and no character development'.[8] It seems that Landau was proved right, despite a continuing affection for the show, which still persists today. It was rumoured that George Lucas visited the set while preparing to shoot *Star Wars* and was very impressed with Johnson and Allder's special effects. Their subsequent, award-winning, big-screen sci-fi work suggests that of all the *Space: 1999* personnel, they were, ultimately, the big winners.

***

When asked, almost a decade on from his final small-screen assignment, for some memories of his seemingly relentless grind on the television treadmill before cinema reclaimed him for one, final, time, Crichton specifically recalled, albeit very briefly, *Danger Man*, *The Avengers* and, most fondly of all, *The Adventures of Black Beauty*. After reciting his regular mantra, 'I needed the money', and admitting that, initially, the idea of making a series inspired by Anna Sewell's 1877 children's classic – 'it had nothing to do with the book' – 'absolutely horrified me', he would admit, 'we had a bloody nice time. I enjoyed it.'[9] Part of that enjoyment must have been the prospect of teaming up again with his old friend, producer Sidney Cole, like Crichton, now well into his sixties but as busy as ever.

A Sunday teatime family fixture on ITV for more than two years in the early seventies, excluding endless repeats down the years, the idea for the series originated with Anthony Gruner, a top television executive, who had loved Sewell's book as a child. 'With acknowledgement to the classic by Anna Sewell', as the opening titles proclaimed, the 'creator' credit went to Ted (Lord) Willis of *Dixon of Dock Green* fame, who invented a number of new main characters for the series, which was set a few years on from the novel, towards the end of the nineteenth century.

The co-producers were Cole and Paul Knight, who, though barely thirty at the time, already had several hours of television under his belt. Knight had never met Crichton before the series started but was quickly won over: 'Sid Cole brought him in, and it's fair to say that everyone loved him. I don't know how he'd be received today, this old bugger;

he was a stickler for discipline and wouldn't take any mucking about. Charlie gave *Black Beauty* a lot of class.'[10] Crichton, easily the oldest of nine directors used on the series, was also its busiest, helming eighteen episodes, three times as many as any of the others on a slate that also included Freddie Francis and Peter Duffell.

Another likely reason for Crichton's enduring affection for the series was the convenience of its basic logistics. The show could effectively be filmed entirely within the confines of a single location discovered by the location manager about half an hour from the centre of London. At Stockers Farm near Rickmansworth, there were rolling fields, lakes and even a quarry, a possible 360-degree pan of nothing but countryside. Even the processing laboratories were only three miles away, at Denham, once Crichton's happy hunting ground. As an added bonus, the farm was situated right next door to some busy stables, run by Reg Dent, a very skilful horse master with on-screen riding experience stretching back more than ten years. Dent provided Black Beauty or, rather, seven versions of the equine star each with an individual skill, ranging from bucking to neighing on cue. Knight amusingly recalled how Dent would call out Beauty's name, and seven pairs of ears would all prick up at the same time.

Crichton's first episode to air, the second in the first season, was 'The Hostage', written by Victor Pemberton and, like the entire series, shot by Ken Higgins, an Oscar-nominated cinematographer (*Georgy Girl*, 1966), working here for the first time with the director. The story is simple enough: Jenny (Judi Bowker) and Kevin (Roderick Shaw), the children of widowed Dr James Gordon (William Lucas), encounter an escaped convict (John Thaw) in their barn while attending to Black Beauty.

Frank Hatherley in the *Stage* of 12 October 1972 devoted an enthusiastic and rather droll column to that particular episode a couple of weeks later:

> *The Hostage* ... was splendidly mounted and guaranteed to raise squeals of juvenile pleasure throughout the land. Mr Pemberton played some neat variations on a well-worn plot. It was the one about the escaped convict using our equine hero to escape, and Charles Crichton directed with considerable energy and style. Filmicly, in fact, *The Hostage* was first-rate. Convict Jack plunged through the woods with kind-but-firm Dr Gordon and a posse of constables with their straining, yelping dogs in hot pursuit. Beauty bucked and kicked. Plucky Kevin fell from a tree and it was touch and go whether help would arrive in time. Jolly exciting stuff.
>
> Black Beauty himself was unable to make much of a contribution to this particular plot. However, he did manage to look (a) disappointed

(b) hostile (c) challenging and (d) happy as the occasion demanded. Clever cutting here. Ken Higgins' excellent photography and Denis King's fine music [his irresistible theme, 'Galloping Home' won an Ivor Novello Award in 1973] added much to Sidney Cole's production.

Hatherley had earlier remarked how simply a 'serial' version might only have stretched to perhaps a dozen episodes whereas 'the series in its current form could, in theory, run forever. In short, *Black Beauty* has now joined the ranks of *Skippy, Flipper* and Co. ...' He concludes: 'Having raised the ghastly spectre of *Skippy* [an Australian kangaroo series that ran for nine years between 1968 and 1977], let me hasten to assure you that *Black Beauty* has left the bathetic bush kangaroo bouncing at the post. Absolutely no contest.'

Crichton divided his episodes equally between the two seasons, which were also necessarily split into two when Bowker, a very young looking seventeen in the first series, was called up by Franco Zeffirelli to co-star as one half of his St Francis of Assisi biopic, *Brother Sun, Sister Moon* (1972). Thus, 'Vicky' became 'Jenny', played by fourteen-year-old Stacy Dorning, daughter of the character actor Robert Dorning.

Paul Knight remembered reading that when Michael Caine decided to return from Los Angeles to live in the UK, he said he had been partly influenced by seeing on TV the 'wonderful countryside' they had shot in *Black Beauty*. He thought it must be 'somewhere in the West Country'. Knight wrote to him to explain it was actually filmed just eighteen miles north-west of London. He never received a reply.

So, for Crichton the memories lingered on, as he agreed with William Lucas when, 'at the end, Bill said that it had become a way of life and it was very funny to be deprived of it'.[11] Cole concurred: 'It was a very agreeable series to make; it was terribly naive and innocent, but that was its attraction, and it communicated itself to the people working on it.'[12]

Could lightning strike twice when Cole, Knight and Richard Carpenter, who had written seventeen of the *Black Beauty* episodes, invited Crichton back five years later to collaborate with them on their latest television creation, *Dick Turpin*? For *Dick Turpin*, the three had formed a new production company Gatetarn and sold the idea to London Weekend Television as a Saturday early evening family adventure in half-hour episodes, with twenty-six plus a full-length feature in total over the next four years, between 1979 and 1982. Inspired by the character of Turpin though set from the year the notorious eighteenth-century highwayman was officially hanged – the fiction suggests that the man executed had merely borrowed Turpin's bad name – the series painted its outlaw as a kind of wronged Robin Hood figure trying to clear his name while righting rustic wrongs. The four main recurring characters were Turpin (Richard O'Sullivan) and his sidekick Nick Swift (Michael Deeks), known as Swiftnick, vying to keep one step ahead of the corrupt duo of Sir John Glutton (Christopher Benjamin) and Captain Nathan Spiker (David Daker).

For *Dick Turpin*, Gatetarn established its base of operations at Ockwells Manor near Maidenhead. The beautiful timber-framed fifteenth-century house and its grounds were, said Knight, rented for a year and all the sets in the series were built there, and many of the *Black Beauty* crew, including Ken Higgins and Reg Dent, back on duty. But the location, recalls Gregory Dark, first assistant director on all Crichton's episodes, also had considerable drawbacks not least of which was its proximity to Heathrow.

> We would probably start shooting around 8.30 in the morning and maybe have to go 12 or 13 takes because of bloody planes. It was seriously frustrating not just for the crew but also for the actors when they had got their performances right. Although the house itself offered us some great things like its baronial hall, it wasn't always easy shooting there because as it was also the base of operations, the phones were ringing constantly, and the old woodwork in the place often creaked.[13]

As well as the usual hurdles when filming period drama such as pylons and television aerials, there was also the matter of the horses. 'There are two things about shooting stuff on horseback,' laughs Dark. 'The first is, very few of the horses have read the script! Also, it was likely that many of the actors had persuaded the casting director that they were Olympic show-jumping standard. We even had one actor who got on a horse facing its bottom.'[14]

After working on *The Professionals* (1977) – which reunited him with Gordon Jackson for the first time since *The Love Lottery* in 1954 – and *Return of the Saint* (1978) – in which Ian Ogilvie had replaced Roger Moore as Simon Templar – Crichton directed ten episodes of *Dick Turpin*, including the opener, 'Swiftnick'. Written by Carpenter, it explained how young Nick Swift came to team up with Turpin, who had returned from military service in Europe to find he had been cheated out of his inheritance by the splendidly named Glutton. From its misty opening titles over a kind of silhouette image of a coach being held up by a masked horseman, the episode perfectly set the tone for the series full of hard-boiled quasi-eighteenth-century dialogue, fast-moving action and hissable villains – Christopher Benjamin in Robert Morley-like mode especially delicious as a bewigged, corrupt toff – crammed into the tightest of running times.

This scene-setting episode was not, however, without its 'teething problems', explains Dark, and did require some reshooting. 'Firstly, because Sid and Paul thought everybody looked *too* clean, which, I have to say, was a perfectly justifiable criticism. The other had to do with the colour of the timbers, which would not have been black at that time. In the end it was decided that once blackened up, they'd just stay black, and we'd die with our secret.' Despite his distinguished track record, Crichton, says, Dark, never made a great thing about it.

> There was nothing grand about him, nor was he pompous. Then, again, he was no shrinking violet. He had an expectation that what he said was law and that was the end of it. First of all, Charlie knew what he was doing, and that wasn't always the case with TV directors. When he gave the actors a note, they certainly listened and absorbed it.
> Mind you he could on occasion be quite exasperating. In those days, you were carting around a three-ring circus and the first decision you had to make was where you were going to park everything up. I'd always say to Charlie, 'Give me a safe spot, somewhere that's not in the direction you're going to shoot.' After the third episode with him, I gave up because I just knew that wherever we put the caravan that's where he'd want the first shot. I'd say to him, 'You said this was the one place you weren't going to shoot.' He'd look at me and reply, 'Well, I'm allowed to change my mind.' Yes, he did have a tendency to 'go over' a bit, but today his overages would be considered coffee money. When Charlie hadn't managed to complete the day's scheduled work, he would go to Sid and Paul's office after shooting finished and say, 'Just reporting for my evening's bollocking.' It could get a bit volatile between them but Charlie always managed to fight his corner, and sometimes mine on occasion.[15]

Said Knight: 'Charlie delivered some brilliant episodes, full of great camera movement. He was a very good scriptwriter too, and contributed "The Judge", an episode in the second series.'[16] With a high comedy content, the story revolved around Turpin posing as a judge he had 'intercepted' in order to best Glutton at a trial involving two of his local friends, including Swiftnick.

This was a typical exchange:

> Turpin (disguised as the judge): 'Who prosecutes? What, you, Glutton?'
> Glutton: 'Aye, my lord.'
> Turpin: 'And who speaks for the defence?'
> Radstock (one of the accused): 'I'm a poor man, my lord. I've no one to speak for me.'
> Turpin: 'Hm, no speech for the defence. In that case, there shall be no speech for the prosecution; that seems only justice.'

Even before *Dick Turpin* had ended its long run on television, Crichton was already embroiled with Gatetarn on yet another half-hour period adventure series, *Smuggler* (1980), set in Cornwall at the turn of the nineteenth century. Against the background of the Napoleonic Wars, the thirteen parter, a UK–Canadian co-production for HTV, followed the swashbuckling fortunes of Jack Vincent (Oliver Tobias, modishly hairy but as wooden as a gangplank), an ex-British naval officer turned smuggler attempting to elude revenue officers as he plies his trade along the south-west coast.

This was film-making on the tightest of budgets – £100,000 per episode – requiring carefully researched locations before the scriptwriting stage so as to accommodate known castles and other period buildings. It also required 'cross-plotting', taking five episodes and scheduling them as though they were one film albeit with the two directors; Crichton had already experienced this as a matter of course on *Space: 1999*.

Cole and Knight prided themselves on not, as before on *Black Beauty* and *Dick Turpin*, having to shoot in a studio. 'Ever since *Black Beauty*,' Knight told *Screen International* at the time, 'we've been literally shooting in barns. There's no need to build great sets. We found all the locations we need round Bristol, North Devon and Wales.'[7] The only exception was a cottage that was specially constructed for the series on a clifftop near Clevedon in North Somerset.

Fast and furious action in the same family-friendly vein as *Black Beauty* and *Dick Turpin*, *Smuggler*, though not nearly as successful, benefited hugely from some splendidly salty locations especially along the coastline below Exmoor. 'Despite his age,' recalls Paul Knight, 'Charlie was up and down those cliffs, some of them very rugged, like a mountain goat. We could hardly keep up.'[8] More interior than most, 'An Eye for an Eye', the final of the three episodes he directed, was surprisingly, and very entertainingly, talky featuring at its heart a potentially violent confrontation between Vincent and two of his former naval shipmates, Agate (Ian Hendry) and Dutchie (Gernot Duda).

In the presence of the series' regulars, Sarah (Lesley Dunlop) and young Honesty Evans (Hywel Williams-Ellis), the gruff pair rake up his foggy past – not yet fully explained in the series – as a warship lieutenant and an ill-fated episode of alleged 'glory-hunting' against the French, which, they claim, led directly to the death of Dutchie's powder-monkey young son, the loss of one of Agate's arms and Vincent's resignation from the service. 'We're debt collectors,' they tell him, with pistols raised, 'and you owe us your life.' Vincent being the series' star is, naturally, innocent of all charges but must prove it to his friends. Agate was one of Hendry's last television roles before dying of alcohol-related illness, and he gives it the full, eye-rolling Robert Newton-style old seadog.

Just turned seventy, Crichton's three episodes of *Smuggler* would be his last, having directed, in total, nearly fifty-five hours of filmed television across a quarter of a century, the equivalent of more than thirty feature-length films in a twenty-five-year span. But given the director's propensity for sub-ninety-minute running times, probably nearer thirty-five.

It is some sort of answer, not by any means perfect or even ideal according to Crichton's own enduring big-screen ambitions, to those who would often continue to ask: just what was he up to between *He Who Rides a Tiger* in 1965 and *A Fish Called Wanda* in 1988?

***

Nearly a decade after an abortive collaboration on *Rentasleuth*, Crichton and John Cleese finally got together in 1977 on a project that would eventually lead to their most successful association of all a further ten years after that. Video Arts was co-founded by Cleese and fellow comedy writer Anthony Jay in 1972 in a bid to inject humour into training films about business management methods. In a reminder of Video Arts' ethos on the fortieth anniversary of the company in 2012, Cleese stated, 'People learn nothing when they are asleep, and very little when they are bored stiff.' By this time, he had sold the company for millions but still continued to appear in some of its training videos.

Since their last encounter towards the end of the sixties, Cleese, now a household name in the wake of *Monty Python's Flying Circus* (1969–74), its first authentic feature spin-off, *Monty Python and The Holy Grail* (1975), and six triumphant episodes of *Fawlty Towers* (1975), suggested to Margaret Tree, Video Arts' joint managing director and programmes' producer, that she might like to seek out Crichton. Tree recalls: 'John was obviously familiar with his work and a great fan, and he thought it was ridiculous Charlie was not still working as a director of both films and television. He said to me that he thought it would really benefit the company if Charlie directed some of our films.'[19]

As Crichton remembered it:

> I think when we were doing *Dick Turpin*, when John rang up Paul Knight, and asked, 'Is he moribund or alive? Is he capable and can he walk?' So Paul gave me a clean bill of health, I suppose, and so I went off and made not a particularly good [first] one for Video Arts. The relationship between John and me grew, and over the years we made many of them together. They had conceived this idea that you can teach more

easily by being amusing than ramming points down people's throats, and they had enormous success as a result.[20]

In fact, Knight suggests instead it was actually Tree, an old friend of his, who first contacted him about Crichton's current state of repair. In any event, Tree met Crichton for the first time when he arrived to direct a 'client' film – another Video Arts speciality – for the *TV Times*. Tree admits that she initially confronted sixty-seven-year-old Crichton,

> with a degree of trepidation because his reputation went before him. One of the most important things about our films was that budgets were always strictly stuck to; in fact, we were always on, or even sometimes under, budget. Now we had got this guy who's more used to films and TV. Will he stick to the budget?
>
> On the first film he did for us, he asked me, 'How many reels of stock to I have?' and I told him that the shooting ratio was 8:1. He replied, 'Oh, what happens if I run out of film?' How I had the nerve to say this, but I told him, 'Well, you stop; the film's over!'
>
> In fact, I needn't have worried because with all the films we did with him, we never went over budget. Never, ever. His ability to shoot at 8:1 or less was quite staggering. Whenever I looked over his shoulder at his script, it was so annotated with things like: what time at what shot, and if we were behind, what shots he could miss out – and still make it. The whole thing was so well prepared and planned. He always had his escape routes if we were behind. Of course, one of the reasons he never went over budget and stuck to the ratio was that he'd been a fine editor, and knew exactly how the thing was going to fit together.[21]

Crichton, who had endured a stroke by this time and walked with a stick, would not have been unfamiliar with the kind of budgets and schedules Video Arts dealt in: around £100,000 for a thirty-minute film (later videotape) on a five-shoot. Most of the films were shot on location but the company also did have use of a 'four-wall' facility – for which they took in all their own paraphernalia, from sparks and lights to catering – at the Hanlon Studios in Acton, West London. Says Tree:

> One of the nicest things about my job was the casting. It was relatively easy to get people to do the films because of John, especially the younger comedians, and also because of Charlie – and we paid well. We were also able to be fairly flexible, which used to drive Charlie a little mad. I would say to him that if we want to get these very starry people, it was better to try and cast at the last moment when they knew they didn't have a big feature film or TV series coming up. If we told them the film was in, say, a couple of weeks' time, they were much more likely to say 'yes' than if it was planned for three months ahead. He put up with it nobly.[22]

THE SEVENTIES: DOWNSIZING 215

Figure 9.1 Crichton with director of photography Peter Middleton (left) on a Video Arts shoot

Between 1977 and 1993 (post *A Fish Called Wanda*), by which time Crichton was well into his eighties, he directed twenty-seven Video Arts titles, including client films for, among others, The Law Society ('Perishing Solicitors'), Midland Bank ('The Safety Catch') and the BBC ('Charter 88'). The training films revelled in such titles as 'More Bloody Meetings', 'The Unorganised Manager', 'If Looks Could Kill' and 'The Dreaded Appraisal'. His cast lists on the various programmes featured the likes of George Cole, Maureen Lipman, James Bolam, Caroline Quentin, Graeme Garden, Tom Bell, Richard Griffiths, Dawn French, Stephen Fry, Jennifer Saunders, Emma Thompson, Rik Mayall, Nigel Hawthorne and, of course, Cleese.

By this time, Crichton's regular props were his pipe, his whisky – or 'my special tea', as he referred to it – and the stick. The last especially sticks in the memory of his regular Video Arts cinematographer, Peter Middleton (Figure 9.1), who recalls:

> I first met Charlie on the first day of a Video Arts shoot. I asked him what he wanted for the first shot. After lining up what I thought he wanted, he looked through the camera and said, 'That's not what I want,' and I immediately felt a blow from his stick, which was to steady him after his stroke. This went on all morning. At lunch, I went to see Maggie [Tree] and told her I didn't like being treated like this. Maggie said that things would sort themselves out, and they did. Charlie and I became good friends over the years – but the stick

rarely stopped. Why did I put up with it? Over time it became a sort of running gag – and less severe!²³

Says Tree: 'I think everybody loved him. One of the nicest things about Charlie was that I never heard him say anything negative about anybody. Occasionally, if I was in trouble with someone else's film, I would speak to Charlie about it, but he would be loath ever to make a criticism.'²⁴

Notes

1 Wesley Hyatt, *Encyclopedia of Daytime Television* (Billboard Books, 1997), p. 211.
2 Lew Grade, *Still Dancing* (Collins, 1987), p. 222.
3 'Shirley's World', Nostalgia Central, https://nostalgiacentral.com/television/tv-by-decade/tv-shows-1970s/shirleys-world (accessed 11 January 2021).
4 'Dragon's Domain', *Moonbase Alpha Space: 1999* wiki, https://moonbasealpha.fandom.com/wiki/Dragon%27s_Domain (accessed 10 September 2020); 'Guardians of Piri, *Moonbase Alpha Space: 1999* wiki, https://moonbasealpha.fandom.com/wiki/Guardian_of_Piri (accessed 10 September 2020).
5 'Space Brain', *Moonbase Alpha Space: 1999* wiki, https://moonbasealpha.fandom.com/wiki/Space_Brain (accessed 10 September 2020).
6 'A Matter of Balance', *Moonbase Alpha Space: 1999* wiki, https://moonbasealpha.fandom.com/wiki/A_Matter_of_Balance (accessed 10 September 2020).
7 https://moonbasealpha.fandom.com/wiki/Moonbase_Alpha_Wiki.
8 Tim Brooks and Earle Marshe, *The Complete Directory to Prime Time Network and Cable TV Shows, 1946–Present* (Ballantine Books, 2003), p. 1107.
9 BEHP.
10 Interview with the author, 27 May 2020.
11 BEHP.
12 *Ibid.*
13 Interview with the author, 3 June 2020.
14 *Ibid.*
15 *Ibid.*
16 Interview with the author, 27 May 2020.
17 *Screen International*, 29 November 1980, p. 11.
18 Interview with the author, 27 May 2020.
19 Interview with the author, 14 May 2020.
20 BEHP.
21 Interview with the author, 14 May 2020.
22 *Ibid.*
23 Email to the author, 21 May 2020.
24 Interview with the author, 14 May 2020.

The eighties: Ealing regained   10

August 1987: less than a month after the start of shooting on *A Fish Called Wanda*, the three-ringed circus that is a film unit settles into Oxford Town Hall, a Grade II listed Victorian building, whose court room is doubling as the Old Bailey. Looking a little like an elderly judge but without a grandiose wig to cover his rather unruly white hair, Crichton, in his seventy-eighth year and perched as ever on a walking stick, is presiding over these particular proceedings with a cheerful vigour that belies his age. He tells me: 'It's only when I look at the stills and see this old man that I have sometimes thought, what an earth am I doing? Honestly, I don't feel my age though I must admit I can't jump up on to rostrums anymore.'[1]

In fact, the ever-present stick, used as much for pointing as walking, though not, one suspects, on this occasion for physically berating the cinematographer, is really the only sign of age as Crichton seems to revel in a hectic schedule that has had cast and crew bounding between locations in and around London as well as in Oxford, the latter just a ten-minute walk from his old university college. The stick is a legacy of his stroke and, subsequently, a chronic bad back, which he later jokily claimed was the result of one of his Video Arts training films some years earlier in which Cleese played 'God'. 'John struck me down for this blasphemous picture and I got this trouble with my back.'[2] To put the record straight, Cleese was actually portraying 'St Peter' giving *The Unorganised Manager* in four-related short films titled, variously, *Damnation*, *Salvation*, *Lamentations* and *Revelations*, a hard time at the gates of Heaven. But you get the point.

While Cleese is plainly, and also publicly, seen as the prime mover of this project, he is happy to be regarded rather as joint ringmaster of the events in Oxford even, on the floor, deferring generously to the man almost thirty years his senior (Figure 10.1). Cleese explains: 'I've always thought this business was seven-eighths mad. People are forever

Figure 10.1 Crichton and John Cleese on the set of *A Fish Called Wanda*

trying to discover "exciting new directors". I do not understand the advantage of youth vis-à-vis direction, It's a phenomenally difficult job. The mechanics, plot, story pace, how actors work, editing. Then, there are the actual logistics of shooting. Frankly, most "exciting young directors" don't know what they're doing.'[3]

Persuading MGM to part with several million dollars' worth of backing for *Wanda*, Cleese told Metro that Crichton was 'simply the best director I've ever worked with'. In Oxford, he continues:

> He's about the only one I've worked with who knows what he's doing. When people have the talent to start with then they know what they're doing. I don't just mean getting someone from the door to a desk. They actually know how to do it best given the context and meaning of the scene in question. In other words, they're no longer operating on logic. It's intuition, and that makes every shot that much better.[4]

As far as Crichton is concerned there seems to be 'no good reason' why there has been such a long gap between features. He offers, wryly, 'The industry seemed to be thinking more and more that as films were being geared to appeal to fifteen-year-olds, they should perhaps have fifteen-year-old directors.'[5] Crichton and Cleese are designated co-directors but, as Cleese is anxious to point out, 'I'm not really co-directing. Putting on my name as co-director is a sort of reassurance for America that shooting could go on if, say, Charlie's back got bad.'[6]

THE EIGHTIES: EALING REGAINED 219

For his part, Crichton firmly contends that Cleese is playing a crucial part behind the camera.

> I've never in my life told an actor how to say a line and so John has been working with the actors a great deal. It is his script after all. I like to think John and I have a shared sense of humour. He has a particular gift for setting up pompous dignity then puncturing it on the spot – one of the things we did so well in those early Ealing days. If he has a fault it is that he tends to see things in brilliant short sketches and so has to be brought back on to the tracks from time to time.

'Discipline,' Crichton smiles, tapping his stick, 'is what we learned at Ealing and I have had to be quite severe with him on several occasions.'[7]

You can perhaps see why, on the first day of shooting, Cleese presented Crichton with a T-shirt that was inscribed, 'Age and Treachery Will Always Overcome Youth and Skill'.

When he and Cleese first talked about making a film together, Crichton admits, 'I never really thought it would happen. John's persistence in getting this going has been quite astonishing, and it's a dream for me. Mind you, you're always terrified. I've never not been terrified, though I'm 20 years terrified on this one.'[8]

***

'What is the Crichton secret?' he was once asked, nearly thirty years before he began collaborating in 1983 with Cleese on the project that would eventually become *A Fish Called Wanda*. 'Well,' the director replied, 'I reckon a good British comedy should have a deep human touch, contain characters who are real people – the sort you meet every day – oh, and yes, be very English in outlook.'[9] On the face of it, *Wanda*, Crichton's twenty-first and final feature film, could hardly be said to have quite substantiated any of those comic criteria that were so clearly evident in Crichton's gently quirky Ealing comedies of the early fifties such as *The Lavender Hill Mob* or *The Titfield Thunderbolt*. Yet, on closer inspection, it turns out that what Cleese and Crichton will manage finally to concoct might, after all, qualify to be in the spirit of Ealing, a black comedy of skewed humanity seasoned with several pinches of the old studio's darker hues evident in the gleeful cruelty of *Kind Hearts and Coronets* and the casual cartoon violence of *The Ladykillers*, the finest hours, respectively, of Crichton's still rather more revered former colleagues, Hamer and Mackendrick.

The long haul of their eventual collaboration, which had its roots in the abortive *Rentasleuth* in the later sixties followed by some of the early Video Arts shorts in the seventies, actually began in earnest poolside in the summer of 1983 at a villa Cleese had hired in the South of France.

Crichton recalled: 'He asked my wife and I to come there and start talking about a picture. So I struggled down and lay on my back beside the swimming pool and we started to swap ideas.'[10]

A clue to what Cleese might have been mulling over at this very early stage can be found in Michael Palin's first ever diary reference, dated 25 April 1983, about a possible future film together: 'J Cleese ... says he's writing his own thing and would I play a man with a stutter.'[11] So later, by the pool, Cleese explained to Crichton that he had this idea about a character with a stutter having to impart some important information. Crichton returned the favour suggesting he would love to have a scene in which a character is run over by a steamroller. The script was off and running. A little over a year after his first diary entry on the subject, Palin wrote, on 15 June 1984, 'Cleese rings. He isn't anxious to become involved in any more films besides ... the film he's been writing for many months with Charles Crichton.'[12] That was to be his last word on the matter for another eighteen months until New Year's Day 1986, when, 'JC takes me aside and asks, almost apologetically, if I mind him writing a part for me in his next film. He says it's a four-hander. Me, Kevin Kline, John, Jamie Lee Curtis.'[13] Two months later, on 24 March, the plot thickens: 'John explains to me his new film "A Goldfish Called Wanda". I am to play a man with a stammer who kills Kevin Kline by running over him with a steamroller.'[14]

So, the two threads from that poolside chat on the Riviera in 1983 had finally been pulled together, and the quartet of eventual stars identified. Cleese had seen and admired Kline in *Sophie's Choice* (1982) and then met him while they both happened to be, separately, in Australia. Serendipitously, they later ended up sharing a condominium towards the end of 1984 when they were co-starring in the western, *Silverado* (1985), during which Cleese learned that Kline was a die-hard Python fan and, discovering that the actor also had funny bones, suggested he might write something for him.

At the turn of 1984, Cleese and his then twelve-year-old daughter Cynthia (by his first wife Connie Booth) went to see the new Eddie Murphy comedy, *Trading Places*, and he was immediately taken with the comic performance of twenty-five-year-old Jamie Lee Curtis, best known at the time as a 'scream queen' in the *Halloween* horror films. A few months on she won the BAFTA for Best Supporting Actress. When Cleese rang her home wanting to speak to her, 'I remember,' she recalled, 'thinking he was mistaken, and that he must have wanted to speak to Chris Guest [she and Guest married later that year] because *This Is Spinal Tap* had just come out.' Later, while lunching together in Hollywood, Cleese told her he was writing a film and that, 'I'd like you to do it. I promise you'll have a great time."[15] Said Crichton: 'John's a very tall man with very long arms and he gathered it together. He began talking to them [Kline and Curtis] about it and he even began to get ideas from them about the characters. Then he'd come back and we'd argue the toss and so on."[16]

Steve Abbott, formerly with Handmade Films (behind *The Life of Brian*) had worked closely with Cleese managing his business affairs since the turn of the eighties,

> It was from about 1980 or 1981 that John started talking about making a comedy film, a sort of equivalent of *Fawlty Towers* in film. Basically, he just wanted to make a very successful film. We were financing the development of the script and the film in all its forms. We flew Kevin and Jamie over, and also paid Charlie a small retainer to get his input. John was confident he could write a hit film. Certainly by 1983/84 the core of the people for *Wanda* were there.

'Then,' explained Abbott, *Wanda* suddenly went into hiatus. 'I would see John pretty much every day on the way to the office. I'd go round to his writing den and we'd do whatever business things were required. Then one day, he said to me, "Remember that film [*Wanda*]? I don't need to do it. How much have we already spent on it? Someone much cleverer than me has already written it." '[17]

He was talking about *Clockwise* (1986), scripted by Michael Frayn, about an obsessively punctual school headmaster whose plans to address an important teachers' conference are thrown into disarray by unforeseen events on a chaotic road trip. Abbott recalls still distinctly being invited with others to watch *Clockwise* when it was still in post-production. 'Afterwards we went to the Café Royal, and it was like a funeral. We knew it wasn't going to work internationally. It was a terrible debrief. The following week, he started talking about *Wanda* again. Whatever we do, he would say regularly, "There's no point making it if it won't open in Chicago; it's got to be able to play everywhere." '[18] That became his refrain. From that moment on, *Wanda* gathered pace.

Said Crichton: 'This script took bloody near four years to develop before the money was found, [but] I think that was very valuable because instead of just sitting down and bang, bang, bang, it went into one's head and was mulled over and reconsidered and reconsidered and reconsidered."[19] Just a month after Palin had noted Cleese's paraphrase of *Wanda*'s plot, he wrote in his diary on 8 April 1986: 'The root of the depression is the recurring Cleese bogey of feeling trapped ... even by the film he's writing for me, Kevin Kline, Jamie Lee Curtis, with Charles Crichton ... "Quite honestly, Mikey, if Charlie Crichton dropped dead tomorrow, I would probably abandon it."'[20] Two months later, on 25 June, Palin recorded, 'The goldfish film seems set for May/June 1987'.[21] Crichton had finally decided to put Cleese on the spot: 'I said if we don't make this film next year [1987], we will never make it at all. He said, "We're going to make it next year", so then he really got down to putting it all on paper, because all the dialogue was, of course, totally his. Then he went to America with the package.'[22]

Abbott admitted that the first time he met Crichton – on a Video Arts set – 'It was a bit of a shock. He'd had his stroke by then and was walking with a stick. He was screaming and yelling, and I remembered thinking at the time, that *Wanda* was going to be a baptism of fire for me. I had literally only met him that once before starting pre-production on the film.'[23]

Palin said:

> John had talked for quite a while about wanting to work with Charlie whom I gathered had said that he'd only do the Video Arts films as long as he and John could do a film together. So when we first met, I wasn't really quite sure about the set-up. Was John just doing this thing for Charlie; was it something that had been fabricated to get him out of an obligation. Of course, it turned out they'd been working on a heist idea for a very long time. I liked Charlie straightaway. He was different, eccentric, always very pleasant, never pushy, not full of the Hollywood banter. He seemed very much his own man. You could say, I was rather intrigued by him. Charlie was not part of the discussions John had with me until we all got together. With Charlie, we went to work fairly quickly on the rehearsal. He didn't have any fancy ideas about method acting or 'getting into the part'. It was more about 'just get on with it'.[24]

According to Abbott, Crichton's age and intermittent infirmity posed no great difficulties when the deal was struck with MGM. 'I had only ever worked before with the Pythons, but I think my naivety was our biggest strength. It was never a question of Charlie being a difficult choice; it was never an issue. This was the team [the actors plus Crichton, Abbott and Cleese as executive producers, Michael Shamberg, an experienced Hollywood 'player', as producer], take it, or leave it!'[25] The insurance people, however, did have some concerns, resulting in Cleese being, at the outset, officially designated 'co-director' with Crichton. Said Cleese: 'They seemed re-assured by this, that if Charlie dropped dead, I would then direct. Of course, I wouldn't have had a fucking clue how to direct it, and wasn't even interested in direction by and large. I would have been in deep water. So, my name was on the slate until, I think, the day we finished shooting when I then took my name off it.'[26]

With 'Goldfish' shortened to, simply, 'Fish', and a joint 'Story' credit for Crichton, the final (though not necessarily) draft of thirteen (eight minor, five major, Cleese told *Vanity Fair*) tells the story of an odd quartet – a stuffy barrister Archie Leach (Cleese, adopting Cary Grant's real name), two expat American con artists, seductive Wanda and certifiable Otto (Curtis, Kline), and a stuttering hitman, Ken Pile (Palin), brought together following a London jewel robbery in a bid to retrieve the hidden loot. It is a very deftly packaged piece of Anglo-American comic 'noir', old-fashioned on the one hand, modishly cynical on the other, a formidable challenge for a septuagenarian film-maker as amid the ensuing mayhem, both sexy and jokily violent, he also has to integrate the acting styles of British stiff upper lip with New York 'method' (Kline) and California cool (Curtis).

Palin had talked about his character with Cleese for up to a year before the cast all met for first day of rehearsals in June 1987, ahead of shooting in July. The first major read-through had been the previous November at Cleese's home. Palin said:

> My interest was that my father had a stammer. John thought there were tremendous comic possibilities for Ken, especially as he is the only one at the end who has the right information and is trying to get it out. John was anxious not to make it just a jokey '*ppp*' type thing but more psychological. Originally, I was quite concerned about the tone. When I first read the script, it seemed very hard in some ways, and some of the characters were pretty unpleasant. As soon as we rehearsed, it was wonderful. Kevin, in particular, just knew how to get the comedy out of it. So my initial reservations disappeared. I quickly got the feeling it was working. With my part, I did have problems, the extent of the stammer and so on. I probably wouldn't have made the film if my father was still alive.[27]

At the June rehearsal, Palin noted Crichton listening, 'wryly interspersing intelligent observations, always with a twinkle in the eye and a generally well-calculated aggrieved air about the way John treats him.'[28] Palin explained how Cleese wanted to be seen

> as the father of the film, but he and Charlie needed each other. John was the one who socialised with the cast, made sure everyone was happy. Charlie was quite respectful on set when John was there. It was all cloaked by a jokey relationship, often bantering rudely with each other. I never felt there was a point where it was going wrong, though I didn't, however, know how it was going to work.[29]

Shooting began in mid-July. Said Palin:

> Charlie had great respect for Kevin, and it was clear from day one that he and Jamie had their own way of approaching things. Kevin would be improvising in the corner with a prop, while Jamie was always fantastically engaged with her part, very articulate, full on.

Hollywood one side, New York the other. There was quite a lot of electricity in the room. Charlie didn't give long notes, while John was more interested in motivation. Charlie was always looking at it with an editor's eye. He kept it moving on and never let a scene become too played or over-rehearsed.[30]

Said Cleese:

> I didn't think Charlie was awfully good directing actors but was, of course, wonderful with the camera, and always knew when it was a good take. 'Do it again' was his basic direction. I was always there to help the actors. For instance, Jamie came to me at the beginning and told me she'd only done six weeks of comedy [*Trading Places*] in her life. So I directed her quite specifically, and taught her a little bit about the metronomic basis of comedy. Then, when we had the romantic scenes, she said to me, 'Now, I'm in charge.'[31]

A week after shooting started, Palin noticed that *The Lavender Hill Mob* was on at one of his local cinemas in North London, and made it in time for the 6 pm screening. 'This must be a sign,' he wrote, on 23 July, 'The film is a delight – played with great humour by basically rather nice characters. Its strengths are amiability and a good pace. I hope that Charlie will be able to inject the same into John's film.'[32]

The film's schedule was designed specifically to accommodate Crichton's age and physical well-being. Abbott explained: 'We never shot beyond 6 pm or 6.30, and never shot weekends. He had a day bed in his dressing room so [he] could have a lie-down at lunchtime. He never looked at rushes during the week. We'd get them to him on tape and he would watch them at weekends. So we really nursed him through it.'[33]

By the time Crichton was reunited on *Wanda* with cinematographer Alan Hume, with whom he had previously worked on various TV assignments in the sixties and seventies, Hume's own career had gone into overdrive, numbering, among his many big screen credits, three Bond films and *Return of the Jedi* (1983), the third in the original *Star Wars* trilogy. Hume's son, Simon, was his father's focus puller on *Wanda*. He recalled:

> My first impression of Charlie was of a rather crusty old gentleman, physically quite delicate who walked with the aid of a stick and talked with a kind of slur one inherits from a minor stroke. I never had the courage to ask. He wore spectacles and a permanent scowl. If you can imagine an old-fashioned tweed-suited granddad character in a Giles cartoon, that pretty much summed him up. His stumbling gait, however, never restricted his ability to take up a permanent position by

the main camera from where he would bark out orders to all involved. Mentally, Charlie was as sharp as a tack and would instantly pick up on misdemeanours in direction or lines. Behind the façade of the grumpy old sod, lay a warm-hearted, caring old man with a wicked sense of humour. I was often entertained by watching any challenges to his authority on set, no matter from whom, which he batted away with his quick wit and sometimes sharp tongue, which gained him huge respect from cast and crew alike. He owned the position of director.[34]

Hume, whose father died in 2010, said that Crichton's authority was complemented by the first assistant director, Jonathan Benson, 'who maintained a gentle and humorous air, relaxing any nerves, which in turn generated the best performances from all concerned'.[35] Before *Wanda*, Benson had in his capacity as an experienced first assistant dealt with everything from the excesses of Ken Russell to the lunacy of Monty Python, not to mention being part of the Oscar-winning team on *Chariots of Fire* (1981). He told me:

> I met Charlie for the first time at the beginning of filming. I thought at first that he was a bit intolerant. Then one day he apologised and said he was sorry for getting impatient and wouldn't be again. After a while, I learned to like him a lot and we became good friends, and from my point of view was the most professional director I ever worked with. He knew his job exactly.[36]

Benson, who died aged eighty-one during the preparation of this book, and Hume both remembered a 'fun' set – not necessarily always the precursor of a successful film – Hume adding, 'the experience was of working with one great big happy family'. Abbott underlined this notion by describing Cleese as 'hosting' the film: 'He had such confidence in us all, and it rubbed off on everyone.'[37]

Palin's favourite memory of Crichton during the shoot was the day he demonstrated to Tom Georgeson, playing the leader of the jewel thieves, how to deliver a tongue-twisting line. Georgeson was having some trouble uttering the tongue-twisting 'Un-be-fucking-lievable,' when Crichton suddenly leapt forward from his position by the camera and said, '"Leave it to me". He flung his stick to one side and bellowed out the line with astonishing energy. It was as if he'd become twenty years younger, just a wonderful moment, and it stopped the show.'[38] There was another, slightly less raucous, intervention by Crichton on Palin's last official day of filming at a pet cemetery in Cobham, as noted in his diary of 11 September: 'Charlie says, "As this is your last day, I am going to show you how to act" and he clambers over the gravestones with complete disregard for their occupants and the little plastic fencing that surrounds them. My last shot is me looking terribly unhappy behind a tree ... Charlie says with quite palpable sincerity, "I think you're quite a good actor".'[39]

Palin, also like others on the film, noted Crichton's penchant for whisky – galore, you might say – his 'special tea': 'He wasn't secretive about it and it never affected his work,'[40] said Palin. Recalled Abbott, 'When we were back at Twickenham Studios, he would come in [associate producer] John Comfort's office after we wrapped for the day and have this huge tumbler of Scotch.'[41] Added Cleese:

> The thing about Charlie was that he was never drunk when he was working but [on location] he was normally drunk by around 9 pm, starting with him and Jonathan Benson having a Scotch together after shooting each day. In the evenings he would get quite merry and sometimes quite truculent. He was one of those ex-public school boys who in those days would show his affection by being quite rude. It's a paradox that an English gentleman is never rude by accident. It means that if you're that class and rude to each other, you're actually fond of each other.[42]

Crichton chose as editor, John Jympson, who had more than thirty-five years' experience dating back to the days when he was an assistant cutter at Ealing, working on films like *Kind Hearts and Coronets* and, later, *The Divided Heart*. Cleese said, 'We cut the film together, then, when it was running 142 minutes, I went on holiday. When I got back it was 118 minutes; Charlie and John had taken 24 minutes out of it. I said, "Don't tell me what you've cut, let me see it first." I saw it and didn't miss anything; it was wonderful.'[43] It was when Cleese met Jympson that he first heard the 'E' word uttered in connection with *Wanda*. Said Cleese, 'I didn't know Charlie had given the script to John, who then said to me, "It's an Ealing comedy," and I yelled, "Yesss!" I hadn't thought of it before like that, but that's exactly what it was.'[44]

After shooting scenes in which in an attempt to kill an elderly lady witness the hapless hitman accidentally slaughters her three dogs instead before the old girl then dies of a heart attack as a result, or running over a man stuck in wet concrete with a steamroller or of colourfully violent dishonour among thieves, how could one not hark back to the gleefully callous *Kind Hearts and Coronets* with its eight bizarre assassinations. Or, for that matter, to the terminally internecine strife of *The Ladykillers* as the gang begin to knock each other off? Stir in some of Crichton's practised skills in puncturing pomposity, and the comparison becomes almost irresistible.

'However,' said Cleese, 'although I knew we had good stuff, we also realised there were things that didn't work, primarily the ending.'[45]

In a version of the script of 27 April 1987 entitled 'Fourth Draft for Logistical Purposes', the final credits start to roll as Archie (Cleese) and Wanda (Curtis) are seated together on board a British Airways flight ahead of take-off.

> WANDA
> Look, Archie ... I have to tell you something ...
>
> She starts to reel off a list of instances when she has misled, or lied to, or tricked, or betrayed, or double-crossed Archie. As the credits end, Wanda concludes her confession. ARCHIE looks at her for some time.
>
> ARCHIE
> Well, don't do it again.
>
> He leans towards her. She moves to embrace him, but he leans past her, picks up her hand luggage, and placed it between them. WANDA smiles. He puts his hand on hers.
>
> FIN

What they actually filmed first was darker and more inconclusive: 'A complete no-no,' said Cleese. 'Jamie and I were on the plane and the camera panned down on the last shot to Jamie's shoes that looked like a shark. That was too weak and too black.'[46] Then the test screenings, or previews, began. Test screenings, especially with comedy in order to gauge where the laughs come – or not – have been common currency ever since, it is said that Harold Lloyd first came up with the idea during the twenties. According to Cleese, there were, depending on which of his accounts you credit, 'ten', or even 'thirteen', such screenings, before invited friends and, simply, impromptu, over the next few months in Hollywood and London. Audiences were particularly uncomfortable not just with the ending but also a scene in which Kline as Otto tortures Palin (to discover the whereabouts of the stashed diamonds) by sticking chips up his nose while he, Otto, proceeds to eat Palin's pet goldfish, also called Wanda, and, not unsurprisingly, with the graphic nature of the dogs' demise.

Cleese seemed happy to take advice from all and sundry.

> I remember having dinner, for instance, with Steve Martin who gave me the most excellent set of notes I've ever had. I also showed it to Robert Towne [Oscar-winning screenwriter of *Chinatown* and, at one time, Hollywood's busiest and highest-paid script 'doctors']. He said that the scene between Jamie and me reduces the warmth between them, so we just cut it.[47]

While you suspect he may have been secretly 'harrumphing' over all this apparent editing indecision, Crichton, always loyal to a fault, 'never queried the process',[48] opined Cleese. Added Abbott: 'I certainly never witnessed John and Charlie fundamentally disagreeing, although I don't think he could quite understand what the fuss was all about.'[49] In a diary entry early in 1988, Palin noted a Wardour Street screening of the film to which Cleese had been invited along a friend in order to have a 'think tank' session afterwards: 'Charlie C abhors them, preferring to rely on professional instinct.'[50]

Crichton himself recalled:

> After we had sneak previews in America, it was quite clear the Americans didn't like the amount of cruel torture that John revels in so we had to cut some of that out, and also the end had to be adjusted because they really wanted a happy ending, Now John and I were slightly wanting a cruel-ish ending. So we had to just soften the character [Wanda] one little bit so they could get together and, possibly, live a few weeks together quite happily.[51]

The result of the process was the need for a few pick-up shots to augment, in some cases soften, existing footage, and for some crucial reshooting, notably the curious case of Kline, apparently arising from the dead, to appear unexpectedly not to say inexplicably, at the window of the plane, *Twilight Zone*-like, as Cleese and Curtis are about to fly off.

Crichton said it came about following 'a preview I think. We were sitting having dinner afterwards with John and some friends, and somebody produced this idea.' Said Palin (thirty-two years on), 'I thought it was horribly incongruous and unnecessary.'[52] Abbott declared it 'daft'. Cleese admitted it was 'ridiculous', but, for audiences, it patently worked. So just who was that 'someone' who produced the idea. In fact, it seems it was none other than Palin according to the concluding paragraph in his diary entry for 13 January 1988, during one of those 'think tank' sessions that he attended at Groucho's along with writers like Michael Frayn and Fay Weldon: 'I think the best suggestion for beefing up the ending is that Otto should appear, cement-clad, at the window ... That's my idea, so perhaps that's why I like it.'[53]

Shortly before Christmas, the team flew to New York for a screening and meetings with the top brass of MGM, including its chairman and chief executive officer, Alan Ladd Jr. Said Abbott:

> This was probably the first time I spent a prolonged time with Charlie, and my recollection was that it was his first time back in the city since the days of Hecht-Hill-Lancaster. I was with him for three days, almost 24/7. He was brilliant company. He got into trouble almost straightaway because he wanted to smoke his pipe in his hotel room on what was probably something like the thirty-third floor. Trying to open the window, the alarm went off, of course, as the hotel people were terrified of jumpers.[54]

Then there was the occasion of dinner hosted by MGM in a very smart restaurant after the screening. Abbott recalled: 'We each had a stretch limo. Charlie simply couldn't understand this and after dinner, by which time it was late evening and he had had enough, asked that his limo be sent away. "Steve," he said, "I'm walking back to the hotel." It was such wonderfully anti-Hollywood-type behaviour. John made me promise to walk with him back the block and a half.'[55]

A Fish Called Wanda opened first in the States, with a New York premiere on 7 July 1988, a Los Angeles premiere following a week later. Two days after that, Vincent Canby in the *New York Times* delivered his verdict – 'a dreadful review,' Cleese remembered, still wincing.[56] He began: 'The best thing about *A Fish Called Wanda* is the anticipation of it.' After that, it was downhill all the way. '[It] sounds great. Yet it plays like an extended lampshade joke ... It's not easy to describe the movie's accumulating dimness or to understand what went wrong. Everyone knocks himself out to be funny. The worse the material becomes, the harder the actors work for increasingly less effect.' He concludes:

> The screenplay doesn't seem to have been thought through ... The movie remains in a limbo halfway between the informed anarchy of Monty Python comedy stripped of all social and political satire, and the comparatively genteel comedy of *The Lavender Hill Mob*. When, toward the end, someone stuffs ketchup-smeared French fries into Mr. Palin's nostrils, *A Fish Called Wanda* seems to have turned into a private joke to be enjoyed only by the members of the cast and crew who made it.[57]

If Cleese, Crichton and Co. felt momentarily floored by Canby's vivisection, then they need only have switched their collective gaze instead to the likes of *Time* magazine, the *Los Angeles Times*, the *Chicago Sun-Times* – whose critic Roger Ebert had, with his television review partner Gene Siskel, also given a double thumbs-up – and *San Francisco Chronicle*, which all delivered almost unblinkingly rave reviews. After describing *Wanda* as 'the funniest movie I have seen in a long time; it goes on the list with *The Producers*, *This Is Spinal Tap*, and the early Inspector Clouseau movies,' Ebert raves on, before generously giving, perhaps of all the US critics, almost too much credit to Crichton:

> Crichton is a veteran of the legendary Ealing Studio, where he directed perhaps its best comedy, *The Lavender Hill Mob*. He understands why it is usually funnier to not say something, and let the audience know what is not being said, than to simply blurt it out and hope for a quick laugh. He is a specialist at providing his characters with venal, selfish, shameful traits and then embarrassing them. And he is a master at the humiliating moment of public unmasking, as when Cleese the barrister, in court, accidentally calls Curtis 'darling'.[58]

By the time the film opened in the UK three months later, it had been a number one box office earner for some weeks in the States and would go on to gross more than $60m in North America alone. *Wanda* was received was no less enthusiastically in the UK by audiences and critics, who might have felt a little aggrieved they had been trumped by their US counterparts and taken it out on the film.

The Times, for example, had no fewer than three excited bites at the film, beginning with Hilary Finch's appreciation following a gala screening at the Edinburgh Film Festival in late August. Finch described it as 'a notable instance of cross-fertilisation ... The torrential comic invention of Cleese is harnessed by Crichton's discipline and craftsmanship.'[59] A week before release, Geoff Brown noted:

> Despite the Britishness of the crazy humour the film is clearly angled towards the US market, and people have been flocking to see it. Crichton had a stab at America over 25 years ago – he was set to direct *The Birdman of Alcatraz* but withdrew after disagreements with Burt Lancaster. Now aged 78 he has finally conquered the country with John Cleese and a fish.[60]

Finally, on 13 October, critic David Robinson added his imprimatur:

> To the Pythons' anarchy and perception of the Alice in Wonderland surreality lurking in English life and society, Crichton adds discipline, story-telling skill and a standard of filmcraft almost extinct today. *Wanda*, boasting both form and style, is a rarity among contemporary comedies ... It is fast and elegant even in its slapstick, and although a little too long, it is streets ahead of most comedies of recent decades.[61]

Not unexpectedly, Crichton's one-time local paper, the *Liverpool Echo*, underlined Jympson's Ealing echo while also referring back to the director's 'past glories': 'It has the look of an Ealing classic eighties style ... The pair of them developed the story which Cleese then scripted. What they have created is true film farce, full of wacky characters and absurd situations. And as in farce at its best, there is a crazy logic to the goings on that the characters are not so much grasping as being swept along by.'

After the turn of the year, 1989, by which time *Wanda* had been denting the box office in a number of major markets with many more to succumb to the film's apparently overwhelming lure over the succeeding months, Palin found himself reunited with Crichton in Brussels for what he would later say provided his most enduring memory of the film-maker, now in his seventy-ninth year. They were there for a screening of *Wanda* at the city's film festival, but, on 12 January, it turned into a double celebration, as, following an interminable speech by the mayor, Crichton was presented with a special medal for his work in celebrating the Resistance, in the form of his film, *Against the Wind*, made more than forty years earlier.

Possibly bemused by all this belated fuss over a long-ago film and, said Palin, 'clearly finding the occasion tedious, Charlie was then asked to speak'.[62] In his very brief response to the award, he recalled that 'on his last trip to Brussels he had a lunch with some army parachutists which began at midday and finished around the same time the following day'. That was about it. 'Next,' said Palin,

> I remember going out on to the town hall's wonderful balcony where Charlie suddenly flicked his cigarette over the side. Like a child, and just after being honoured. We then had to do a press conference at which the foreign press seemed disinclined to ask Charlie any questions. I said that they should ask him something. Rather reluctantly they did. He gave good crisp replies which none of them could understand. I thought to myself at the time, 'You're wicked, high-risk company.' It was like being with Terry Jones when he was on form. Charlie had that lovely, mischievous attitude in his reaction to a rather pompous, formal occasion.[63]

That same month, the awards season began badly for *Wanda* at the Golden Globes, with no reward from three nominations – film, actor (Cleese), and supporting actress (Curtis), all in the comedy or musical category. It is an old saw that comedy rarely takes the big prizes, with a mere handful in history earning best film at the respective Academy Awards on either side of the Atlantic; unless, in the case of the BAFTAs, you happen to be Woody Allen who had won three.

Ahead of the forty-second BAFTAs, held at the Grosvenor House Hotel on 19 March, it looked brighter for Cleese and Co. with no fewer than nine nominations including film, original screenplay and direction. On the night, Cleese, vying with Kline, Robin Williams (*Good Morning, Vietnam*) and Michael Douglas (*Fatal Attraction*), won best actor, while Michael Palin was named best supporting actor, overhauling Peter O'Toole (*The Last Emperor*), Joss Ackland (*White Mischief*) and David Suchet (*A World Apart*).

Cleese was in Los Angeles to receive his mask, and remained an active spectre via satellite at the feast when, towards the end of the evening, Crichton became the eleventh and oldest ever recipient to date of the Michael Balcon Award for Outstanding British Contribution to Cinema (a year after the Pythons had taken the prize). Crichton tottered up to the stage with his stick to accept his award from Ben Kingsley, before, in a clear voice, declaring,

> I did not expect to be here at this moment. I am. John Cleese manipulated it so that after doing all that other stuff I eventually did *Wanda* for which I thank him very much. I have a big message for young directors who are trying to get into the business. Do not work with all those talented artists because you get on the floor in the morning, you know what you're going to do, you've got it all worked out, and then they have all sorts of ideas and you're absolutely lost. Never mind, I finished on schedule, and MGM, Michael Shamberg and various other people were quite pleased with that.

They then cut back to LA with Cleese, on a big screen, still reading out *Wanda*'s long list of credits on a tiny piece of paper. 'Finally,' he said, 'I'd like to thank Charlie Crichton again, a wonderful old man, a great director because he is an artist to his fingertips. His ego never obtrudes on the screen. You're a wonderful old man, Charlie.' To which a delighted audience could hear Crichton barking into his microphone, 'I'm not old!'

There was, surely, a delicious irony in the fact that Crichton's award was in the name of his old Ealing boss whose puritan streak would never back in the day have ever countenanced a film like *Wanda* that, despite latter-day claims for its Ealing kinship, almost wallowed in its exuberant, albeit jokey, '15'-rated sex, violence and bad language.

Ten days later, the *Wanda* team had moved on to the Shrine Auditorium in Los Angeles for the sixty-first Academy Awards, at which Crichton had been named in two categories: best film, alongside Michael Shamberg, and best original screenplay, jointly with Cleese. A third nomination was for Kevin Kline and he eventually triumphed over Alec Guinness (*Little Dorrit*) – another Ealing echo – Martin Landau (*Tucker: A Man and His Dream*) and River Phoenix (*Running on Empty*). Kline's role as the outrageous, psychopathic Otto was far and away the film's showiest while at the same time most hilariously unpredictable thanks in part to various bits of business that the actor himself devised during shooting (Figure 10.2). Having also been promised years earlier a likely comic tour de force by Cleese, he grabbed the chance with both hands and a relentlessly foul mouth to chew up and spit out the writer's sharp anti-British American barbs. But in between the colourful effing and blinding were two even more memorable, non-expletive bits of Otto; his firm belief that the London Underground was a political movement, and, much more dangerous, 'Don't call me stupid!'

THE EIGHTIES: EALING REGAINED   233

Figure 10.2 Kevin Kline menaces Michael Palin in *A Fish Called Wanda*

Kline, in gentler, more reflective mode, concluded his short, polite acceptance speech with a final thank you to Crichton, 'who proves there's no such thing as growing old when you have a dream'. A sweet sentiment until you read Palin's diary entry for 9 April: 'Kevin K. calls from Tacoma, Washington ... Kevin is funny about his Oscar speech. Apparently something about "Charlie Crichton – one man and his dream" was censored by Hollywood. He'd originally written "one man and his drink".'[64] Crichton's sudden and stunning reappearance in the mainstream of film-making after more than twenty years prompted considerable buzz from the newer generation of Hollywood movie executives some of whom, Cleese heard via a friend, enquired at a meeting, 'Who's this exciting new director?'

While he may have missed out in BAFTA's specific categories, there was some domestic consolation for Crichton at the annual *Evening Standard* film awards where *Wanda* won best film and, more personally, he was given the Peter Sellers Award for Comedy, twenty-eight years after he had worked for the one and only time with the late actor.

The film also made Crichton a comparatively rich man. According to Abbott, who had designed the deal, he 'broadly had 10% of the profits'. *Wanda* cost $7.5m and its gross, worldwide rentals were just shy of $178m ($338m in today's money). It got to number one at the box office in every major territory apart from, curiously, Portugal and Japan. It is, Abbott added, 'the gift that keeps on giving'.[65] With some of his earnings, Crichton bought a plot of land at Kirkmichael in Perthshire and had constructed a Scandi-style lodge, which he and Nadine named 'Tarka' (after the otter). Nearby was the River Ardle on which, then approaching eighty, and with his Scottish heritage reclaimed, he could continue to indulge a love of fly-fishing.

If for Crichton, at what would be a triumphant climax to his film-making career, there was ever a better moment for turning one of Cleese's funniest, most self-deprecating *Wanda* lines on its head, it was right now: 'You have no idea how awful it is being British, You have to apologise all the time.'

***

Dividing his time between Scotland and a comfortable flat in South Kensington, Crichton still had no thoughts of giving up work and continued to direct occasional client and training films for Video Arts. He was also pinning his hopes on being asked by Cleese to collaborate on what had been mooted as some sort of *Wanda*-related/sequel project – *Death Fish 2* was one of the droller titles being bandied about – reuniting the main quartet of actors. Palin's first reference to such a possibility was noted in his diary of 8 March 1991: 'A film to be about the importance of humour v bigotry and prejudice,' adding, ominously, 'not with Charlie. He [Cleese] found it heavy going with Charlie towards the end of *Wanda*, especially, JC says, in the editing stage.'[66] The start date was likely to be autumn 1992.

In the event, *Fierce Creatures*, about a giant multinational planning to turn a small English zoo into a money-making theme park replete with the eponymous beasts at the terminal expense of gentler fauna, did not begin filming until May 1995. Then following a hiatus and change of director midstream, more shooting and some reshooting was required until January 1997. The $25m 'equal', as Cleese dubbed it, to *Wanda*, proved a giant flop. Said Cleese: 'I had told Charlie I wanted to do a film with him again and this time it would be one for all the family. I think I carried on talking to him about it a few times but I soon began to see that by then he'd be too old. I remember saying that once to him and Nadine, and she was very disappointed because Charlie was at his happiest directing.'[67] Although Palin had referred to possible tensions during the editing of *Wanda*, he said later, 'I really do think John was more worried about Charlie's age. There was, after all, going to be quite a long gap between films. That certainly worried John. Maybe he rationalised it as being about the editing rather than age.'[68]

THE EIGHTIES: EALING REGAINED   235

Palin's final and, as ever, affectionate diary reference to Crichton is dated 23 June 1995 during the first part of shooting *Fierce Creatures*, in this case on a Pinewood Studios zoo set.

> Enlivened by the arrival ... of Charlie Crichton and Nadine. Charlie, his strong, long, handsome face well-tanned, looks very little different from the way he was eight years ago ... Charlie is set down in front of the leopard's cage, and various members of the old Wanda team are ushered into or a trifle shyly approach his presence, as if he were ancient royalty – a revered icon. Amanda, John's assistant, brings him a large scotch in a small, chunky glass tumbler, which he takes in his badly shaking hands. He's still the same slightly prickly, mischievous self, though. His face breaks easily into a smile, and he grips his walking stick with reassuring strength.[69]

Abbott explained how life with and around Cleese changed dramatically from 1992 after he married his third (now ex-) wife Alyce Eichelberger, an American psychotherapist. 'I think,' said Abbott, 'she had her eyes set on John's fortune and wanted to isolate him from everyone around him, from his bank manager, to his lawyer, to his agent, as well as me and the management team. She possibly saw Charlie in the same light; certainly, he and Nadine felt they had been hung out to dry by John.'[70]

The year 1992 was also the year that Crichton, at eighty-one, began his final creative collaboration, adapting for the cinema a Noel Coward play, *Hay Fever*, with Robert McKee, thirty years his junior. Detroit-born McKee had, by the turn of the nineties, become best known as a screenwriting 'guru', whose story seminars around the world attracted endless aspiring film-makers including, on four separate occasions, John Cleese. McKee, also an experienced scenarist in his own right, had been summoned to the Noel Coward Suite at the Savoy where a 'wannabe producer', one of McKee's former students, had taken up residence after raising, he claimed, some millions in seed money from the chief executive officer of a major pharmaceutical company to make a film version of *Hay Fever*. There, he met Crichton for the first time. 'How did Charlie first strike me?' said McKee, 'Sharp as a razor and like a smoking chimney – if it wasn't his pipe it was cigarettes'.[71]

What Crichton did not know was that McKee was already a huge fan of his work dating back to boyhood days in the States when,

> I saw every Ealing comedy that was ever made. By the time we met I had been doing a full-day lecture on comedy, crowned by *Wanda*.
> As a comic piece, it absolutely demonstrates every single brilliant principle of comic execution, from the bottom up. It's a brilliant satire of middle-class people trying to be criminals with a superb rom-com that

touches your heart. Wanda drives the story through the first four acts but for the fifth act, Archie takes over and drives it to the climax. In fact, I've been teaching it now for thirty years because I need an example that illustrates *every* aspect of comedy.[72]

McKee discovered that Crichton had

> basically said 'no' to directing *Hay Fever*. He didn't think it was a film. I then read it and said the same thing. Charlie, of all people, would know the difference between a homage to Coward by filming his play and a true film. It was all very well for Coward lovers to go and enjoy it, but what about all those people who don't know who he is, especially in the States.

Shades of Cleese's *Wanda* refrain, 'There's no point making it if it won't open in Chicago; it's got to be able to play everywhere.' Said McKee: 'Charlie and I connected straightaway. And we both knew why: there is no spine to the play; it's really just a collection of subplots.'[73]

Hay Fever revolves around the antics of four members of the Bliss family whose smug, self-satisfied and selfish behaviour drives away their weekend guests without, amid the familial turmoil, their even realising it. Written in 1924, it is generally regarded among the most enduring of Coward's works. Indeed, just as McKee and Crichton were having their first discussions, the play was enjoying yet another successful West End run, starring Maria Aitken, who had played Cleese's cuckolded wife, Wendy, in *Wanda*. Said McKee, 'We were asking ourselves, "Why isn't it a film", so Charlie suggested, "let's go and see it."'[74] As a result, McKee felt he could now devise from the material what he regarded as a suitable 'spine', a sort of central plot, which would make the subject more cinematic. 'If you can do that,' Crichton told him, 'I'm in.'[75] Although neither seemed to have much faith in the producing credentials of McKee's former student, their hopes principally resided with the project's co-producer, John (Lord) Brabourne, who had thirty years' worth of experience including the successful Agatha Christie film adaptations of the seventies and eighties.

So McKee, by this time living in London, and Crichton, ensconced in South Kensington when he wasn't flitting to fly fish in Perthshire, began their collaboration. Said McKee:

> I would write, submit pages and then get notes. Charlie couldn't write in a literary sense, but his judgment and his sense of what works and what doesn't as comedy was genius, so the note you'd get 90 per cent of the time was 'Not funny!' We'd also talk about the motivation of the characters, the usual story stuff. But in the end it came down to, 'Is the

scene funny? Are the action and turning points surprising? Did they give you an instant rush? Was the dialogue witty?' When I was done with the draft, people to whom I also showed it couldn't tell what was Coward and what was me.[76]

Despite some interest from actors like Albert Finney and Maggie Smith, the project finally floundered when it turned out that the supposed 'seed' money had all been frittered away, mostly, said McKee, on the Savoy lifestyle, while the ever-honourable Brabourne simply could not find enough interest elsewhere to help finance a £5m film.

During their working association, McKee would go round to Crichton's flat at around 3 pm where

> in his little sitting room, he had his chair with its back to the wall. He would have what was left of that day's bottle of scotch and then maybe a bottle of red and we'd go through what I'd done on the script. Come 6 pm or 7 pm, Nadine would call us into the kitchen where she'd cooked salmon – it was always salmon – and we'd drink some white. That was our regular routine until we felt we'd got the script down.[77]

Their get-togethers coincided with Cleese beginning active 'prep' for *Fierce Creatures*, which, according to McKee,

> Charlie assumed he would direct and, I believe, was still fully loaded to direct. Yes, he was in his eighties; and yes, he had lung cancer, which eventually killed him. He was still sharp, though, and demanding, and had taste. That's why *Wanda* was so hysterically funny. It was because Charlie wouldn't let any soft stuff get by. All he knows is, 'Not funny'. I remember asking him one day, 'How do you know it's not funny?' He replied: 'Simple. Laughter is involuntary. If what you had written was funny, I would have laughed, but I didn't laugh, so it's not funny.' Basic stuff.[78]

Steve Abbott was another regular visit to the flat in those final years:

> My career path has been blessed by luck, which included working with a director of such genius and experience. We were from different eras and there was nothing particular to bond us – for instance, I could never explain to Charlie the mysteries of football while he couldn't explain fly fishing to me – yet, as he became a bit more decrepit, a friendship blossomed as we shared our enthusiasm for cinema.[79]

Charles Crichton died, aged eighty-nine, on 14 September 1999. A fortnight or so later, in *The Times* of 1 October, Michael Palin contributed a heartfelt tribute to the film-maker under the headline 'Farewell to the Admirable Charlie'. He began: 'He was a true original, a twenty-four-carat gold character, an individual of such rich quirkiness that whenever I was with him I felt, this was what the Monty Pythons might be like when they get old.'

He recalled Crichton and Cleese's 'rather amiable father–son relationship – with John as the father and Charlie as the son' and his deceptive physical frailty. 'Charlie wielded his stick like William Wallace his claymore or Moses his rod. He'd strike the floor so hard while making a point that you expected water to spring forth.'

He noted Crichton's particular 'dislike of the formal and anything verging on the pompous was almost pathological and evidently he maintained it to the end, leaving instruction that there was to be no memorial service for him'. For Palin, 'he was always the admirable Crichton, keeping alive a spirit of youthfulness and irresponsibility way into old age. He was a man who understood and delighted in the comedy of being British.'[80]

Notes

1 Interview with the author, *The Guardian*, 5 November 1987.
2 BEHP.
3 Interview with the author, *The Guardian*, 5 November 1987.
4 *Ibid*.
5 *Ibid*.
6 *Ibid*.
7 *Ibid*.
8 *Ibid*.
9 *Uxbridge and West Drayton Gazette*, 5 March 1954.
10 BEHP.
11 Michael Palin, *Halfway to Hollywood: Diaries 1980–88* (Weidenfeld & Nicolson, 2009), p. 273.
12 *Ibid.*, p. 349.
13 *Ibid.*, p. 429.
14 *Ibid.*, p. 445.
15 Darryn King, ' "Just a Concoction of Nonsense": The Oral History of *A Fish Called Wanda*'. *Vanity Fair*, 12 July 2018.
16 BEHP.
17 Interview with the author, 26 March 2020.
18 *Ibid*.
19 BEHP.
20 Palin, *Halfway to Hollywood*, p. 448.
21 *Ibid.*, p. 462.
22 BEHP.
23 Interview with the author, 26 March 2020.
24 Interview with the author, 11 February 2020.
25 Interview with the author, 26 March 2020.
26 Interview with the author, 14 August 2019.
27 Interview with the author, 11 February 2020.

28 Palin, *Halfway to Hollywood*, p. 541.
29 Interview with the author, 11 February 2020.
30 *Ibid.*
31 Interview with the author, *The Guardian*, 5 November 1987.
32 Palin, *Halfway to Hollywood*, pp. 550–1.
33 Interview with the author, *The Guardian*, 5 November 1987.
34 Interview with the author, April 2020.
35 *Ibid.*
36 Interview with the author, 25 March 2020.
37 Interview with the author, 26 March 2020.
38 Interview with the author, 11 February 2020.
39 Palin, *Halfway to Hollywood*, p. 560.
40 Interview with the author, 11 February 2020.
41 Interview with the author, 26 March 2020.
42 Interview with the author, *The Guardian*, 5 November 1987.
43 *Ibid.*
44 *Ibid.*
45 *Ibid.*
46 *Ibid.*
47 *Ibid.*
48 *Ibid.*
49 Interview with the author, 26 March 2020.
50 Palin, *Halfway to Hollywood*, p. 587.
51 BEHP.
52 Interview with the author, 11 February 2020.
53 Palin, *Halfway to Hollywood*, p. 587.
54 Interview with the author, 26 March 2020.
55 *Ibid.*
56 Interview with the author, *The Guardian*, 5 November 1987.
57 *New York Times*, 15 July 1988.
58 *Chicago Sun-Times*, 29 July 1988.
59 *The Times*, 22 August 1988.
60 *The Times*, 8 October 1988.
61 *The Times*, 13 October 1988.
62 Interview with the author, 11 February 2020.
63 *Ibid.*
64 Michael Palin, *Travelling to Work: Diaries 1988–98* (Weidenfeld & Nicolson, 2014), p. 41.
65 Interview with the author, 26 March 2020.
66 Palin, *Travelling to Work*, p. 174.
67 Interview with the author, *The Guardian*, 5 November 1987.
68 Interview with the author, 11 February 2020.
69 Palin, *Travelling to Work*, p. 374.
70 Interview with the author, 26 March 2020.
71 Interview with the author, 20 November 2019.
72 *Ibid.*
73 *Ibid.*
74 *Ibid.*
75 *Ibid.*
76 *Ibid.*
77 *Ibid.*
78 *Ibid.*
79 Interview with the author, 26 March 2020.
80 Michael Palin, 'Farewell to the Admirable Charlie', *The Times*, 1 October 1999.

Appendix 1: An attitude to direction

The following is an essay by Charles Crichton dated December 1971. Its provenance is unknown, but it is reproduced by kind permission of the Crichton family.

The techniques of direction are simple and easily learned. How they are applied is a personal matter and, as in any other form of expression, distinguishes between the artist and the hack. Rules are made to be broken but it is only the good director who knows when to break them and why. Definitive statements trail behind them a multitude of exceptions and qualifications. Bresson may assert categorically that truth is destroyed by the use of trained actors, and in terms of his own work he must be right. As a generalisation such a statement is untenable.

My own generalisation is that paradoxically the more selfless a director may be, the more forcefully will his personality emerge on the screen. The novice director is sometimes confused by his reverence for the *cinema d'auteur* and feels that it implies a need to exercise a tyrannical control over his colleagues. But I take it that *cinema d'auteur* is a term used to describe a film dominated by the creative vision of one personality in contradistinction to the slick machine-made picture that used to come from the Hollywood factory.

This vision is not impressed upon the film by the use of strong-arm methods. Film is a gregarious medium and the director should be sensitive to the artistry of others and create for them a sense of freedom so that their talents can be fully expressed within the framework of his conception of the whole.

The importance of personal relationships becomes apparent from the very onset. The script is no more than the blueprint of a film and because he must interpret it, the director should play a part in its conception. He may of course be the sole author in which case there is no problem, or he may be working in harness with a writer. To put it crudely, who then is the boss? The question should never arise, for if each is thinking only of the final work they will find a level at which each can contribute. It may be that the director's visual sense complements the writer's ability to draw character or the director may act as a catalyst or he may simply reach a deep understanding of the writer's intentions.

Whatever the level of the collaboration, the two must achieve a mutual respect and find the temperature at which their individual contributions will fuse together. There is no room for egotism in cinema. Most writers know this and even those who have achieved renown in other spheres recognise that they must change gear, as it were, when scripting and they welcome collaboration, knowing that only a miracle can give the work importance if writer and director have not dreamed the same dreams together.

The frontiers of each man's job and the processes by which a film is brought to the floor tend to overlap. While the script is still being hammered out, the director should also be working with the art director. He should be casting and planning practical details with the production crew. Possibly his most fascinating task at this time is to research the subject in depth. If a leading character is a coal miner he must learn about mining, go down a pit, taste coal dust in his mouth, feel the grit in his eye and know what daylight looks like after a long shift underground. By examining the outward aspect of things he will come closer to inner truths.

This applies to comedy as much as it does to straight drama, for however far comedy reaches towards farce it always starts off from reality and we laugh most when we recognise the truth hidden in an absurdity. A film is a vast mosaic composed of thousands of tiny parts and each part must be true in itself and in its relationship to the whole. The more conscientiously a director works on the detail, the more each detail will enrich his understanding of the whole.

There may be directors who even before they start shooting can see the finished work in some sort of inspired flash. I am not one of them. At the very least one should be able to feel the mood, style and pace of the film and before tackling any particular scene on the floor, one should be able to hold it in the head in its entirety.

A useful exercise is to make small thumbnail sketches of every intended set-up. Some directors employ sketch artists to draw the entire film out for them and the result is displayed on the walls of an office or in a corner of the studio. I distrust this method as it means that the director has not himself gone through the process of visualising each shot. Furthermore, because the sketches are probably beautifully executed, they begin to take on a restrictive authority, they become a sort of corset stifling the talents of actors and crew and of anyone else with something creative to contribute. The sketches work best when they are 'all one's own work'. They stimulate the imagination, act as shorthand notes and etch the scene clearly in the mind. They can be kept strictly secret.

Try to get these drawings made before consultations begin with the art director. They help to pinpoint physical requirements in the set design that may not be evident from the script. The script might read 'JOHN opens the door and sees MARY climbing out of the window'. If the director wants a dramatic angle, a low set-up from behind John, using a wide-angle lens, then the relationship of door to window and the height of the window wall or the need for a ceiling piece will all affect the design of the set. On the other hand, the art director may produce a brilliant design, which will be ruined if detailed specifications are slavishly followed. Work back over the sketches, adjusting them to take advantage of what the art director has offered.

I don't suppose a director really directs in the aggressive sense of the word. He shapes and reshapes, pushes and prods, coaxes and persuades, and of course he selects.

It is to be hoped that the lighting cameraman has attended the meetings with the art director. The image that will eventually appear on the screen will take its form as much from the play of light as from set design. Thus the first contacts are made between cameraman and director and the first dialogues take place about what the picture is going to look like.

The choice of locations requires as much care as the design of the sets and preferably it should be made in the company of the cameraman and his operator. Perhaps the script mentions a specific location, such as the Tower Bridge, in which case it must be carefully studied in relation to the scene. It sometimes happens that a study of the location will suggest improvements in the action.

More often the script will call for something in vaguer terms, perhaps a beach beneath rocky cliffs, three such locations are found each with excellent though different dramatic possibilities. To choose between them is an agony. The first must be discarded because it presents overwhelming practical difficulties – it will be impossible to get a generator within reasonable distance of the site or the time taken to get crew and equipment into position will eat up a large part of the shooting day. The other two locations remain and seem equally attractive. Study each in turn, squat on them, learn their moods in different weathers and at different states of the tide. Whichever beach is chosen, the memory of the jilted one will remain to haunt and torment the mind.

APPENDIX 1: AN ATTITUDE TO DIRECTION

The first day of shooting can be frightening. One seems to be engulfed by a sea of expectant faces all waiting for the miracle, which will make the blueprint come to life. First-day nerves are understandable, but fortunately they are quickly lost in the excitement of work. It is as well to follow a routine on the floor.

Careful organisation makes for speed, and speed is important not just because it saves money but because it keeps everybody's interest at a high pitch and their work is correspondingly better. I assume that before this first day interpretation of character has been discussed with the artistes. A well-known actor once remarked that this should be unnecessary if the script were properly written but I cannot agree. Shakespeare gets reinterpreted with every passing year. The actor concerned may have been jealously guarding the freshness of his own conceptions and such protective instincts must be respected. Artistes are sometimes vain and need to be 'loved up'. They are sometimes complacent and need to be jolted. Sometimes a head-on collision is unavoidable and stimulating, but whatever happens an artiste's confidence should never be destroyed. One must tread with care for the act of creation can be a lonely and very personal affair.

I have never found that it has been much help to read the script through with the cast before starting to shoot. Readings do not allow one to probe deeply enough into the heart of the matter. Real working rehearsals, however, can bring great rewards. Usually it's impossible to hold these on the actual sets because they have not yet been built, but a large bare room where the dimensions can be chalked on the floor and a few pieces of appropriate furniture can be introduced will serve very well. The experience gained may indicate flaws in the script. It will certainly deepen the understanding between the cast and director, will enlarge their appreciation of character and theme and during the days that intervene before shooting, the subconscious will be at work sorting, analysing and creating afresh from the knowledge gained. Such rehearsals can be dangerous if the actors are pushed so far that they become stale. They should be stopped at a point when one feels that the scene still has something new to reveal.

If extensive pre-rehearsals are not possible it is good to rough out each day's work ahead with the cast, but not at first with the technicians. This does not necessarily mean sending the unit away for a cup of tea, as will be explained later. Suppose that the scene under consideration is an emotional one – a key scene that is going to tax the artistes to the utmost. To give them the best possible chance, the director may have planned an intricate pattern of moves for camera and cast that makes it possible to play the whole scene through in one long flowing set-up.

There will be three or four close-ups to be picked up afterwards. In these circumstances my own routine would be as follows:

1. Rehearse the scene without the crew. This is a time when unexpected attitudes to characterisation may crop up and it is good to be able to sort them out without the unit standing around gawping. Make sure that the artistes are happy in the moves that have been previously worked out. An actor should never feel that a move has been devised for the sake of composition. On the contrary, he must feel that the camera is there for his benefit. If an actor doesn't like a move he probably has good reason, anyway give him the benefit of the doubt and adjust the shot accordingly. An inspired conception from one of the players may require a big alteration in the design of the shot. It must be made. At this juncture, the artistes will be just walking through their parts, fitting themselves into them, measuring themselves against the other players.
2. Bring the unit on to the floor and let them watch a mechanical rehearsal. Discuss the pattern of shots and indicate how it will be broken into its component angles and the most economical order of shooting. You may see a gleam in the eye of the lighting cameraman. Find out what is exciting him. If his idea is good, grab it. These excitements are the stuff from which films are made and if you have done your preparatory work properly you can quickly incorporate them without destroying your overall conception. There should be an intuitive accord between director and camera crew. They are his eyes.
3. Mark out the first major set-up using the viewfinder only. The various positions of the actors and camera are chalked on the floor. The camera on its dolly is cumbersome and its use at this stage will only lead to delays and frustration.
4. Go away and let the unit get on with its work. The time can be well spent rehearsing the next scene in the schedule, that is to say in doing the work suggested in [point] 1.
5. When the crew is ready for you, return to the floor and run through the scene to check all the mechanics, the camera moves, lighting, focus, mike positions. Usually some adjustments will have to be made. Let the unit have whatever time it needs because, once these changes are done, the floor must be dedicated to artistes and director.
6. Now is the time for total involvement. The scene has to come to life. The actor is now so familiar with lines and moves that he no more thinks about them than a man walking considers where he will put his foot. He has all the outside trappings of the part and must now dig deeply into the emotions. Start shooting before the cast has reached its peak. Some actors never give their best until they

know the camera is running – like horses in a western who refuse to move until they hear the sound of the clapperboard. The business of bringing a number of the actors to the boil at the same time can be tricky. An artiste trained on the stage can sustain a performance but one who has worked exclusively in films tends to reach his zenith and then starts to lose his magic. Actors are sensitive to the problem and the faster worker will usually pace himself to the needs of the slower.

I do not know how anyone can direct sitting down. You cannot feel when sitting down. Standing beside the camera you can sense the harmony growing between artistes and crew, you feel the rise in temperature, the air is charged and then, suddenly, you know the miracle has happened. The scene has come to life. If the operator feels he has bungled or the cameraman looks sour or the sound man grumbles, print the take anyway. It is a hundred to one that the emotion you felt as the scene played has been captured on the celluloid and far transcends any minor mechanical defect.

7. Quickly cover any remaining angles. Presumably they will be simple static shots and can be set up directly through the camera.

This rather elaborate routine is by no means always necessary, and where it is possible to simplify it is right to do so. Artistes and crew get quickly bored and resentful if you wrap the work around with too much mystique. It may be that the director has decided that the drama of the scene will best be conveyed by carefully studied static compositions and that this need outweighs considerations of continuity in performance. Even so, the artistes must not feel that they are being pushed into unnatural positions for the sake of the camera, and it is as important as ever to rough out the whole conception before starting work on any particular set-up. The more clearly artistes and crew understand the scene, the more they will be able to contribute.

The locations and the hazards of weather or the difficulties of terrain may be the factors that govern the working method. It is no good working with deliberation in a howling blizzard – best to have a quick conference in the warmth of a car and then rush out and get the work done as quickly as possible. In any case the rigours of the weather and the speed of working can give a sharp edge to performances and for this one can be truly thankful. In exterior work chance plays the part of the gods, snatching away triumph at one moment and bestowing unlooked for bounties at another. But chance favours the director who is the best prepared and who can the most quickly adapt himself to circumstances. A scene originally visualised in brilliant sunshine may achieve added charm when played under a dripping umbrella.

I have only used improvisation when it has been forced upon me, in the kind of scene where dialogue and action depend on uncontrollable events – for instance a boat landing in a rough sea. Cover the scene with as many cameras as possible.

While it is all happening try to watch for the essential points of the scene and if there is any doubt as to whether they have registered, cover those sections again in close shot. Presumably true improvisation aims at approaching very close to reality and by forcing the players to speak and react spontaneously it attempts to probe into subconscious layers of character. I prefer to believe that the controlled creative talents of writer and artistes have more to offer.

The approach to documentary is no different in essence to the approach to a fiction film. Intensive research and preparation are essential and this is true even if the director takes the view that the material must speak for itself and that he must not allow himself to impose his own attitudes on the film.

In fact the moment the director points the camera or selects an angle he is making a conscious choice, and is therefore making a personal statement. It is best to be honest and admit that this is inevitable and right. Once this is accepted, it seems obvious the director should plan as carefully as he would for any other kind of film. He should steep himself in his subject, work out his sequences with infinite care, know the kind of angles he will use and why and he should hold in his head the pattern and rhythm of his shots.

Armed with this blueprint he can then take full advantage of the unexpected and can be as delicate as he wishes in revealing his own point of view. Such self-abnegation is not necessarily commendable. A study of the work of one of the greatest documentary directors, Robert Flaherty, shows that he patently wished his attitude to be revealed and that he must frequently have gone to great lengths to stage the action of his films.

Whatever kind of film a director makes, whether it is fiction or documentary, there should come a time when he finds that his subject has attained a will of its own and is dictating decisions to him just as authors sometimes find that their characters are writing their own dialogue. When this happens he knows that the work is good. It can only happen after long and arduous preparation. It is often said that inspiration is 90 per cent perspiration. It certainly does not come unwoved out of the empty air.

Appendix 2: Memories of a mentor

After quitting law studies and his native Argentina during the military junta, Miguel Pereira took a film course at the University of Minnesota before moving to London where he enrolled at the London International Film School (LIFS). Pereira, aged sixty-three at the time of writing this book, whose debut feature, La deuda interna (1988), *also known as* Verónico Cruz, *won prizes at Berlin and Chicago, recalls his days at the LIFS learning his craft from, among others, Charles Crichton.*

In 1982, I was graduating in the art and technique of film making at the LIFS. Almost at exactly the same moment, the armed forces of my country, Argentina, were recapturing the Malvinas. As we all know, this action started a brief but bloody war. In my case, it ended in an abrupt way one of the best periods of my life. All of a sudden, from being a happy young film student, I became an 'enemy' living in London.

In 1966, television arrived in Jujuy, the small city where I was born and raised. In between series about cowboys and policemen that kept us glued to the small screen, there was one show in particular that felt quite different from the American offerings. It was *The Avengers*, a British series, and it attracted me immensely.

At the time, I couldn't tell why the tone, the humour, the action and even the sexual tension between the two main characters, seemed different from the rest. Little did I know then, that, many years later, Charles Crichton, who directed some of the episodes, was going to become my film teacher at the LIFS, and a decisive influence on my career.

My film course in Minnesota allowed me to see a huge number of films, including many of the classics. But I also discovered something new: documentary film. The films of John Grierson and Robert Flaherty took a deep grip showing me you could tell stories with real people, in real places. But it was in my student apartment, on an old

TV set, that I discovered the BBC with its wonderful documentaries on nature, peoples of the world and ancient cultures. I was mesmerised by its programming. Another light went on. I was going to become a documentary film-maker.

With this in mind, I left for the UK, hoping to continue my film studies there, where, to my knowledge, the best documentaries in the world were produced. The LIFS was renowned for its teaching excellency and had no quota for foreign students, with many starting to flock there from around the world. For me, this was a blessing in disguise, as I could share my passion for cinema with students from every continent.

It was at the LIFS that I finally came face to face with Charles Crichton. Our school year at the LIFS was divided into terms, six of them for the full duration of the course. As it was a 'hands-on' method of teaching, we were making short films from the very beginning, using all kind of film equipment from the first to the sixth term. We started with very simple, mute, black-and-white shorts and, gradually, term after term, more complex elements were added until we finished the course with a fully-fledged 35 mm colour sync sound film.

Charles was our tutor in the fourth term, when we had to write a script for a black-and-white short fiction, shot in a studio. This was the first time that we were using a 35 mm blimp camera, as the sound was synchronised, and we were using professional actors.

As I did with all my previous films, I chose to be the lighting cameraman. I thought that I was building myself a good reputation in that area, as many students asked me to do the photography on their films. This was an excellent opportunity to practise under all light conditions as I still wanted to shoot my own documentaries. But this time, it was all about *mise en scène*, and Charles was a true master of it.

During our lessons, I started to realise that Charles not only had directed a myriad of films in his already long career, but also, to my surprise, many episodes of TV series such as *The Avengers*. There he was, standing in front of me, smoking his pipe, always humble, patient and generous with his advice. This was a director who, without him knowing it, gave me a different sense of cinema, and taught me that one could tell stories in a different way than Hollywood.

We interacted with Charles quite intensely for the three months of the fourth term. Although this seemed like a short period, I was lucky enough to strike up a warm friendship with him. Some evenings, when the school closed its doors, we used to go for a pint to the Seven Dials, a pub in the corner of Shelton Street. Obviously, we talked about cinema at length until the bartender shouted for the last calls. I was fortunate to have these chats with Charles, as I learned first-hand about his films and many anecdotes of British cinema.

There, in the noisy atmosphere of a typical English pub, we recognised in each other that, despite the difference in our age and backgrounds, we shared the same passion for making films. But then his face turned more serious and after an interminable pause, he said: 'Miguel, forget about being a lighting cameraman or a camera operator. You have seen and done many things at your young age. You have things to tell. You must become a writer and a director.'

Those words still resound in my memory.

After we finished the fourth term, our course director had to write some comments on our performances in the film that we had completed. This is what Charles had to say about me: 'A likeable character who devoted an unselfish energy to the film he was working on. His performance as lighting cameraman was no more than satisfactory and I suspect that his talents lie in the area of writing and directing rather than in photography. He is both inquisitive and perceptive and I hope he will get a chance to prove himself before his course is finished.'

Time went on and I submerged myself in the last remaining six months of the course. Charles was also busy with the new group of students in his term, so we didn't get to see each other very often. We shared the occasional coffee at the school cafeteria, and he was always pushing me to write a script for a feature film.

After the Falklands War was over, my English girlfriend, Vivien, travelled to Argentina and became my wife. We decided to return to England where I started to work as a freelance camera assistant for the BBC. When my wife, who was a nurse, had to work night shifts, I would write page after page of my first script. In my mind, I could hear Charles whispering in my ear to get on with it.

That script became *Verónico Cruz*, as it was called in the UK, my first feature as a director, and I got an invitation to screen it at the Edinburgh Film Festival in 1988. There was quite a buzz in the city about a new comedy film directed by a famous old British director, who was making his comeback after many years.

After I left my suitcase in the room, I came down to the hotel lobby to get my accreditation for the festival. The place was bubbling with guests, film critics, journalists and film buffs. A circle had formed around this man who was answering questions and chatting to everyone. I stood there looking at him as many warm memories of my old teacher came flooding back.

Charles seemed happy and in good shape, as if youth had got a new grip on him. Suddenly, he made eye contact with me, a big smile crossed his face and, raising both his arms, he shouted: 'Miguel!' Everybody turned heads looking for this 'Miguel' whom Charles was calling so effusively. My eyes clouded with tears, I walked up to him and we hugged. It was teacher and pupil again. Then, he whispered in my ear, mischievously: 'Didn't I tell you that you should write and direct?'

Filmography

As director

For Those in Peril, 1944, 77 mins, b/w

Production company: Ealing
Producer: Michael Balcon
Associate producer: S.C. Balcon
Screenplay: Harry Watt, J.O.C. Orton, T.E.B. Clarke, story by Richard Hillary
Cinematographer: Douglas Slocombe (exteriors), Ernest Palmer (interiors)
Editor: Erik Cripps
Art direction: Duncan Sutherland
Music: Gordon Jacob
Leading players: David Farrar (Murray), Ralph Michael (Rawlings), Robert Wyndham (Leverett), John Slater (Wilkie), John Batten (wireless operator), Robert Griffith (Griffiths), Peter Arne (junior officer), James Robertson Justice (operations room officer)

Painted Boats (aka Girl of the Canal), 1945, 63 mins, b/w

Production company: Ealing
Producer: Michael Balcon
Associate producer: Henry Cornelius
Screenplay: Stephen Black with Micky McCarthy; commentary by Louis MacNeice
Cinematographer: Douglas Slocombe
Editor: Leslie Allen
Art direction: Jim Morahan
Music: John Greenwood
Leading players: Jenny Laird (Mary Smith), Bill Blewitt (Pa Smith), May Hallatt (Ma Smith), Robert Griffith (Ted Stoner), Harry Fowler (Alf Stoner), James McKechnie (narrator)

252 FILMOGRAPHY

Dead of Night, 1945, 102 mins, b/w segment – 'Golfing Story'

Production company: Ealing
Producer: Michael Balcon
Associate producer: Sidney Cole, John Croydon
Screenplay: John V. Baines, Angus MacPhail; additional dialogue by T.E.B. Clarke
Cinematographer: Douglas Slocombe, Stan Pavey
Editor: Charles Hasse
Art direction: Michael Relph
Music: Georges Auric
Leading players: Basil Radford (George Parratt), Naunton Wayne (Larry Potter), Peggy Bryan (Mary Lee)

Hue and Cry, 1947, 82 mins, b/w

Production company: Ealing
Producer: Michael Balcon
Associate producer: Henry Cornelius
Screenplay: T.E.B. Clarke
Cinematographer: Douglas Slocombe
Editor: Charles Hasse
Art direction: Norman G. Arnold
Music: Georges Auric
Leading players: Harry Fowler (Joe Kirby), Frederick Piper (Mr Kirby), Vida Hope (Mrs Kirby), Douglas Barr (Alec), Jack Warner (Nightingale), Alastair Sim (Felix H. Wilkinson), Jack Lambert (Ford)

Against the Wind, 1948, 96 mins, b/w

Production company: Ealing
Producer: Michael Balcon
Associate producer: Sidney Cole
Screenplay: T.E.B. Clarke, Michael Pertwee (adaptation), Paul Vincent Carroll (additional dialogue)
Cinematographer: Lionel Banes
Editor: Alan Osbiston
Art direction: J. Elder Wills
Costume designer: Anthony Mendleson
Music: Leslie Bridgewater
Leading players: Robert Beatty (Father Philip), Simone Signoret (Michele), Jack Warner (Cronk), Gordon Jackson (Duncan), Paul Dupuis (Picquart), John Slater (Emile Meyer), James Robertson Justice (Ackerman)

Another Shore, 1948, 77 mins, b/w

Production company: Ealing
Producer: Michael Balcon
Associate producer: Ivor Montagu
Screenplay: Walter Meade
Cinematographer: Douglas Slocombe
Editor: Bernard Gribble
Art direction: Malcolm Baker-Smith
Music: Georges Auric
Leading players: Robert Beatty (Gulliver), Moira Lister (Jennifer), Stanley Holloway (Alastair), Michael Medwin (Yellow), Sheila Manahan (Nora), Irene Worth (Bucksie Vere-Brown)

Train of Events, 1949, 88 mins, b/w segment – 'The Composer'

Production company: Ealing
Producer: Michael Balcon
Associate producer: Michael Relph
Screenplay: T.E.B. Clarke
Cinematographer: Douglas Slocombe
Editor: Bernard Gribble
Art direction: Malcolm Baker-Smith
Costume designer: Anthony Mendleson
Music: Leslie Bridgewater
Leading players: Valerie Hobson (Stella), John Clements (Raymond Hillary), Irina Baronova (Irina Norozova), John Gregson (Malcolm Murray-Bruce), Gwen Cherrell (Charmian)

Dance Hall, 1950, 80 mins, b/w

Production company: Ealing
Producer: Michael Balcon
Associate producer: E.V.H. Emmett
Screenplay: E.V.H. Emmett, Diana Morgan, Alexander Mackendrick
Cinematographer: Douglas Slocombe
Editor: Seth Holt
Art direction: Norman Arnold
Costume designer: Anthony Mendleson
Leading players: Natasha Parry (Eve), Jane Hylton (Mary), Diana Dors (Carole), Petula Clark (Georgie), Donald Houston (Phil), Bonar Colleano (Alec), Douglas Barr (Peter)

The Lavender Hill Mob, 1951, 78 mins, b/w

Production company: Ealing
Producer: Michael Balcon
Associate producer: Michael Truman
Screenplay: T.E.B. Clarke
Cinematographer: Douglas Slocombe
Editor: Seth Holt
Art direction: William Kellner
Costume designer: Anthony Mendleson
Music: Georges Auric
Leading players: Alec Guinness (Holland), Stanley Holloway (Pendlebury), Sidney James (Lackery), Alfie Bass (Shorty), Marjorie Fielding (Mrs Chalk), Edie Martin (Miss Evesham)

Hunted, 1952, 84 mins, b/w

Production company: BFM/Independent Artists
Producer: Julian Wintle
Screenplay: Jack Whittingham
Cinematographer: Eric Cross
Editor: Geoffrey Muller
Art direction: Alex Vetchinsky
Music: Hubert Clifford
Leading players: Dirk Bogarde (Chris Lloyd), Jon Whiteley (Robbie), Elizabeth Sellars (Magda Lloyd), Kay Walsh (Mrs Sikes), Frederick Piper (Mr Sikes), Geoffrey Keen (Det. Inspector Deakin)

The Titfield Thunderbolt, 1953, 84 mins, colour

Production company: Ealing
Producer: Michael Truman
Screenplay: T.E.B. Clarke
Cinematographer: Douglas Slocombe
Editor: Seth Holt
Art direction: C.P. Norman
Costume design: Anthony Mendleson
Music: Georges Auric
Leading players: Stanley Holloway (Valentine), George Relph (Weech), Naunton Wayne (Blakeworth), John Gregson (Gordon), Godfrey Tearle (The Bishop), Hugh Griffith (Dan)

The Love Lottery, 1954, 89 mins, colour

Production company: Ealing
Producer: Monja Danischewsky

Screenplay: Harry Kurnitz, Monja Danischewsky (additional dialogue)
Cinematographer: Douglas Slocombe
Editor: Seth Holt
Art direction: Tom Morahan
Costume design: Anthony Mendleson
Music: Benjamin Frankel
Leading players: David Niven (Rex Allerton), Peggy Cummins (Sally), Anne Vernon (Jane) Herbert Lom (Amico), Charles Victor (Jennings), Gordon Jackson (Ralph)

The Divided Heart, 1954, 89 mins, b/w

Production company: Ealing
Producer: Michael Truman
Screenplay: Jack Whittingham, Richard Hughes
Cinematographer: Otto Heller
Editor: Peter Bezencenet
Art direction: Edward Carrick
Costume design: Anthony Mendleson
Music: Georges Auric
Leading players: Yvonne Mitchell (Sonja), Cornell Borchers (Inga), Michel Ray (Toni), Armin Dahlen (Franz), Alexander Knox (Chief Justice), Liam Redmond (First Justice), Eddie Byrne (Second Justice), Theodore Bikel (Josip)

The Man in the Sky, 1957, 87 mins, b/w

Production company: Ealing/MGM
Producer: Michael Balcon
Associate producer: Seth Holt
Screenplay: William Rose, John Eldridge
Cinematographer: Douglas Slocombe
Editor: Peter Tanner
Art direction: Jim Morahan
Music: Gerard Schurmann
Leading players: Jack Hawkins (John Mitchell), Elizabeth Sellars (Mary Mitchell), Walter Fitzgerald (Conway), John Stratton (Peter Hook), Eddie Byrne (Ashmore), Lionel Jeffries (Keith)

Law and Disorder, 1958, 76 mins, b/w

Production company: Paul Soskin Productions/British Lion
Producer: Paul Soskin
Screenplay: T.E.B. Clarke, Patrick Campbell, Vivienne Knight
Cinematographer: Ted Scaife

256 FILMOGRAPHY

Editor: Oswald Hafenrichter
Art direction: Allan Harris
Music: Humphrey Searle
Leading players: Michael Redgrave (Percy Brand), Robert Morley (Judge Sir Edward Crichton), Ronald Squire (Colonel Masters), Elizabeth Sellars (Gina Lasalle), Joan Hickson (Aunt Florence), Lionel Jeffries (Major Proudfoot), Jeremy Burnham (Colin Brand)

Floods of Fear, 1958, 84 mins, b/w

Production company: Rank Organisation
Producer: Sydney Box
Screenplay: Charles Crichton, Vivienne Knight (additional dialogue)
Cinematographer: Christopher Challis
Editor: Peter Bezencenet
Art direction: Cedric Dawe
Costume design: Joan Ellacott
Music: Alan Rawsthorne
Leading players: Howard Keel (Donavan), Anne Heywood (Elizabeth), Cyril Cusack (Peebles), Harry H. Corbett (Sharkey), John Crawford (Murphy), Eddie Byrne (Sheriff), John Phillips (Dr Matthews)

The Battle of the Sexes, 1960, 84 mins, b/w

Production company: Prometheus Film Productions
Producer: Monja Danischewsky
Screenplay: Monja Danischewsky
Cinematographer: Freddie Francis
Editor: Seth Holt
Art direction: Edward Carrick
Costume design: Vi Murray
Music: Stanley Black
Leading players: Peter Sellers (Mr Martin), Constance Cummings (Angela Barrows), Robert Morley (Robert Macpherson), Jameson Clark (Andrew Darling), Ernest Thesiger (Old Macpherson), Donald Pleasence (Irwin Hoffman), Moultrie Kelsall (Graham)

The Boy Who Stole a Million, 1960, 84 mins, b/w

Production company: Fanfare Films/George H. Brown Productions
Producer: George H. Brown
Screenplay: Niels West-Larsen, Charles Crichton, John Eldridge
Cinematographer: Douglas Slocombe
Editor: Peter Bezencenet
Art direction: Maurice Carter
Music: Tristram Cary

Leading players: Virgilio Teixeira (Miguel), Maurice Reyna (Paco), Marianne Benet (Maria), Harold Kasket (Luis), Curt Christian (Currito), Bill Nagy (Police chief), George Coulouris (Bank manager)

The Third Secret, 1964, 103 mins, b/w

Production company: Hubris Productions
Producer: Robert L. Joseph
Screenplay: Robert L. Joseph
Cinematographer: Douglas Slocombe
Editor: Frederick Wilson
Art direction: Tom Morahan
Wardrobe supervisor: John McCorry
Music: Richard Arnell
Leading players: Stephen Boyd (Alex Stedman), Jack Hawkins (Sir Frederick Belline), Richard Attenborough (Alfred Price-Gorham), Diane Cilento (Anne Tanner), Pamela Franklin (Catherine Whitset), Paul Rogers (Dr Milton Gillen)

He Who Rides a Tiger, 1965, 103 mins, b/w

Production company: British Lion/David Newman Productions
Producer: David Newman
Screenplay: Trevor Peacock
Cinematographer: John von Kotze
Editor: Jack Harris, John N. Smith
Art direction: Seamus Flannery, Richard Harrison
Costume design: Joanna Wright
Music: Alexander Faris
Leading Players: Tom Bell (Peter Rayston), Judi Dench (Joanne), Paul Rogers (Supt Taylor), Kay Walsh (Mrs Woodley), Jeremy Spenser (The Panda)

A Fish Called Wanda, 1988, 108 mins, colour

Production company: MGM/Michael Shamberg Productions/Prominent Features/Star Partners Limited Partnership
Producer: Michael Shamberg
Screenplay: John Cleese, Charles Crichton
Cinematographer: Alan Hume
Editor: John Jympson
Art direction: Roger Murray-Leach
Costume design: Hazel Pethig
Music: John Du Prez
Leading players: John Cleese (Archie Leach), Jamie Lee Curtis (Wanda Gershwitz), Kevin Kline (Otto), Michael Palin (Ken Pile), Maria Aitken (Wendy), Tom Georgeson (Georges Thomason)

As assistant editor/editor

For Korda

Wedding Rehearsal (1933, assistant editor)
Men of Tomorrow (1933, assistant editor)
Cash (1933, assistant editor)
The Girl from Maxim's (1933, assistant editor)
The Private Life of Henry VIII (1933, assistant editor)
Sanders of the River (1935, editor)
Things to Come (1936, co-editor)
Elephant Boy (1937, editor)
21 Days (1940, editor)
Prison Without Bars (1938, editor)
The Thief of Bagdad (1940, editor)
Old Bill and Son (1941, editor)

For Ealing, as editor

Young Veteran (1940, short)
Yellow Caesar (1941, short)
Guests of Honour (1941, short)
Find, Fix and Strike (1942, short)
The Big Blockade (1942)
Greek Testament (1943, short)

As associate producer

Nine Men (1943)

Television credits (as director)

The Wild Duck (ITV Play of the Week)	1957
Man of the World (ITV – three episodes)	1962–63
Danger Man (ITV – two episodes)	1964
The Human Jungle (ITV – one episode)	1964
Man in a Suitcase (ITV – six episodes)	1967–68
The Avengers (ITV – five episodes)	1965–69
Strange Report (ITV – five episodes)	1969
Here Come the Double Deckers (BBC – one episode)	1970
Shirley's World (ITV – one episode)	1971
The Adventures of Black Beauty (ITV – eighteen episodes)	1972–74

The Protectors (ITV – five episodes)   1973–74
Space: 1999 (ITV – fourteen episodes)   1975–76
The Professionals (ITV – one episode)   1978
Return of the Saint (ITV – two episodes)   1978–79
Dick Turpin (ITV – ten episodes)   1979–82
Smuggler (ITV – three episodes)   1981

Video Arts (as director)

Commissioned/client programmes/release dates

TV Times
Truth and Logic   November 1977
Hip Hip Hooray   June 1979

Law Society   November 1982
Perishing Solicitors

Schulenburg Technical Services   June 1984
Goddamn Schlumberger

Midland Bank   October 1990
The Safety Catch

NCR Corporation   July 1991
Stuck on Quality

Charter 88 BBC   1994
One of six episodes

Training programmes/release dates

The Unorganised Manager   March 1983
Part 1: Damnation
Part 2: Salvation

Success at Selling   October 1983
Part 3: Difficult Customers

More Bloody Meetings   March 1984

260 FILMOGRAPHY

Success at Selling   September 1984
Part 4: Closing the Sale

The Unorganised Manager   July 1985
Part 3: Lamentations
Part 4: Revelations

If Looks Could Kill   February 1986
(The Power of Behaviour)

Managing Problem People   August 1988
Rule-Bound Reggie
Big-Mouth Billy
Moaning Minnie
Wimpey Wendy
Lazy Linda
Silent Sam   October 1988

An Inside Job   May 1990
(The Internal Customer)

The Dreaded Appraisal   October 1990

The Paper Chase   December 1991
Cutting Back the Paperwork

The Best of Motives   1993

Selected bibliography

This bibliography is by no means a complete record of all the works and sources consulted during the writing of this book. It is intended to serve as a resource for readers who wish to pursue further study of the life and works of Charles Crichton.

Aldgate, Anthony and Richards, Jeffrey, *Britain Can Take It*, Basil Blackwell, 1986.
Annakin, Ken, *So You Wanna Be a Director?*, Tomahawk Press, 2001.
Balcon, Michael, *Michael Balcon Presents a Lifetime of Films*, Hutchinson, 1969.
Baker, Roy Ward, *The Director's Cut*, Reynolds & Hearn, 2000.
Barr, Charles, *Ealing Studios*, Studio Vista, 1993.
Bogarde, Dirk, *Snakes and Ladders*, Chatto & Windus, 1978.
Box, Betty, *Lifting the Lid*, Book Guild, 2000.
Branaghan, Sim, *British Film Posters: An Illustrated History*, BFI, 2006.
Brooks, Tim and Marshe, Earle, *The Complete Directory to Primetime Network and Cable TV Shows*, 8th ed., Ballantine Books, 2003.
Brown, Geoff and Kardish, Laurence with Puttnam, David and Mancia, Adrienne, *Michael Balcon: The Pursuit of British Cinema*, Museum of Modern Art, 1984.
Buford, Kate, *Burt Lancaster: An American Life*, Aurum Press, 2008.
Cardiff, Jack, *Magic Hour*, Faber & Faber, 1996.
Clark, Jim with Myers, John H., *Dream Repairman*, Landmarc, 2010.
Clarke, T.E.B., *This Is Where I Came In*, Michael Joseph, 1974.
Cleese, John, *So Anyway*, Arrow Books, 2014.
Cohen, J.M. and Cohen, M.J., *The Penguin Dictionary of Quotations*, Penguin, 1960.
Coldstream, John, *Dirk Bogarde*, Phoenix, 2004.
Cooper, Nick, *The Shaping of Things to Come*, Network, 2007.
Cushnan, Joe, *Stephen Boyd: From Belfast to Hollywood*, Feedaread.com, 2012.
Danischewsky, Monja, *White Russian – Red Face*, Gollancz, 1966.
Dean, Basil, *Mind's Eye*, Hutchinson, 1973.
Drazin, Charles, *The Finest Years: British Cinema of the 1940s*, André Deutsch, 1998.

SELECTED BIBLIOGRAPHY

Drazin, Charles, *Korda: Britain's Movie Mogul*, I.B. Tauris, 2011.
Duffell, Peter, *Playing Piano in a Brothel*, BearManor Media, 2011.
Duguid, Mark, Freeman, Lee, Johnston, Keith M. and Williams, Melanie (eds), *Ealing Revisited*, BFI, 2012.
Falk, Quentin, *The Golden Gong*, Columbus Books, 1987.
Falk, Quentin, *Travels in Greeneland: The Cinema of Graham Greene*, UPNG, 2014.
Francis, Freddie with Dalton, Tony, *The Straight Story from Moby Dick to Glory*, Scarecrow Press, 2013.
Gifford, Denis, *British Cinema*, Zwemmer, 1968.
Gifford, Denis, *The British Film Catalogue, 1895–1985*, David & Charles, 1986.
Grade, Lew, *Still Dancing*, Collins, 1987.
Greene, Graham, *The Pleasure Dome: The Collected Film Criticism 1935–40*, Secker & Warburg, 1975.
Guinness, Alec, *Blessings in Disguise*, Fontana/Collins, 1986.
Guinness, Alec, *My Name Escapes Me: The Diary of a Retiring Actor*, Hamish Hamilton, 1996.
Hardy, Phil (ed.), *Horror*, Aurum Press, 1985.
Harper, Sue and Porter, Vincent, *British Cinema of the 1950s: The Decline of Deference*, Oxford University Press, 2003.
Hawkins, Jack, *Anything for a Quiet Life*, Coronet, 1973.
Hawkins, John and Hawkins, Ward, *The Floods of Fear*, Eyre & Spottiswoode, 1957.
Hetherington, S.J. and Brownrigg, Mark, *Muir Mathieson: A Life in Film Music*, Scottish Cultural Press, 2006.
Hinxman, Margaret and D'Arcy, Sue, *The Films of Dirk Bogarde*, Literary Service & Production, 1974.
Holden, Anthony, *The Secret History of Hollywood's Academy Awards*, Little, Brown, 1993.
Holloway, Stanley, *Wiv a Little Bit O' Luck*, Leslie Frewin, 1967.
Hyatt, Wesley, *The Encyclopedia of Daytime Television*, Billboard Books, 1997.
Keel, Howard with Spizer, Joyce, *Only Make Believe: My Life in Showbusiness*, Barricade Books, 2005.
Kemp, Philip, *Lethal Innocence: The Cinema of Alexander Mackendrick*, Methuen, 1991.
Korda, Michael, *Charmed Lives*, Random House, 1979.
Lejeune, C.A., *Thank You for Having Me*, Tom Stacy, 1964.
Lewis, Roger, *The Life and Death of Peter Sellers*, Applause, 1997.
Lord, Graham, *Niv: The Authorised Biography of David Niven*, CB Creative Books, 2013.
McFarlane, Brian, *An Autobiography of British Cinema*, Methuen, 1997.
McFarlane, Brian, *The Encyclopedia of British Film*, Methuen, 2003.
McFarlane, Brian, *Real and Reel*, Manchester University Press, 2012.
Mackendrick, Alexander, *On Film-Making*, Faber & Faber, 2004.
Mackenzie, S.P., *British War Films 1939–1945*, Hambledon & London, 2001.
Miller, John, *Judi Dench: With a Crack in Her Voice*, Orion, 2004.

SELECTED BIBLIOGRAPHY 263

Mitchell, Yvonne, *Actress*, Routledge & Kegan Paul, 1957.
Murphy, Robert, *British Cinema and The Second World War*, Continuum, 2000.
Murphy, Robert (ed.), *Directors in British and Irish Cinema*, BFI, 2006.
Murphy, Robert, *The Third Secret: A Startling Journey into 'A World of Nightmare'*, Indicator, 2019.
Neame, Ronald with Cooper, Barbara Roisman, *Straight from the Horse's Mouth*, Scarecrow Press, 2003.
Newman, David, *Three Men Went to War*, New English Library, 1978.
Norman, Barry, *And Why Not? Memoirs of a Film Lover*, Pocket Books, 2003.
Palin, Michael, *Halfway to Hollywood: Diaries 1980–88*, Weidenfeld & Nicholson, 2009.
Palin, Michael, *Travelling to Work: Diaries 1988–98*, Weidenfeld & Nicholson, 2014.
Pendreigh, Brian, *On Location: The Film Fan's Guide to Britain and Ireland*, Mainstream, 1995.
Perry, George, *Forever Ealing*, Pavilion, 1981.
Petrie, Duncan, *Bryanston Films: An Experiment in Cooperative Independent Film Production and Distribution*, Routledge, 2017.
Powell, Michael, *A Life in Movies*, Faber & Faber, 1986.
Richardson, Michael, *Bowler Hats and Kinky Boots*, Telos, 2014.
Rotha, Paul, *Robert J. Flaherty: A Biography*, University of Pennsylvania Press, 1983.
Scott, Peter, *Gentleman Thief: Recollections of a Cat Burglar*, HarperCollins, 1995.
Sellers, Robert, *The Secret Life of Ealing Studios*, Aurum Press, 2015.
Sikov, Ed, *Mr Strangelove: A Biography of Peter Sellers*, Sidgwick & Jackson, 2011.
Silverman, Stephen M., *The Fox That Got Away: The Last Days of the Zanuck Dynasty at 20th Century Fox*, Lyle Stuart, 1988.
Spicer, Andrew, *Sydney Box*, Manchester University Press, 2006.
Sutherland, Jon and Canwell, Diane, *The RAF Air Sea Rescue Service 1918–1986*, Pen & Sword, 2010.
Sutton, Paul, *Six English Filmmakers*, Buffalo Books, 2014.
Sykes, Christopher, *Evelyn Waugh*, Collins, 1975.
Thomas, Nicholas (ed.), *International Directory of Films and Filmmakers: Films*, St James Press, 1990.
Tynan, Kathleen, *The Life of Kenneth Tynan*, Methuen, 1987.
van Gelder, Peter, *That's Hollywood*, HarperCollins, 1990.
Warner, Jack, *Jack of All Trades*, W.H. Allen, 1975.
Warren, Patricia, *British Film Studios: An Illustrated History*, Batsford, 2001.
Winnington, Richard, *Film Criticism and Caricatures 1943–1953*, Elek Books, 1975.
Wood, Linda, *British Films 1927–1939*, BFI, 1986.
Wright, Basil, *The Long View*, Paladin, 1976.

Index

20th Century Fox 173
21 Days 25–7

Abbott, Steve 221, 222, 224, 225, 226, 227, 228, 233, 235, 237
ABPC Elstree 145, 183
Academy Awards 14, 99, 231, 232
Adventures of Black Beauty, The 4, 207–9
Against the Wind 3, 66–73, 77, 82, 109, 128, 231
Agate, James 56
Aitken, Maria 236
Aked, Muriel 77
Allder, Nick 205
Allegret, Marc 28
Amalgamated Studios 143
Anderson, Gerry 204
Anholt, Tony 204
Annakin, Ken 148
Another Shore 74–8, 82, 111
Anstey, Edgar 42
Arnell, Richard 180
Asquith, Anthony 9, 52
Associated-Rediffusion 141, 157
Astley, Edwin 181
Attenborough, Richard 174, 180
Auric, Georges 61, 130, 132
Avengers, The 4, 192–6, 247

Bain, Barbara 205
Balcon, Sir Michael 3, 12, 35, 40, 43, 57, 59, 63, 78, 79, 85, 93, 101, 120, 121, 122, 125, 134, 135, 157, 166, 170
Balcon, S.C. 46
Banes, Lionel 46, 72, 151, 196, 252
Banks, Leslie 16, 26
Barker, Felix 190
Baronova, Irina 80
Barr, Charles 40, 42, 60, 66, 101, 115, 130, 133, 157, 158, 164
Barr, Douglas 62, 86
Barry, Christopher 121
Bass, Alfie 97
Battle of the Sexes, The 4, 157–65
BBC 135, 202
BBFC 151
Beatty, Robert 68, 72, 75, 77, 88
Bell, Monta 23
Bell, Tom 187, 190, 191
Bells Go Down, The 43
Benjamin, Christopher 210
Bennett, Compton 37, 40, 147
Benson, Jonathan 225
Berger, Ludwig 28, 29
Bernstein, Shirley 178
Betts, Ernest 152
Bezencenet, Peter 148
Big Blockade, The 38, 39, 40
Birdman of Alcatraz, The 155–7, 172
Birkin, Andrew 178
Biro, Lajos 16, 20
Black, Stephen 50
Blewitt, Bill viii, 42, 49, 50, 251
Bliss, Sir Arthur 22

Blue Lamp, The 69, 92
Bogarde, Dirk 101, 104, 105, 107
Borchers, Cornell 126, 133
Borradaile, Osmond 23, 29
Botting, Josephine 119, 121
Boulting Brothers, the 136, 142, 143
Bowker, Judi 208
Box, Sydney 147, 148
Boy Who Stole a Million, The 108, 165–71
Boyd, Stephen 173, 180
Brabourne, Lord John 236
Bradford, Richard 196, 197
Brandt, Bill 81
Bridge, Joan 113
Bridgewater, Leslie 81
British Academy Film Awards (BAFTAs) 99, 133, 137, 138, 231, 232
British & Dominions (B & D) Studios 11
British Lion 100, 136, 142, 144, 157, 165
Brook, Clive 25
Brown, Geoff 230
Brown, George H. 166, 170
Browning, 'Kits' 176
Bruce, Keith 162
Bryan, Peggy 54
Bryanston Films 157, 165, 166, 170
Buford, Kate 156
Burnham, Jeremy 144, 195, 256
Buss, Robin 72
Butler, Lawrence 29
Byrne, Eddie 126, 139, 150, 255, 256
Byrne, Johnny 206

Caine, Sir Michael 209
Campbell, Patrick 144
Camps, Dr Francis 199
Canby, Vincent 191, 229
Captive Heart, The 63, 67
Carmichael, Ian 136
Carpenter, Freddie 119
Carpenter, Richard 209, 210
Carrick, Edward 159

Carroll, Paul Vincent 68
Cash 12
Catbird Seat, The 154, 155
Cavalcade 14
Cavalcanti 1, 5, 35, 36, 42, 43, 54, 57, 59, 60, 71, 81
Challis, Christopher 148, 151
Chapman, Graham 200
Chesterton, G.K. 22
Churchill, Winston 21, 30, 109
Cilento, Diane 174, 180
Clair, René, 5, 9, 13, 52, 61
Clark, Jim 201
Clark, Petula 86, 89
Clarke, T.E.B. 43, 54, 61, 64, 67, 81, 92, 96, 99, 109, 110, 135, 143, 154, 203
Cleese, John 2, 200, 213, 214, 217, 218, 219, 222, 224, 226, 227, 229, 231, 233, 234, 238
Clemens, Brian 192, 193, 194, 195
Clements, John 80, 141
Clockwise 221
Cole, Sidney 41, 54, 70, 72, 79, 80, 108, 181, 182, 196, 207, 209, 212
Colleano, Bonar 88
Collier, John 23
Cooper, Nick 20, 21
Cornelius, Henry 60, 65, 143, 251, 252
Counsel's Opinion 12
Coxhead, Elizabeth 116
Crichton, David 28, 35, 174
Crichton, Hester 5, 8
Crichton, John Douglas 8
Crichton, Nadine 171, 234, 235, 237
Crichton, Nicholas 47
Crichton, Patrick 5
Crichton, Pearl 24, 28, 35, 171
Crown Film Unit 35, 41
Crowther, Bosley 100
Croydon, John 170
Cruel Sea, The 67, 109
Cummings, Constance 158, 164
Cummins, Peggy 118, 121
Curtis, Jamie Lee 220, 221, 223
Cusack, Cyril 149

266 INDEX

Dahlen, Armin 126
Daker, David 210
Dalrymple, Ian 31
Dance Hall 4, 85–92, 97, 106
Danger Man 4, 181–2
Danischewsky, Monja 44, 78, 118, 120, 157, 158, 159
Dark, Gregory 210, 211
Davis, Sir John 67, 134
Dead of Night 53–7, 79, 119
Dean, Basil 25, 26
Dearden, Basil 1, 40, 43, 79
Deeks, Michael 210
Dell, Jeffrey 16, 17
Dench, Dame Judi 174, 175, 176, 188, 191
Denham Film Studios 2, 7, 13, 20, 23, 28, 30, 32, 36
Dent, Alan 99, 131, 140
Dent, Reg 208
Dick Turpin 209–11
Dickinson, Thorold 43
Dighton, John 43, 74
Distilling Whisky Galore 79
Divided Heart, The 3, 5, 124–35, 226
Donat, Robert 9, 12
Dorning, Stacy 209
Dors, Diana 86
Dowling, Joan 64
Drazin, Charles 12
Drifters 9
Duffell, Peter 197, 208
Duguid, Mark 37, 114
Dunlop, Lesley 212

Ealing Studios 1, 36, 40, 42, 57, 81, 91, 100, 141
Ebert, Roger 2, 229
Edinburgh Film Festival 230, 249
Eldridge, John 92, 108, 137, 167
Elephant Boy 7, 15, 22–5
Emmett, E.V.H. 86

Farrar, David 45, 48
Fawlty Towers 221

Fenton, Lynn 191
Fierce Creatures 234, 237
Film Society, the 9, 74
Finch, Hilary 230
Finch, Peter 149
Find, Fix and Strike 37, 41
First Love 155
Firth, Peter 202
Fish Called Wanda, A 1, 2, 5, 196, 201, 213, 217–34
Flaherty, Robert 7, 22
Floods of Fear 4, 147–52
Foot, Michael 36
For Those in Peril 43–8
Foreman Went to France, The 38
Fowler, Harry 51, 62, 64
Francis, Freddie 164, 208
Frank, Nino 101
Franklin, Pamela 174, 178, 199
Freeman, Lee 67
Freiberger, Fred 206
French, Sir Henry 121
French, Philip 56
Frend, Charles 3, 38, 39, 54, 157
Frost, David 200

Galsworthy, John 25
Garas, Kaz 198
Gatetarn Productions 209, 212
Gaumont-British 12, 43
Gentle Sex, The 53
Georgeson, Tom 225
Ghost Goes West, The 13
Gibbs, Gerald 199
Gilmore, Eddy 172
Girl From Maxim's, The 12
Golden Globes 231
Golden Laurel Award 134
Goldhawk Studios 190
Gone With the Wind 30
GPO Film Unit 35
Grade, Lord Lew 171, 196, 203, 204
Graham, Morland 31
Grant, Elspeth 152, 162, 163, 170
Greatorex, Wilfred 182

INDEX   267

Greek Testament 37
Green Grow the Rushes 100
Greene, Graham 24, 26, 32, 76, 161
Gregson, John 110, 203
Grierson, John 5, 9, 35, 108
Griffith, Hugh 110
Griffith, Robert 49
Group 3 108, 137
Gruner, Anthony 207
Guests of Honour 37
Guinness, Sir Alec 94, 96, 99, 101, 117, 138, 163
Gulston, Peter 185
Gwenn, Edmund 12

Halfway House, The 44, 53
Hall, Mordaunt 13
Hallatt, May 51, 53
Hamer, Robert 1, 40, 54, 65, 76, 81, 89, 219
Hardwicke, Sir Cedric 21
Harman, Jympson 133, 162
Harper, Sue 114, 134, 143
Harrison, Stephen 12
Hasse, Charles 37
Hatherley, Frank 208
Hawkins, Jack 135, 137, 138, 140, 174, 177, 180
Hay Fever 235–7
He Who Rides a Tiger 4, 213
Hecht, Harold 154, 155, 156
Hecht-Hill-Lancaster 154, 228
Heller, Otto 126
Hendry, Ian 212
Henson, Gladys 90
Hepburn, Audrey 97, 149
Here Come the Double Deckers 202–3
Heywood, Anne 149
Hickson, Joan 144, 182, 256
Higgins, Ken 208
Hillary, Richard 43
Hobson, Valerie 80
Holloway, Stanley 75, 77, 94, 110
Holt, Paul 120

Holt, Seth 136, 159, 176, 253, 254, 255, 256
Hornbeck, William 15, 16, 23, 30, 36
Houston, Donald 87
Hudd, Walter 23
Hue and Cry 1, 60–6, 67, 85, 98, 105, 202
Hughes, Richard 109, 125
Human Jungle, The 182–3
Hume, Alan 194, 195, 203, 224, 257
Hume, Simon 224
Hunt, Gareth 205
Hunted 4, 101–8
Hylton, Jane 86

Illing, Peter 68
ITC Productions 171, 204

Jackson, Gordon 42, 68, 70, 71, 128, 210, 252, 255
James, Sidney 97, 110
Jay, Anthony 213
Jeayes, Allan 23
Jenkins, Megs 139
Johnson, Brian 205
Johnston, Dr Keith 49, 53
Joseph, Robert L. 172, 179, 180
Justice, James Robertson 68
Jympson, John 226, 230

Kalmus, Natalie 30
Keel, Howard 149, 151
Keen, Geoffrey 126
Kellino, Roy 46
Kelsall, Moultrie 102, 158, 256
Kemp, Philip 1, 74, 79, 85, 89
Kersh, Gerald 41
Kind Hearts and Coronets 3, 65, 76, 115, 219
King, Denis 209
Kipling, Rudyard 22
Kline, Kevin 220, 221, 223, 232
Knight, Paul 207, 209, 210, 211, 212, 213

Knight, Vivienne 136, 148, 255, 256
Korda, Sir Alexander 2, 7, 10, 19, 25, 29, 30, 32
Korda, Michael 16, 22, 23, 31
Korda, Vincent 12, 15, 28, 29, 31, 33
Korda, Zoltan 11, 15, 17, 30, 33
Kruse, John 183
Kulik, Karol 10, 11, 12, 16, 17, 27, 31, 32
Kurnitz, Harry 118

Ladykillers, The 3, 65, 98, 219
Laird, Jenny 49, 53, 251
Lancaster, Burt 154, 156
Landau, Martin 205, 206
Lane, Anthony 163
Langhammer, Dr Claire 90
Laughton, Charles 13
Lavender Hill Mob, The 1, 85, 92–101, 107, 196, 200, 219, 224
Law and Disorder 4, 142–7, 182
Laxdale Hall 108
Le Million 9
Lee, Bernard 183
Lee, Christopher 195
Leicester Square Theatre 17, 21
Leigh, Vivien 26
Lejeune, C.A. 99, 106, 120, 140
Leonard, Sheldon 203
Les Enfants du Paradis 91
Linklater, Eric 108
Lister, Moira 75
Locarno International Film Festival 107
Lockhart, Freda Bruce 91
Lom, Herbert 119, 183
London Films 10, 13
London International Film School 5, 180, 247
London Weekend Television 209
Lord, Graham 115
Love Lottery, The 115–22
Lucas, George 207
Lucas, William 208, 209
Luchaire, Corinne 27

Lucky Jim 136
Lyon, Francis 15

McCarthy, Michael 50, 102
McGahan, Katy 36
McGoohan, Patrick 181, 182
McKechnie, James 50
McKee, Robert xi, 5, 235, 236, 237
Mackendrick, Alexander 1, 40, 65, 74, 78, 86, 89, 219
Mackenzie, Sir Compton 78
Mackenzie, Paul 41
McKinney, Nina Mae 17
MacLaine, Shirley 202, 203
Macnee, Patrick 192, 193
MacNeice, Louis 50
MacPhail, Angus 43, 78, 81
Majdalany, Fred 98
Major and The Private, The 156
Man in a Suitcase 196–8
Man in the Sky, The 108, 135–41
Man in the White Suit, The 3, 65, 99
Man of the World 171
Man Who Could Work Miracles, The 7
Mann, Ned 20
Marshall, Roger 194
Martin, Edie 97, 110
Martin, Vivienne 144
Marylebone Studios 188, 190
Massey, Raymond 20
Mathieson, Muir 28, 148
Maxted, Stanley 119
Meade, Walter 74
Mellor, Roger Philip 91
Men of Tomorrow 10–11, 258
Menzies, William Cameron 20, 29
Merseyside Film Institute 92, 96
MGM ix, 26, 35, 135, 140, 173, 181, 218, 222, 228, 229, 232, 255, 257
MGM British Studios 135
Michael Balcon Award, the 231
Michael, Ralph viii, 46, 188, 251
Middleton, Peter 215

INDEX 269

Millar, Sir Ronald 81
Millions Like Us 53
Mills, John 31
Mitchell, Yvonne 127, 129, 132, 133, 134
Moholy-Nagy, Laszlo 20
Montagu, Ivor 74
Morgan, Diana 86, 89
Morley, Robert 144, 145, 146, 158, 160, 164
Morse, Barry 205
Mosley, Leonard 73
Mousehole 8, 49
Murphy, Professor Robert 71, 141, 175, 179

Neal, Patricia 174
New College, Oxford 8
Newley, Anthony 86
Newman, David 187, 188, 190
Newton, Robert 26
Next of Kin 43
Nine Men 41–3
Niven, David 115, 117, 120, 121

O'Connor, John J. 205
O'Sullivan, Richard 210
O'Sullivan, Tim 114
Oberon, Merle 10
Ockwells Manor 210
Old Bill and Son 31
Olivier, Sir Laurence 26, 32
Orton, J.O.C. 43
Oundle 8
Overlanders, The 78
Owen, Frank 36

Painted Boats 48–53, 61, 102
Palin, Sir Michael 2, 220, 221, 222, 223, 225, 230, 231, 235, 237
Parry, Natasha 86, 87
Passport to Pimlico 115
Peacock, Trevor 186, 187, 189, 191
Penfold, Christopher 205
Pereira, Miguel 5, 247–50

Périnal, Georges 13, 29, 31
Perry, George 85, 115, 130, 135
Pertwee, Michael 68
Peter Sellers Award for Comedy, the 233
Petrie, Professor Duncan 161, 165, 170
Pinewood Studios 28, 79, 105, 135, 147, 169, 196, 205, 235
Piper, Frederick 42, 188
Pitt, Ray 37
Pool of London 92
Porter, Nyree Dawn 204
Porter, Vincent 114, 134, 143
Powell, Dilys 133
Powell, Michael 13, 29, 87
Priggen, Norman 159
Prison Without Bars 27
Private Life of Henry VIII, The 10, 12–14, 28
Protectors, The 204
Prudential Assurance Company 13
Psycho 172
Pulver, Andrew 136

Quayle, Anna 194
Quayle, Sir Anthony 198, 199

Radford, Basil 54, 55
Rank Organisation 28, 60, 67, 82, 149
Rattigan, Terence 52
Rawsthorne, Alan 148
Ray, Michel 127, 129, 131, 134
Reddin, Kenneth 74
Redgrave, Sir Michael 40, 144
Relph, George 110, 141
Relph, Michael 110
Rentadick 201
Rentasleuth 200–1, 213, 219
Reyna, Maurice 166, 168–70
Richards, Dick 152, 191
Richardson, Michael 193, 194, 195, 197
Richardson, Sir Ralph 20

Rigg, Diana 192
Roberts, Andrew 67
Roberts, Denys 144
Robeson, Paul 17, 18, 28
Robinson, David 230
Ronay, Edina 188, 189
Rose, William 137, 138
Rowan, Roy 124
Rózsa, Miklós 29
Russell, Billy 49

Sabu 23, 24, 29, 30
Sagan, Leontine 10, 11
St Piran's 8
Sanders of the River 15–18, 28
Saraband for Dead Lovers 72
Scott of the Antarctic 70
Seaholme, Jeff 65
Sellars, Elizabeth 106, 137, 140, 145, 254, 255, 256
Sellers, Peter 158, 160, 161, 162, 163
Sellers, Robert 121
Setton, Maxwell 157
Shamberg, Michael 222, 232
Shaw, Roderick 208
Shepperton Studios 141, 171
Sherrin, Ned 201
Shipman, Kenneth 170
Shirley's World 203
Signoret, Simone 68, 70
Sikov, Ed 161
Sim, Alastair 62
Siskel, Gene 229
Slater, John 44, 68, 251, 252
Slocombe, Douglas 46, 63, 72, 96, 109, 111, 112, 119, 137, 139, 166, 176
Smart, Ralph 181
Smuggler 212–13
Soskin, Paul 143
Sous les toits de Paris 9
Space: 1999 4, 204
Spicer, Professor Andrew 147
Spoliansky, Mischa 28
Stafford, Brendan J. 182
Stephens, Martin xi, 132, 145

Sterling, Joseph 79
Stevens, Craig 171
Stoke Bruerne 52
Strange Report 198–200
Strauss, Oscar 28
Sundays and Cybele 178
Sutton, Dudley 183
Swaffer, Hannen 17

Tanner, Peter 79, 193
Tate, Nick 205
Technicolor 28, 29, 30, 109, 113, 116, 120, 121
Ten Little Niggers 52
Thaw, John 208
Thesiger, Ernest 20, 158
Thief of Bagdad, The 28–31
Things to Come 15, 19–22, 31
Third Secret, The 172–80
Thompson, Howard 107
Thomson, David 1
Thorson, Linda 195, 196
Thurber, James 157, 161
Titfield Thunderbolt, The 6, 85, 109–15, 219
Tobias, Oliver 212
Toeplitz, Ludovico 13
Tolnay, Akos 24
Train of Events 53, 79, 91
Tree, Margaret 213, 214
Trevor-Owen, Mark 200
Trubshawe, Michael 145, 203
Truman, Michael 92, 94, 109, 115, 126
Turpin, Gerry 183, 193
Turville 56
Tutin, Dorothy 141
Twickenham Studios 190
Tynan, Kenneth 125

Vaughn, Robert 204, 206
Veidt, Conrad 29
Vernon, Anne 119
Verónico Cruz 247
Video Arts 3, 213–16, 217, 234
von Kotze, John 190, 191

Walker, Alexander 5, 140, 152, 179
Wallace, Edgar 15
Wallace, Martin 147
Wallasey 8, 30, 35, 92, 116
Walsh, Dermot 88
Wanamaker, Sam 159
Ward Baker, Roy 183
Warner, Jack 63, 68
Warren, Patricia 23
Watt, Harry 40, 41, 42, 43, 78, 251
Waugh, Evelyn 32
Way to the Stars, The 52, 88
Wayne, Naunton 54, 110
Webb, Steven 190
Wedding Rehearsal 11
Weiler, A.H. 146, 163, 166
Wells, H.G. 19, 22, 31, 54, 99
Went the Day Well? 43, 56, 71
West-Larsen, Niels 167
Whelan, Tim 29
Whisky Galore 78–9, 108, 157
White, Valerie 64
Whiteley, Jon 102, 104, 105, 106, 131

Whitley, Reg 73
Whitney, Jack 29
Whittingham, Jack 102, 125, 127, 131, 254, 255
Wild Duck, The 141–2
Williams-Ellis, Hywel 212
Willis, Lord Ted 207
Wills, Anneke 198
Wills, J. Elder 67
Winnert, Derek 91
Winnington, Richard 56, 82
Wintle, Julian 102, 182, 192, 254
Worton Hall Studios 16, 21
Wright, Basil 60
Wyndham, Robert 46
Wyver, Professor John 142

Yellow Caesar 37
Young Veteran 36–7
Young, Harold 11, 12, 14

Zanuck, Darryl F. 175
Zech, Harry 20

EU authorised representative for GPSR:
Easy Access System Europe, Mustamäe tee 50,
10621 Tallinn, Estonia
gpsr.requests@easproject.com

www.ingramcontent.com/pod-product-compliance
Ingram Content Group UK Ltd.
Pitfield, Milton Keynes, MK11 3LW, UK
UKHW021304180326

11351UKWH00004B/2597